Deep Roots in a Time of Frost
Essays on Tolkien

Patrick Curry

Deep Roots in a Time of Frost

Essays on Tolkien

2014

Cormarë Series No. 33

Series Editors: Peter Buchs • Thomas Honegger • Andrew Moglestue • Johanna Schön

Series Editor responsible for this volume: Thomas Honegger

Library of Congress Cataloging-in-Publication Data

Patrick Curry:
Deep Roots in a Time of Frost. Essays on Tolkien
ISBN 978-3-905703-33-7

Subject headings:
Tolkien, J.R.R. (John Ronald Reuel), 1892-1973
Nature
Criticism
Enchantment
The Lord of the Rings
The Hobbit
The Silmarillion

Cormarë Series No. 33

First published 2014

© Walking Tree Publishers, Zurich and Jena, 2014

Cover illustration 'Green Pietà' by Patrick Curry

Set in Adobe Garamond Pro and Shannon by Walking Tree Publishers
Printed by Lightning Source in the United Kingdom and United States

Acknowledgments

I would like to thank Taylor & Francis, Routledge, Wiley Blackwell, Walking Tree Publishers, The Tolkien Society, Bloomsbury, West Virginia University Press and HarperCollins for permission to re-publish the respective essays. The original places of publication are given on the first page of each essay.

For their support and suggestions, I am very grateful to the following: David Abram, David Doughan, Sonia Fargue, Verlyn Flieger, John Garth, Margarita Carretero González, Liz Greene, Ursula Le Guin, Sean Kane, Marek Oziewicz, Clay Ramsay, Marlene Roeder, Suzanna Saumarez, Guglielmo Spirito and Martin Sternberg.

I would also like to thank Stratford Caldecott, David Gransby, Nick Groom, Graham Harvey, Thomas Honegger, Franco Manni and Eduardo Segura, the editors of various collections, for their invitations to present or contribute papers.

I also want to thank these people in particular:

Thomas Honegger, for all his work and help with editing and publishing this collection.

Charles Noad, for his peerless proof-reading.

Susan Peters, for her kind, generous and unflagging encouragement throughout.

Tom Shippey, for his counsel, not only learned but wise, over the years.

And Michael P. Winship, with whom I discovered Middle-earth at the same time and place, Millbrook N.Y. in the autumn of 1966. It has been my pleasure and privilege to take part in an ongoing conversation with him, on all such matters, throughout the succeeding years (now numbering nearly fifty – something that makes no sense to me at all, but then numbers never did). Thank you, Michael.

London, October 2014
Patrick Curry

Contents

Introduction

Deep roots in a time of frost, then. Or, as seems more likely, fire. But in either case, the roots of J.R.R. Tolkien's work run deep indeed. It will outlive that of most of his contemporaries and successors, and promises give succour to people we will never know in their own dark times. My own concern is with one aspect in particular: its enchantment, both as a theme in the work itself and as an effect on its readers. I have gone into some detail about enchantment in the essays that follow which I won't repeat here, but you won't go far wrong if you remember that it is first and foremost about wonder. (I'm sorry for some repetition in the essays themselves, by the way, but it's unavoidable when they often address and return to the same themes.)

Enchantment was also a prime concern for Tolkien, and he contrasted it sharply with magic, or will. With good reason, the Ring of Power is a magic ring, and the most powerful magician in Middle-Earth was, of course, Sauron. He was also the most technologically advanced one. There is no contradiction here; "our" magic is modern technoscience. (Magic and machine most probably share the same root in Proto-Indo-European: *magh*, meaning 'to have power'.)

Tolkien's term for enchantment was Faërie, meaning both the place where you go when you are enchanted and the state you are in when you find yourself there. It is a fundamentally non-modern place and experience.[1] And the central figure in and of Faërie is the Elf. Indeed, he asserted that "the Elves are there (in my tales) to demonstrate the difference between the two", that is, magic and enchantment.[2] The Elves not only practise enchantment as their art, they embody it.

---

[1] See my essay "Enchantment and Modernity", pp. 76-89 in *PAN: Philosophy, Activism, Nature* 9 (2012), accessible at http://arrow.monash.edu.au/vital/access/manager/Repository/monash:85446 (click on 'View').

[2] J.R.R. Tolkien, *The Letters of J.R.R. Tolkien*, ed. Humphrey Carpenter, with the assistance of Christopher Tolkien. London: HarperCollins, 2006, p. 146.

Now it is interesting to speculate on the Elves' mythic and literary provenance, and as a practising Catholic, Tolkien was brave to give a major role to such theologically ambiguous beings, "perhaps the only creatures to whom the [Christian] Model does not assign, as it were, an official status", as C.S. Lewis put it.[3] Certainly they are radically different from the diminutive wingèd imps of Shakespeare and J.M. Barrie, being "a race high and beautiful […] the People of the Great Journey, the People of the Stars."[4] But my chief interest has always been not origins or influences but something Tolkien reminded us not to forget in his essay on fairy-stories: "the effect produced now by these old things in the stories as they are."[5]

I can certainly recall their initial effect on me. I enjoyed the early chapters of *The Lord of the Rings* (perhaps having been prepared unawares by reading The Hobbit at an early age), but the first moment of enchantment was the Company's, and my, encounter with Glorfindel. Meeting Gildor earlier provided a foretaste, of course, but this was the full-blown thing, attended by that strange sensation of deep familiarity with someone or something new. Flickering, flashing, shimmering and, in the final test, shining: these are all phenomena, I subsequently discovered, that often attend enchantment. But why did Glorfindel, and later Elrond and Galadriel, affect me so strongly? And why did I so readily recognise it?

One way to understand the importance of Elvish enchantment is negatively, where they are reduced to a caricature or absent altogether. The Elves in Peter Jackson's films are the former: almost without exception camp, Aryan and slightly fascist, more arrogant than wise and self-important than dignified. Overall I must reluctantly agree with Christopher Tolkien's melancholy verdict on the films: "They eviscerated the book by making it an action movie for young people aged 15 to 25 […] The chasm between the beauty and seriousness of the work, and what it has become, has overwhelmed me. The commercialisation has reduced the aesthetic and philosophical impact of the

---

3 *The Discarded Image*, quoted in Laura Miller, *The Magician's Book: A Skeptic's Adventures in Narnia*. New York: Little, Brown, 2008, p. 272.
4 *The Lord of the Rings*, Appendix F.
5 J.R.R. Tolkien, *The Monsters and the Critics and Other Essays*, ed. Christopher Tolkien. London: HarperCollins, 2006, p. 128.

creation to nothing."[6] Orcs and wargs are inflated into grotesque monsters but apparently we aren't ready for Faramir as genuinely noble, nor Treebeard as genuinely wise. And then there is Jackson's clumsy meddling with not only characters but plot, even when it wasn't needed in order to convert the books into films. Did he actually think he was a better storyteller than Tolkien? Or was he simply determined to leave his "mark" all over it?[7]

As for absence, consider the TV series of "Game of Thrones", based on the books by George R.R. Martin. It supposedly shares the same genre as *The Lord of the Rings*, and it does indeed share skilled storytelling, but there is no equivalent to Elves in "Game of Thrones". Not coincidentally, it is obsessed instead with will, including magic, power – political, social and sexual (the misogyny is breathtaking) – and violence, culminating in sadism and torture. The same is true of countless other "fantasy" books, TV series and video games. Now these things are present in Middle-earth too, albeit less crudely; but they are not there nihilistically, for their own sake. Rather they coexist, to quote one of Tolkien's definitions of enchantment, with "a love and respect for all things, 'animate' and 'inanimate', an unpossessive love of them as 'other'."[8] The contrast is the point, and without it there is no point.

But isn't there something stupendous about what "Game of Thrones" shows us? To be sure. It is the sheer intensity, scale and consequences of our own restless and unappeasable desires: for security, for power, for status, for sensation. But after these have been denied or even fulfilled (although never for long or enough), without that unpossessive love like grace, which cannot be managed or controlled, somewhere in our lives, everything else threatens to become meaningless.

In his conversation with the wise-woman Andreth, the Elf Finrod Felagund tells us how our disenchanted obsession with use, method and technique (whether material or spiritual) appears to Elves. He asks her, "do you know

---

6 In an interview in *Le Monde* on July 9, 2012: http://www.worldcrunch.com/culture-society/my-father-039-s-quot-eviscerated-quot-work-son-of-hobbit-scribe-j.r.r.-tolkien-finally-speaks-out/hobbit-silmarillion-lord-of-rings/c3s10299/#.UXMsj0qCVBl (accessed 6 July 2014).

7 It's true that Cate Blanchett, Vigo Mortensen and Ian McKellen are excellent, but they are excellent actors.

8 J.R.R. Tolkien, *Smith of Wootton Major*, extended edition, ed. Verlyn Flieger. London: HarperCollins, 2005, p. 101.

that the Eldar say of Men that they look at no thing for itself; that if they study it, it is to discover something else; that if they love it, it is only (so it seems) because it reminds them of some other dearer thing? Yet with what is this comparison? Where are these other things?"[9] Where indeed? For there is another world, but as the enchanted realise, to quote the poet Paul Valéry, it is in this world, and only there. Or rather, here. Thus what the Elves, as enchantment, have most to offer in healing the Earth's wounds, not least those resulting from the domination of Men, is "the restoration of the *love of Arda*".[10]

There is no point in repeating anything here that is in the essays, but there are a few things I want to add. One is that I have known for some time that Tolkien's distinction between magic (including modern science) and enchantment, although fundamentally sound, needs more work.[11] In particular, does it leave the old Earth magic of healing, nurturing and protecting life in the same category as the biotech industry, Big Pharma and so on? That doesn't seem right.

I think the answer is that they do indeed have something in common, namely to effect a change (or stop one) in the primary world. Beyond that, though, they diverge sharply. For example, a shaman and a wildlife management biologist both want to ensure the well-being of a population of animals. But the former does so through techniques of focussed empathy and draws upon local knowledge and tradition which respect those animals as fellow-subjects and independent agents, whereas the latter works through objectifying the animals and drawing upon scientific knowledge (statistical, biological, ecological) that treats them as purely instances of universal laws.

Another example: a biodynamically-grown tomato results from working with the natural world, respectfully and with minimal interference in its own intentions and processes. (Intentions need not be conscious, let alone solely human.) A

---

9   J.R.R. Tolkien, *Morgoth's Ring*, ed. Christopher Tolkien. London: HarperCollins, 1994, p. 316.
10 *Morgoth's Ring*, p. 343; author's emphasis.
11 As Geoffrey Cornelius, John Michael Greer, Liz Greene, Clay Ramsay, Marlene Roeder and Suzanna Saumarez have always said. I'm grateful for their persistence. Tolkien himself was aware of this point; see *Letters*, p. 199.

genetically-engineered tomato, in contrast, results from treating it as a thing to be manipulated entirely for our benefit in ways whose only limits are technical.

Working with nature allows room for relationships with it, so questions of ethics are present from the start. So is the potential for enchantment, reveal. ing the intrinsic value of those other beings and processes. Dominating and exploiting nature as a mere object for us to treat in any way we want starts with disenchanting it, and destroys any wonder of the other that may inconveniently arise along the way.

The first approach to the world is also open to enchantment in another way. In order to experience the world as a reindeer does, and thus know what a reindeer knows, the shaman becomes one while also remaining a man. That is pure metaphor, the royal road to enchantment. And eating a biodynamic tomato invites you into the ancient story of life on Earth, including humans, alongside her many other hungry children. The GM tomato, on the other hand, enrols you willy nilly in the modern narrative of humans as masters and conquerors of life on Earth, who is now to be their slave. Not much enchantment there.

I believe this difference is another version of the old distinction between *magia* ("natural" or "white" magic) and *goeteia* (necromantic or "black" magic). Both are still magic, but very different kinds.

I also want to mention something important which nonetheless took me an embarrassingly long time to realise. (There is a character in José Saramago's novel *All the Names* who is lying on his bed having a conversation with the ceil-ing, as you do, and at one point he says, "I'm not stupid", to which the ceiling replies, "No, you're not, it's just that you take a long time to understand things, especially simple things …") I mean the internal and essential link between enchantment and what Tolkien identified as his story's real theme: "Death and the desire for deathlessness".[12] This is what prevents a concern with enchant-ment from becoming ultimately frivolous.

What is the nature of the link? Respecting both death and enchantment, it consists of learning to let go – or refusing to let go. Tolkien contrasts the exis-

---

12 *Letters*, pp. 246, 262.

tential situation of humans as "the mystery of the love of the world in the hearts of a race 'doomed' to leave and seemingly lose it", as against that of Elves: "the anguish in the hearts of a race 'doomed' not to leave it, until its whole evil-aroused story is complete". The temptation facing us humans is therefore what Tolkien called "serial longevity", or trying to literally live forever, and confusing that with the immortality that may or may not await us on the other side of the grave. And it is a mark of Tolkien's humility that of the latter there is only, he writes, "Hope without guarantees".[13]

That's not enough for those who demand certainty and security, of course, and the dream of "endless serial living" haunts Western culture well beyond a few cryogenic, cyborg and transhumanist extropian fantasists.[14] It terminates in the ghastly unlife of a Ringwraith, virtually disembodied, hopelessly endless, fearing death yet craving it: not the fulfilment of immortality, but its parody.

The common ground shared by enchantment and death is suggested by the fact that when the One Ring of Power is destroyed, the Three Rings of healing also fade. A friend insisted that I get to grips with this the strange and counter-intuitive connection, and then I read and grasped Verlyn Flieger's point that "*The Lord of the Rings* is, among other things, a story about the ability to let go." The Ring, as she says, is the obvious example, but the "timeless beauty of Lórien is the deeper example."[15] And life itself is the ultimate instance. This is what links Tolkien's three great themes of death, enchantment, and magic.

In the meanwhile, the situation while we live is just as described in the opening of *The Lord of the Rings*: the Elves are still passing over the Sea, enchantment is always leaving us, power-magic is threatening to dominate everything, and we are constantly faced with the joyless prospect of the Dominion of Men. So we must learn to be able to live in the "grey and leafless world" of disenchantment if and when need be. It's not easy, but unless we can both welcome enchantment without perverting it with any agenda (Boromir's

---

13 In this paragraph, *Letters*, pp. 246, 284, 237.
14 *Monsters*, p. 153. For a brilliant analysis of this dream-cum-nightmare in Western philosophy, see Adriana Cavarero, *In Spite of Plato: A Feminist Rewriting of Ancient Philosophy*, transl. Serena Anderlini-D'Onofrio and Aine O'Healy. New York: Routledge, 1995.
15 The friend was Michael Winship. Verlyn Flieger, *A Question of Time: J.R.R. Tolkien's Road to Faërie*. Kent OH: Kent State University Press, 1997, p. 112.

mistake) and let go when the time comes, it is not safe with us, nor we with it. As Aragorn warns Boromir, it is what we bring to enchantment that makes it dangerous.

Third, a word on the limits of enchantment. It is highly significant that the fate of the world at the end of the Third Age turns not on Elves, or even Men, but on hobbits. True, Frodo and Sam are unusual hobbits, even Elf-friends, while Gollum is barely still a hobbit at all. (Gollum is surely Tolkien's contribution to the cast of the most distinctive characters in twentieth-century fiction.) But taking hobbits for the moment to be "a diminutive branch of the human race",[16] they – and more to the point, we – are not Elves, and cannot finally live as them. We may visit Faërie and be visited by it, if so blessed, but we cannot stay there.

The final question regarding enchantment then becomes: what is a way of life that makes it welcome and honours its presence, but also recognises that it (or we) cannot stay for long, and helps us to let go and live without it when necessary? This is where the hobbits – loving embodied and embedded life in all its messy, imperfect glory, capable of defending it with "courage in a tight spot", preferring peace to explosions and green to black-or-white – come into their own.[17] We moderns have a great deal to learn from them, starting with the urgent need to "go back, slow down".[18] Hobbits were into Slow Food, and all the other Slows, well before they were a movement.

Finally, I want to clarify the connections between the sections that follow. It is my perception that all enchantment is ultimately rooted in nature. I mean the living more-than-human natural world which includes, but vastly exceeds, ourselves. To justify this claim would take far more time and room than I have here, but enchantment is always an embodied and emplaced experience. At the same time, it is also completely spiritual and mysterious. The result is wonder in, and as, sensuous particularities, or what Max Weber called "concrete magic".[19]

---

16 *Letters*, p. 406.
17 Courage: what the hobbits suspected Saruman lacked, compared to Gandalf. See my reflections on the hobbits as "domestic" in "Enchantment in Tolkien and Middle-earth" below.
18 Teresa Brennan, *Globalization and its Terrors. Daily Life in the West*, London: Routledge, 2003, p. 39.
19 H.H. Gerth and C. Wright Mills (eds.), *From Max Weber: Essays in Sociology*. London: Routledge, 1991, p. 282.

So too, properly understood, is nature. Fittingly, Tolkien described Elves as not supernatural but "natural, far more natural" than ourselves.[20] As the Elves are of Arda, so is enchantment of the Earth.

What of the section on literary criticism? The critical hostility and incomprehension that Tolkien's work has largely met with, in such striking contrast to its popular reception, stems from what I call "modernism". Ironically for a worldview that prides itself on being rational, modernism is viscerally suspicious of enchantment. Like Gollum upon tasting the life-giving Elven waybread, its adherents splutter, "Ach! No! You try to choke poor Sméagol. Dust and ashes, he can't eat that." For, confirming the elective affinity of enchantment and nature, the modernist is equally allergic to the experience and even concept of the natural world as alive, animate, and a subject in its own right. It is only allowed to have meanings that we humans deign to give it.

Meanwhile, those with power – the corporate warlocks, technoscientific wizards and spokesmen for "Knowledge, Rule, Order"[21] – set about remaking the living world in just that disenchanted image: meaningless but useful, a thing to be manipulated for profit but without its own intrinsic value. But this is also why so many readers love Tolkien's work: it awakens us, with a thrill, from the deadening spell of modernism. Modernist disenchantment is the real fantasy, compared to which Middle-earth is reality itself.

---

20 *Monsters*, p. 110.
21 The mantra of the collaborator Saruman, evidently the model for so many of our politicians.

fect produced *now* by these old things in the stories as they are." Besides, it is both boring and pointless to spill ink establishing whether Tolkien was "reactionary" or "progressive". Neither can the work itself be pigeonholed in such a way – as if its meaning was forever fixed, and not whatever it presents itself as, in ways that cannot be predetermined. I am going to argue that the *The Lord of the Rings* has a life of its own in ways beyond what Tolkien himself could have anticipated, and which are a part of the explanation of its enduring appeal.

Let us look at that appeal for a moment. English-language sales for *The Hobbit* total 29 million (ahead of any other single work of fiction of this century); for *The Lord of the Rings*, 18.5 million. And that only covers up till 1989. Tolkien's global popularity is well-known, from the "Middle-earth Libre" graffiti in Quebec to the adoption of his work (I am told) by an Italian anarchist group. It is also attested to by the 30-odd translations, an early and possibly fabulous example being that into Vietnamese in 1969. (A South Vietnamese army division immediately, and rather perceptively, adopted the Eye of Sauron as their emblem.) There is even an area of submarine features off the South-West coast of Ireland named after Tolkien characters (hence "Gollum's Channel", and so on). So no one could argue that all this was a flash-in-the-pan phenomenon, riding on the heels of the 60s counter-culture; sales in the 90s remain brisk.

Yet this extraordinary popular success has been accompanied by relentless critical hostility. Beginning with Philip Toynbee's sneers and Edmund Wilson's rant in the 1950s, it has never flagged. The general view was perhaps best summed up by the poet John Heath-Stubbs: "A combination of Wagner and Winnie-the-Pooh." Given that criticism from the left tends to be more social and political, that's what I intend to concentrate on here. Amid all the critical rubbish, there are a few serious points. First, however, let's get the rest of it out of the way. Catherine R. Stimpson brought up several common refrains in 1969. "An incorrigible nationalist," she wrote, Tolkien "celebrates the English bourgeois pastoral idyll. Its characters, tranquil and well fed, live best in placid, philistine, provincial rural cosiness" (or would prefer to). His language reveals "class snobbery" (both trollism and orcism, in fact). His characters are cleanly divided into "good and evil, nice and nasty" (notwithstanding the fact, which she notes, that almost all the races are a collection of good, bad and indifferent individuals; and completely overlooking the inner struggles of Gollum, Boromir, Denethor and Frodo himself. This is *not* a serious point).

Finally, "[b]ehind the moral structure is a regressive emotional pattern. For Tolkien is irritatingly, blandly, traditionally masculine [...]. He makes his women characters, no matter what their rank, the most hackneyed of stereotypes. They are either beautiful and distant, simply distant, or simply simple." Here it is tempting to reply, guilty as charged. Even with the characters of Galadriel, Éowyn and Shelob – without whom *The Lord of the Rings* would be seriously impoverished, and who are more complex than Stimpson allows – Tolkien's paternalism if not patriarchy is unmissable. Yet it is too easy to ask a work to be something it isn't, or its author to do something he or she didn't set out to do. Indeed, maybe we should be grateful that Tolkien *didn't* attempt a more feminist Middle-earth. Consider the ghastly results, for example, when two otherwise superb writers, John Fowles and Dennis Potter, tried to place female characters centre-stage in *The Mantissa* and *Blackeyes* respectively. Just imagine what Tolkien might have wrought! Some of these points were recently recycled in the *New Statesman and Society* (Kaveney): Tolkien's emphasis on social hierarchies (no mention however of "the hour of the Shire-folk, when they arise from their quiet fields to shake the towers and counsels of the Great"); the fact that "praise of Tolkien has often been the cover for a broadside attack on modernism and even on realism" (is nothing sacred?); and a putative link between Tolkien's cult following and "the authoritarian direction taken by much American commercial fantasy and science fiction." (He really should have anticipated that, back in 1937.) The author concludes that Tolkien is "worth intelligent reading, but not passionate attention." Clearly, this town isn't big enough for both of us.

It is true that Tolkien's evil creatures are frequently "swart, slant-eyed", foul-mouthed and apparently poorly educated, and tend to come from the south ("the cruel Haradrim") and east ("the wild Easterlings") – both threatening directions in Tolkien's "moral cartography". It is also true that black is a terrible colour, especially when contrasted with white. It must be admitted that Tolkien is drawing on centuries of such moral valuation (not unrelated to historical experience) attached to his chosen setting, in order to convey something immediately recognisable in the context of his story, without attempting to mitigate the possibility of racist interpretation. (I say "possibility"; it is grossly insulting to his readers to assume they automatically transfer their feelings about orcs to all the swart or slant-eyed people they encounter in the street.) Thus as Clyde Kilby (1977) recounts, when Tolkien was once asked what lay east and south of the Middle-earth of *The Lord of the Rings*, he replied:

> "Rhûn is the Elvish word for east. Asia, China, Japan, and all the things which people in the West regard as far away. And south of Harad is Africa, the hot countries." Then Mr. Resnick asked, "That makes Middle-earth Europe, doesn't it?" To which Tolkien replied, "Yes, of course – Northwestern Europe ... where my imagination comes from."

(In which case, as Tolkien also admitted, Mordor "would be roughly in the Balkans.") However, he reacted sharply to reading a description of Middle-earth as *Nordic*:

> Not *Nordic*, please! A word I personally dislike; it is associated, though of French origin, with racialist theories [...] The North-west of Europe, where I (and most of my ancestors) have lived, has my affection, as a man's home should [...] but it is not "sacred", nor does it exhaust my affections.

It is also, I believe, more Tolkien's material than his message. Consider that the races in Middle-earth are most striking in their variety and autonomy. Without suggesting that a clear-cut choice exists, is this an instance of ethnocentrism, or multiculturalism? Or even, given that most of the races are closely tied to a particular geography and ecology, and manage to live there without exploiting it to the point of destruction – bioregionalism? Again, one of the subplots of *The Lord of the Rings* concerns an enduring friendship between members of races traditionally estranged (Gimli and Legolas); and the most important wedding in the book, between Aragorn and Arwen, is an interracial marriage. As usual, the picture is a great deal more complex than the critics perceive.

It is also true that Tolkien was deeply hostile to "modernity". I am as grateful as anyone for the benefits of modernity, but it is becoming very hard to celebrate their undiluted beneficence; to that extent, Tolkien's diagnosis, at least, is starting to look increasingly prescient. In any case, there is certainly no reason whatsoever to automatically associate modernity with progressive politics. So let's turn now to some more serious charges, beginning with Tolkien's central and most unique characters: the hobbits.

II

With this audience, of all people, I don't need to catalogue the traits of hobbits: their fondness of food and drink, closeness to the land, hostility to machines, intellectualism and inarticulateness. Though I will remind you of what one famous hobbit almost replied, when asked, "What is finer than flying?" Bilbo only allowed his native tact, not to mention caution, to overrule suggesting, "A warm bath and late breakfast on the lawn afterwards". "Nonetheless," their chronicler notes, "ease and peace had left this people still curiously tough." This being, in Shippey's words, "the notorious Anglo-hobbitic inability to know when they're beaten."

As Tolkien notes, Bilbo and Frodo were exceptional in many ways: their wealth, bachelorhood, and aestheticism. Sam, as a recently and exceptionally lettered gardener, was far more typical, or as Tolkien put it, "the genuine hobbit". But your behaviour had to be extreme to land you in any real trouble; for "The Shire had hardly any 'government'." The only real officials were the Mayor of Michel Delving, Postmaster and First Shirriff, plus various hereditary heads of clans.

Now it doesn't take any great perceptiveness to see in "these charming, absurd, helpless" (and not-so helpless) hobbits a self-portrait of the English, something which Tolkien even admitted, in an unguarded moment, to Clyde Kilby. Take the view in 1940 by George Orwell, and still instantly recognizable (albeit sadly altered in some respects), of a conservative people neither artistically nor intellectually inclined, though with "a certain power of acting without thought"; taciturn, preferring tacit understandings to explication; endowed with a love of flowers and animals, valuing privateness and the liberty of the individual, and respecting legality; not puritanical and without definite religious belief, but strangely gentle (and here we feel our losses in the 1980s), with a hatred of war and militarism that coexists with a strong unconscious patriotism. Orwell sums up English society as "a strange mixture of reality and illusion, democracy and privilege, humbug and decency."

With apologies to Tolkien, *plus ça change*. True, these attributes are inextricably mingled with ones (some) English have *wanted* to find in the mirror; none are eternal and immutable. Because they constitute a national fantasy, however, it does not follow that they have no social reality. Also, if I may be so bold, Tolkien's portrait is not altogether a flattering one; it includes greed, small-mindedness and philistinism.

But the kind of Englishness the hobbits embody is more particular than that. Although identifiably modern in many respects – and as several commentators have noticed, it is crucial that Bilbo and Frodo *be* modern, in order to mediate between ourselves and the ancient and therefore somewhat foreign world they inhabit – they also represent, as David Harvey puts it, "the archetypal pre-Industrial Revolution English yeomen," but even more specifically pre- the Conquest of 1066, before the hated Norman Yoke imposed centralized autocratic government, a foreign language and an alien cultural tradition, and the rootless cosmopolitanism of an elite Latin education – which, as Shippey has pointed out, culminated in, among other things, the creation of a "distinctive literary caste": the same caste that harried Tolkien throughout his life and after.

But whether Anglo-Saxon, feudal or modern, the hobbits' "bucolic" and organic "naturalness" clearly falls within the long tradition in English letters of nostalgic pastoralism or ruralism, celebrating a time "long ago in the quiet of the world, when there was less noise and more green." Listen to some of these titles and remarks, from the nineteenth and early twentieth centuries: Tennyson's English *Idylls* – William Morris's "fair green garden of Northern Europe" – the Poet Laureate Alfred Austin's *Haunts of Ancient Peace* (1902) (that could easily be a song by Van Morrison today: no coincidence) – Ford Madox Ford's *The Heart of the Country* – Henry Newbolt's *The Old Country* – Kipling's "Our England is a garden" – Maurice Hewlett's *Song of the Plough* – and there are many more, but you get the idea. In other words, there has long been a deep cultural gulf between England's (southern) "green and pleasant land" and her (northern) "dark satanic mills"; or as Martin Weiner (1985) puts it with an aptness all the better for my case because it is (presumably) unintentional, "[t]he power of the machine was invading and blighting the Shire."

Of course the irony here is that by 1851 England was already the world's first urban nation, with over half the population living in towns. This has led many critics to see ruralism as *simply* a fantasy (in the unkind sense) – "a psychic balance wheel," in Weiner's words. But nothing, I'm afraid, is that simple.

The fount for social criticism of this sort is *The Country and the City*, by Raymond Williams (1985). It is an important and influential book, but one which I dislike. Let's try to put it to work in understanding Tolkien. Williams says that nostalgic "celebrations of a feudal or aristocratic order" embody values that "spring to the defence of certain kinds of order, certain social hierarchies and moral stabilities," which he implies act in defence of social injustices, and even fascism. Perhaps this is the place, therefore, to consider the politics (in the narrow sense) of Middle-earth. Tolkien described his own political opinions as leaning to "Anarchy (philosophically understood, meaning abolition of control, not whiskered men with bombs) – or to 'unconstitutional' Monarchy." "I am not a 'socialist' in any sense", he wrote, "because the 'planners', when they acquire power, become so bad [...] the spirit of 'Isengard', if not of Mordor, is of course always cropping up. The present design of destroying Oxford in order to accommodate motor-cars is a case. But our chief adversary is a member of a 'Tory' Government." (The proposal referred to was a so-called relief road through Christ Church meadow – a very contemporary ring to that.)

Anarchism or libertarianism has a left/right instability that has always irritated both those wings, who like to have these matters cut-and-dried. No socialist, nor even democrat then, but neither is there in Tolkien a whiff of "blood and soil" fascism. And that is what we find in Middle-earth. One might say "subsidiarity rules OK" – that is, decisions seem indeed to be taken at the lowest possible level, closest to those who are most affected by them. Indeed, the Shire functions by a sort of municipal democracy. None of this, of course, applies to Mordor – an utterly authoritarian regime with a slave-based economy featuring intensive industrialism and agribusiness.

Raymond Williams continues:

> In Britain, there is a precarious but persistent rural-intellectual radicalism: genuinely and actively hostile to industrialism and capitalism; opposed to commercialism and the exploitation of the environment; attached to country ways and feelings, the literature and the lore.

This sounds generous, but here comes the big Reservation:

> in every kind of radicalism the moment comes when any critique must choose
> its bearings, between past and future […]

Furthermore, "[w]e must begin not in the idealisations of one order or another, but in the actual history to which they are only partial and misleading responses." Thus myth and revolution are *alternative*, not complementary responses to crisis.

This is nonsense: positivist about "history", essentialist in holding the political character of traditions to be inherent and fixed, and intellectualist in thinking that ideological and factual criticism is a sufficient basis for a political programme. Most unforgivably, it ignores the massive lesson that the left, by now, should have learned from Gramsci (or, failing him, Mrs Thatcher); that people do not live by factual and historical bread alone, but also by ideas, values and visions of alternatives. The past feeds the future, as *myth* does revolution: something that Orwell understood better than many who have patronized him since.

What really matters now about the image of pre-Conquest England "as a free and equal rural community" benefiting from "a primitive freedom" and "the perpetual impulse of 'Nature'" (in Williams's excellent description) is not the extent to which things were actually otherwise – which is itself an interpretation rather than a fact, and may become mobilised as a resource in one political direction or another – but rather the *use* of such an image in the present. Within his own remit, Tolkien himself – old reactionary though he undoubtedly was, in the true meaning of the word – saw this very clearly. Indeed, his anti-positivism is bizarrely in tune with the best and most refreshing aspects of postmodern philosophy. "History often resembles 'Myth'," he wrote, "because they are both ultimately of the same stuff."

Of course, it is true that the defence of the "vanishing countryside" can become deeply confused with the defence of the old rural order. But it certainly *need* not. As Weiner notes, there have been "variants of ruralism to suit all political inclinations […] Conservatives and Imperialists, anti-Imperialists, Liberals and Radicals." The meaning of such a myth is not written on stone. Today it is standing up to the bulldozers in Twyford Down and Oxleas Wood, while simultaneously encouraging defenders of the corrupt and undemocratic "Mother of Parliaments" that has sent them in; in the struggle between landowners and ramblers, it is claimed on both sides.

One contemporary writer, Fraser Harrison, goes straight to the heart of the matter:

> While it is easy to scoff at the whimsicality and commercialism of rural nostalgia, it is also vital to acknowledge that this reaching-out to the countryside is an expression, however distorted, of a healthy desire to find some sense of meaning and relief in a world that seems increasingly bent on mindless annihilation.

Accordingly, says Harrison, "it becomes meaningful to talk of 'radical nostalgia'". (The word itself means precisely *homesickness*.) It does express a truth of its own, which reflects an authentic and deeply felt emotion. The pastoral fantasy nostalgia invented is after all an image of a world in which men and women feel at home with themselves, with each other and with nature, a world in which harmony reigns. It is an ideal.

Tolkien himself listed as a primary function of fantasy *Recovery*, which he defined as the "regaining of a clear view." In a nice twist, his wonderful discussion of *escapism* in "On Fairy-Stories" even turns the tables on his "progressive" critics, who are confusing, he writes, and

> not always by sincere error, the Escape of the Prisoner with the Flight of the Deserter. Just so a Party-spokesman might have labelled departure from the misery of the Führer's or any other Reich and even criticism of it as treachery [...]

> For a trifling instance: not to mention [...] electric street-lamps of mass-produced pattern in your tale is Escape (in that sense) [...] out comes the big stick: "Electric lamps have come to stay," they say ... "The march of Science, its tempo quickened by the needs of war, goes inexorably on ... making some things obsolete, and foreshadowing new developments in the utilization of electricity": an advertisement. This says the same thing only more menacingly.

Tolkien has put his finger here on the deep complicity of *social realists*, and socialist thought in general, with the scientific/technological/managerial state and its ideology which it professes to be contesting. And given the nature of this monster, is it any surprise that by way of metaphoric contrast, Tolkien and so many other people have turned to nature?

III

That point brings me to the borders of the Shire. But we are still in Middle-earth. As Gildor said to Frodo, "it is not your own Shire. Others dwelt here before hobbits were; and others will dwell here again when hobbits are no more. The wide world is all about you: you can fence yourselves in, but you cannot for ever fence it out." And as Tolkien himself commented, "hobbits are not a Utopian vision, or recommended as an ideal in their own or any age. They, as all peoples and their situations, are an historical accident – as the Elves point out to Frodo – and an impermanent one in the long view."

What is most striking about this larger world, that, notwithstanding the ignorance of the hobbits about its reality and importance, encloses and sustains the Shire in space, as well as precedes and follows it in time? Certainly the variety, richness and consistency of its sense of place is extraordinary. The fact is that Middle-earth is more real to me (and I am certainly not alone in this) than many "real" places; and if I should suddenly find myself there (which would of course astound me – but not utterly) I would have a better idea of how to find my way about than if I had been dropped in, say, central Asia or South America. But what is most striking about Tolkien's world – and this has been noticed by many readers, and even some literary critics – is its profound feeling for the natural world: geography and geology, ecologies, flora and fauna, the seasons, weather, the night-sky, and the Moon in all its phases. The experience of these phenomena as comprising a living and meaningful cosmos saturates his entire story. Even the various races of people are rooted in, and unimaginable (both to themselves and us) without, their natural contexts. As Sam said of the Elves in Lothlórien, "Whether they've made the land, or the land's made them, it's hard to say".

Tolkien obviously had a particular affection for flora. I counted 64 species of non-cultivated plants specifically mentioned in *The Hobbit* and *The Lord of the Rings* – surely an unusual number for any work of fiction – in addition to his own nine invented (or discovered) kinds. But pride of place, obviously, goes to trees. Every forest in Middle-earth has its own unique personality. And none more memorably than the green city of Caras Galadhon in Lothlórien.

Tolkien does not romanticize nature, however. Angela Carter points out in another connection that the wood in Shakespeare's *A Midsummer Night's Dream* is

> *the* English wood. The English wood is nothing like the dark, necromantic forest in which the Northern European imagination begins and ends, where its dead and the witches live [...] For example an English wood, however marvellous, however metamorphic, cannot, by definition, be trackless [...] But to be lost in the forest is to be lost to *this* world, to be abandoned by the light, to lose yourself utterly, an existential catastrophe. Nineteenth-century nostalgia disinfected the wood, cleansing it of the grave, hideous and elemental beings with which the superstition of an earlier age had filled it. Or rather, denaturing those beings until they came to look like those photographs of fairy folk that so enraptured Conan Doyle.

All good stuff, but its interest here lies in how it *doesn't* apply to Middle-earth. In fact, such "denaturing" of Elves was exactly what Tolkien held against Shakespeare. The hobbits may go rambling through an English wood of a day's outing, but as any reader of *The Hobbit* could tell you, wandering off the path in Mirkwood definitely amounts to an "existential catastrophe". Tolkien made no attempt to prettify "the hearts of trees and their thoughts, which were often dark and strange, and filled with a hatred of things that go free upon the earth."

Individual trees figure importantly too: the Party Tree, Old Man Willow, the White Tree in Minas Tirith – to say nothing of the two cosmogonic trees of Telperion and Laurelin. And, of course, hobbits were not Tolkien's only unique creation; he also gave us Ents, and Treebeard. When asked the cardinal question in any kind of war – in fact, the question that is itself (however discreet) the first act of war (however polite): "Whose side are you on?" – Treebeard replies,

> I am not altogether on anybody's *side*, because nobody is altogether on my *side*, if you understand me: nobody cares for the woods as I care for them, not even Elves nowadays.

It is easy to hear the voice of Tolkien himself here. He freely acknowledged his own "tree-love", writing – perhaps in view of his own "totem tree", a birch in his front yard – to the *Daily Telegraph*, not long before his death, that "[i]n all my works I take the part of trees as against all their enemies."

He even referred to *The Lord of the Rings* as "my own internal Tree." But not the only one. "I have among my 'papers'," he once wrote, "more than one version of a mythical 'tree'." The reference, or application, to his Niggle's surviving painting "Leaf", but a tiny fragment of the Great Tree of his ambition, is obvious.

He was well aware, of course, of the hallowed place of trees in mythology and folk-lore everywhere. But his personal involvement with trees, combined with their mythic resonance, produced an extraordinarily vivid depiction. Tolkien's trees are too vulnerable ever to be *just* symbols.

And there was an historical dimension too. He would have been well aware that (as W.G. Hoskins put it), "From rising ground England must have seemed one great forest before the fifteenth century, an almost unbroken sea of tree-tops with a thin blue spiral of smoke rising here and there at long intervals." Middle-earth's own Old Forest was itself already only a survivor of vast forgotten woods … And at the opening of the story in *The Lord of the Rings*, even such remnants are on the edge of doom. Fangorn is threatened by Saruman, who "has a mind of metal and wheels, and does not care for growing things." And if that were not enough, "it seems that the wind is setting East, and the withering of all woods may be drawing near." For in what remains of the green garden of Middle-earth has re-appeared the Ring of Power. "The Ring! What shall we do with the Ring, the least of rings, the trifle that Sauron fancies?" Elrond alone permits himself any irony, even as he too, as do all the good and great, acknowledges his helplessness.

Here we must tread carefully, for Tolkien has warned us repeatedly against an allegorical topical reading of his story. (I'm sure you all know his words well. He also once wonderfully complained: "To ask if the Orcs 'are' Communists is to me as sensible as asking if Communists are Orcs.") And he is right. He had worked hard to create a literary artefact that precisely *isn't* "allegorical or topical" – and very wisely, as we shall see. Without suggesting that the meaning of the Ring is thereby exhausted, however, I shall avail myself of my right as a reader to perceive "applicability" – a particular application that is, I believe, forcing itself upon us daily.

Consider that the Ring epitomises the strongest economic and political form of power in Middle-earth, which threatens to dominate all others in one vast autocratic realm. There are apparently no limits to its power in the material realm; true, it cannot create beauty or understanding or healing, but it rules over the three Elven Rings that can. And from *their* point of view, its transformative power is entirely destructive. Furthermore, this potential will be realised to the full once the Ring is entirely under the control of Sauron. Needless to say, if "the Ring is taken, then the Shire will be no refuge." Indeed, in the first book of *The Lord of the Rings*, it becomes apparent that Tom Bombadil alone is unaffected by it. Although not (in my opinion) Tolkien's most felicitous character, Tom Bombadil clearly represents, in Tolkien's own words, "the spirit of the (vanishing) Oxford and Berkshire countryside." But the point about him here is that as Galdor says: "Power to defy our Enemy is not in him, unless such power is in the earth itself. *And yet we see that Sauron can torture and destroy the very hills.*" That fact becomes brutally clear in Frodo and Sam's agonizing journey to Mordor. I will spare you the full description of the desolation before Mordor: "a land defiled, diseased beyond all healing," where, in Frodo's words "earth, air and water all seem accursed."

Do we not see just this blighted industrial wasteland today in Eastern Europe and Russia? And could we not find its equivalents elsewhere: in poisoned rivers and even whole seas; clear-cut and slashed and burned acres that were once rainforest, richest in life anywhere on the planet; smoking, reeking cities where life, by contrast, is cheap? This process has a name, by the way. The Greek *oikos*, which gives us *eco*, means "house" or "abode"; the Latin *caedere*, "to kill". Hence, *ecocide*. (And the combination of Greek and Latin only confirms that no good can come of it.)

Professor Shippey (1982) has observed of the Ring that "it is a dull mind which does not reflect, 'Power corrupts, and absolute power corrupts absolutely'." And he shrewdly reminds us that the Ring is addictive in a very modern way. But this interpretation can be further tightened up with no loss of meaning, indeed with some gain. It needs no allegorical special pleading or stretch of the imagination to see that our Ring is that malevolent contemporary amalgam of three things: the power of the nation-state – capitalism in the form of transnational economic muscle – and scientism, or the monopoly of knowledge by modern technological science. Like Tolkien's Ring, there are apparently no limits to its potential mastery of nature (certainly not those of Mercy); and once it is on the finger of its collective principal servants – that is, completely removed from any democratic accountability – there will be no way to control it at all. (Those servants have no wish to control it; rather, to feed it.) There is precious little control as things are, of course. Sporadic public protest and non-governmental organisations worry away at its edges and fight "the long defeat", but always under the shadow of "that vast fortress, armoury, prison, furnace of great power, Barad-dûr […] secure in its pride and its immeasurable strength." (And not the least because, in a twist even Sauron never thought of, almost everybody – even those who will suffer the most by its adoption, even those who are already living in ways that constitute the solution to its terrible problems – seems so seduced by the monster's hand-maidens in advertising and the media that they can hardly wait to sign up. Addictive indeed.)

Tolkien has been accused of a simple-minded moral Manicheism, simply pitting good against evil. This charge is bizarrely wide of the mark. One of the glories of Middle-earth is its messy pluralism; the alliance against Mordor is only just cobbled together (thanks mainly to Gandalf) among people with drastically different agenda. *The Lord of the Rings* celebrates difference and defends neutrality. These are precisely the things that are jeopardised by Sauron, who seeks to turn all Middle-earth into one vast and homogenous entity, under his all-seeing Eye that might remind us not only of "single vision", in Blake's words, but Foucault's alarm-call about the insidious growth of institutionalised knowledge-as-power: "Where religions once demanded the sacrifice of bodies, knowledge now calls for experimentation on ourselves, calls us to the sacrifice of the subject of knowledge." (And let us recall that Saruman's thirst for knowledge at all costs was precisely what baited Sauron's trap in which he was caught.)

The social and human brutalization this entails absolutely cannot be separated from the ecological. Sauron's own strategy recognises this fact: be sure to destroy your victims' natural habitat, and with it their way of life, before remaking it and them in your own terrible image. Such deprivation is of course proceeding apace. At home, it's true, our rivers haven't yet started catching fire, like the pitiable Cuyahoga in Cleveland; but "[t]hey're always a-hammering and a-letting out a smoke and a stench, and there isn't no peace even at night in Hobbiton. And they pour out filth a purpose; they've fouled all the lower Water, and it's getting down into Brandywine." When, that is, rivers and streams aren't disappearing altogether, due to overabstraction (an apt word for it!) by the water companies newly privatised and protected by the government.

Given that trees were Tolkien's special concern, however, I will merely note that whereas forests once covered sixty percent of the earth's land surface, they now cover less than six – and in England, roughly *half* of the already decimated ancient woodlands still present in 1945 have since been destroyed. But for anyone who knows hobbits reasonably well, I think I can bring it still closer to home. There was an obscure report last year, tucked away in one of the Sunday broadsheets, entitled "Wild fungi face extinction as pollution threat increases." It seems that wild mushrooms are dying out across Europe; in Holland 91 species have disappeared and another 182 are on the verge of extinction; in Germany the number of chanterelles taken annually has dropped from several thousand pounds to a few hundred, while in Britain the once common cep can now only be found in remote parts; ditto the wood blewits. The cause? Increased levels of nitrogen and sulphur in the air, and heavy metals leaching into the soil. One ecologist said "mass extinctions" were now imminent, and that the consequences for trees, vital symbiotes for fungi, were unknown, but he feared the worst. Given that the New World Order can apparently dispense with the material attributes of nature, what hope for moral or aesthetic arguments? As Richard Mabey writes, these "are now seen as, at their best, sentimental and impractical, and at their worst – it is a favourite phrase – 'purely subjective preferences'. Somewhere along the line many deep and widely shared human feelings have become regarded as a devalued currency." Or as Fraser Harrison powerfully puts it,

> throughout these years, nature has nevertheless prevailed as the richest source of metaphor concerning the human condition. It is in this sense that I believe we can claim to have our own indispensable *cultural* need of conservation Apart from all other consequences, the loss of each species or habitat from the countryside amounts to a blow struck at our own identity.

Yet such a position continues to be the target of critical cynicism. Keith Thomas, for example, has written that "the cult of the countryside" beginning in the eighteenth century was "in many ways a mystification and an evasion of reality [...] The irony was that the educated tastes of the aesthetes had themselves been paid for by the developments which they affected to deplore." And the historian Ludmilla Jordanova goes farther. Western capitalist society, she argues, sentimentalises animals and plants in order to systematically destroy them without facing the fact. "'Man' never left centre stage; nature has never been, and will never be, recognised as autonomous."

A gloomy outlook indeed! But it should be possible, without being branded a traitor, to reply, "It ain't necessarily so." That is, cultural conservationists are *not* necessarily cultural conservatives (in the pejorative sense). In fact, not even cultural conservatives are. Tolkien's position, for example, has acquired a new and distinctly radical meaning – or at the very least, potential meaning – as the crisis which partly motivated its writing has deepened and widened.

So a little humility seems in order. Can one really comfortably speak for *reality*, and dismiss all outrage at the desecration of nature by those of middle-class provenance as necessarily *affectation*? (I myself cannot deny such origins; nor that I never feel so sane and reverential as when I am in the company of broad-leaved trees, the taller and older the better. But I would utterly deny anyone else's right or ability to infallibly disqualify my experience in such a way.) And in any case, wasn't the overall social *reality* one of all-too-human inconsistency, paradox and confusion, as well as (rather than simply) unadulterated hypocrisy? I would also question (except of course as a bold rhetorical move) the use of the word *never*. If "never has been" is already debatable, how much more so is "never will be"!

Ironically, the permanent human possession of centre stage is increasingly coming under question. In the struggle over the fate of irreplaceable primary old-growth forests in North America, for example, the contestants are increasingly polarised between "humanists" (in this case the logging industry and its supporters) and "deep ecologists" (often under the aegis of the organisation Earth First!). For the former, as Robert Pogue Harrison so elegantly writes, rather belying the messiness of the fight, two activists for Earth First! have already been blown up by a car bomb, apparently planted by a Christian fundamentalist pro-logger

> there can be no question of the forest as a consecrated place; as a place of strange or enchanting or monstrous epiphanies; as a natural sanctuary. There can be only the claims of human mastery and possession of nature – the reduction of forests to utility.

John Fowles has put it more bluntly:

> We shall never fully understand nature (or ourselves), and certainly never respect it, until we dissociate the wild from the notion of usability – however innocent or harmless the use.

(And even more certainly, I would add, never revere it.) Nor is Tolkien wanting here, for that is just what Frodo experienced in Lórien: "He felt delight in wood and the touch of it, neither as forester nor as carpenter; it was the delight of the living tree itself." Or as Gimli rhetorically asked Legolas: "Do you cut down groves of blossoming trees in the spring-time for fire-wood?" Sadly, we do.

Such an insight or plea is a hard one to make, in the face of more obvious, powerful and immediate considerations. One is easily accused of "indulging in fatuous romanticism." But the survival of anything worth the name "nature" – and therefore of whatever it means to be human in relation to nature – looks increasingly likely to depend on the success of just such a case. With the entry of this dimension, however, we are at the very edge of Middle-earth. To be precise, we are still in Tolkien's world, but we have been brought up short by the Sea.

IV

This shore marks the literal and symbolic limit of both the natural world – itself enfolding the Shire, of course – and the domination, actual or potential, of the Ring. Thus, as Legolas recalled when he first heard the gulls at Pelargir: "The Sea! [...] Alas! for the gulls. No peace shall I have again under beech or under elm." Or as Frodo replies, when Sam comments of Rivendell that "[t]here's something of everything here", "Yes, something of everything, Sam, except the Sea." As Tolkien himself said:

> There are other things more grim and terrible to fly from than the noise, stench, ruthlessness, and extravagance of the internal-combustion engine. There are hunger, thirst, poverty, pain, sorrow, injustice [...] And lastly there is the oldest and deepest desire, the Great Escape: the Escape from Death.

And in a letter:

> there is I suppose applicability in my story to present times. But I should say, if asked, the tale is not really about Power and Dominion: that only sets the

wheels going; it is about Death and the desire for deathlessness. Which is hardly more than to say it is a tale written by a Man!

Part of his "message", he once added, was "the hideous peril of confusing true 'immortality' with limitless serial longevity. Freedom from Time, and clinging to Time [...] Compare the death of Aragorn with a Ringwraith." "Endless serial living" – what a wonderful phrase! especially in its chilling kinship, unforeseen by Tolkien, with the "serial killing" of our own day. And from the same land comes its perfect embodiment, the practice of cryogenics – that is, freezing the body immediately after physical death, in the morbid hope of subsequent revival, thanks to the literally unstoppable "progress" of science. (As someone who shares with Tolkien "a heartfelt loathing" for Disney and all his works – but also because the point would have been useful, as a marker of the vast difference between their works – I recently learned with regret that the tale of Walt Disney's frozen head is apocryphal.)

Of course, it is one thing to assert and appreciate the profound value of limits (as unfashionable in this century as it is prescient), and quite another to do so when faced with the ultimate personal Limit (so far as most of us know). Tolkien was very well aware of this, and in fact saw it as one of the keys to his beloved *Beowulf*. He called it

> the theory of courage, which is the great contribution of early Northern literature [...] It is the strength of the northern mythological imagination that it faced this problem, put the monsters in the centre, gave them victory but no honour, and found a potent but terrible solution in naked will and courage [...]

As a Christian, of course, Tolkien believed that the victory of the monsters was illusory, or at least, not final. *The Lord of the Rings* contains repeated hints about "more than one power at work," beyond even that of the greatest in Middle-earth, namely Sauron; that Bilbo was *meant* to find the Ring; about "chance-meetings", and "luck". But as Shippey says, "Mordor and 'the Shadow' are nearer and more visible." There is no question of luck or chance interfering with the exercise of free will, and at almost any point in *The Lord of the Rings*, things could have gone disastrously wrong. Indeed, what finally gave this power the opportunity to intervene at the crucial last hurdle, when Frodo is standing at the Crack of Doom, was his and Sam's stubborn persistence; plus their free exercise (and Bilbo's before them) of "Pity and Mercy". Without that, there would have been no Gollum, and Frodo would have claimed the Ring.

"Pity and Mercy" sum up why I have chosen to call this third sphere (after culture and nature) ethics. They also bring us to the question of the Christian (or otherwise) nature of *The Lord of the Rings*. Of Tolkien's own Christianity there is no doubt, but the uncomfortable relationship between that religion and nature – no time for that. The important differences between Catholicism and Protestantism – nor that. Only what Tolkien described as the "monotheistic world of natural theology" of Middle-earth. He maintained that *The Lord of the Rings*

> is of course a fundamentally religious and Catholic work; unconsciously so at first, but consciously in the revision. That is why I have not put in, or have cut out, practically all references to anything like "religion", to cults or practices, in the imaginary world. For the religious element is absorbed into the story and the symbolism.

Now it is a curious and important question why Tolkien should have *wanted* to cut out all references to religion in "a fundamentally religious work"; we shall return to it. First, and at the risk of impertinence, I want to contest this description of *The Lord of the Rings* as economical with the truth; or at least, seriously inadequate.

True, it is nominally monotheistic. At the top is God, called "the One". But as Tolkien admits, He "indeed remains remote, outside the World, and only directly accessible to the Valar or Rulers. These take the place of the 'gods', but are created spirits [...]" The One only directly intervened in history once, and that was in the momentous reshaping of the world in the Second Age. There is never the slightest suggestion that He would do so again.

The Valar, also described as "the Guardians of the World" and (interestingly) as "powers", are somewhat more present. They have at least visited Middle-earth, and one in particular – Elbereth – is the object of song, prayer and supplication in *The Lord of the Rings*. This, it seems to me, introduces a real element of polytheism into the picture, which therefore cannot, by definition, be *fundamentally* Christian.

Other aspects of *The Lord of the Rings* point to the same conclusion. For example, there is evidence of an active animism: the manifestation of the mountain

Caradhras's displeasure in snow; the herb *athelas*, that makes the air sparkle with joy; the reflection of Sauron's attack in a great engulfing cloud, and the subsequent change in the winds prefiguring the turn of the tide in the battle for Minas Tirith … This, and much else, is contained in one of Tolkien's most marvellous passages, when the Captain of the Nazgûl confronts Gandalf before the ruined gates of Minas Tirith, in the moment when the cock crows, welcoming only the morning, and "as if in answer there came from far away another note. Horns, horns, horns. In dark Mindolluin's sides they dimly echoed. Great horns of the North wildly blowing." And after the battle, "A great rain came out of the Sea, and it seemed that all things wept for Théoden and Éowyn, quenching the fires in the City with grey tears." The "as if" and "it seemed" here are plainly a sop to rationalists. When Tolkien writes that "[t]ree and stone, blade and leaf were listening," he does *not* mean it metaphorically.

Polytheism and animism are, of course, pagan by (Christian) definition, and the celebrations of 1420 are a veritable pagan feast. (One could almost say "orgy".) On Midsummer eve – not just any old day in the year –"the sky was blue as sapphire and white stars opened in the East, but the West was still golden, and the air was cool and fragrant." This is the setting for the symbolic marriage (and its subsequent consummation) of the King and his bride, Arwen Evenstar. It comes as no surprise that 1420 became famous for its weddings, and in an inverse "wasteland" effect the land too is restored to fertility. Young hobbits, you will recall, sat on the lawns under the plum-trees and ate, "until they had made piles of stones like small pyramids, or the heaped skulls of a conqueror, and then they moved on."

There are other interesting complications I can't go into: the practice of reincarnation among the Elves, for example, which Tolkien defended in reply to a Christian reader who felt he had "overstepped the mark." True, quasi-Christian grace and prophecy appear in *The Lord of the Rings*, along with tantalising traces of Christ-like attributes on the part of Gandalf and Frodo. But divination, long a *bête noir* of the Church, figures too; and in any case, all these things have far older lineages than their relatively recent Christian versions. That also applies to Eärendil. As the Morning and Evening Star, the brightest *star* in the heavens – namely, Venus – and the emblem and icon of Elbereth, his goddess of feminine compassion, Eärendil has antecedents considerably older and more precise than either angels or Mary.

It could even be said that Tolkien's religious mythology is, in one major respect, not supernatural at all, but humanistic. As Zipes has pointed out (1979), "Tolkien raises the small person, the Hobbit, to the position of God, that is, he stands at the centre of the universe [...] The spiritual world manifests itself through the actions of the redeemed small person."

None of this is intended to denigrate the Christian elements in Tolkien's work. Indeed, none of the elements I have found should be taken as somehow trumping or cancelling out the others. (I am not suggesting, for example, that *The Lord of the Rings* is either "really" or "unconsciously" pagan.) The point is the extraordinary richness and complexity of the work. And when we turn to how and why Tolkien wrote what he did, the point emerges clearly that its syncretism, including (indeed requiring) the elimination of "practically all references to anything like religion" (as we now understand it) was a conscious and deliberate decision.

The clue to this lies in Tolkien's old exemplar, the author of *Beowulf.* In his British Academy lecture (1936), Tolkien characterised the poem as "a fusion that has occurred at a given point of contact between old and new, a product of thought and deep emotion." Living in such a time, when paganism (including its "Northern courage") was succumbing to the new religion – but unevenly, and unpredictably – its author had responded to this dilemma by suppressing the specifically Christian. Is it surprising, then, that Tolkien should decide to emulate the *Beowulf*-poet, and see to it that "the religious element is absorbed into the story and the symbolism"? For he was undoubtedly keenly aware that he too lived at a given point – the other end of the same historical epoch, the "post-Christian" to *Beowulf*'s "pre-", when once again there was no single clear and over-arching set of values. Christian, pagan, humanist and many other values mix and collide; there is no single criterion by which to judge between them that is even nearly universally accepted, yet none of them is unaffected by the others. (For that reason one cannot meaningfully speak of a "return" to any of them.) And the same applies politically, socially, philosophically ... If there is one dictum that sums up this situation – and incidentally suggests a positive response – it must be Joseph Schumpeter's: "To realize the relative validity of one's convictions and yet stand for them unflinchingly is what distinguishes a civilised man from a barbarian." And it is entirely fitting, if ironic, that it is Schumpeter's civilised man, not his barbarian, who now embodies the pagan virtue of "Northern courage" that Tolkien so admired. As part of the same process, the green of leaves which used to signify barbarism is now well on its way to becoming the sign of a society sufficiently civilised to value nature.

Tolkien "realized the absurdity in post-Christian days", in Richard L. Purtill's words, "of attempting original myth." His solution was to attempt a re-creation through literary myth. In some remarks in a letter about the Arthurian myth, he finds it (he says) not only "imperfectly naturalised" (more British than English) and over-generous with *Faërie*, but

> [f]or another and more important thing: it is involved in, and explicitly contains the Christian religion.
>
> For reasons which I will not elaborate, *that seems to me fatal* […] (I am speaking, of course, of our present situation, not of ancient pagan, pre-Christian days […])

Thus Tolkien needed Frodo and the hobbits not only to give his disabused modern readers access to the ancient heroic world of Middle-earth but also as a mediation, like *The Lord of the Rings* as a whole, "between pagan myth and Christian truth" – and between that Truth and modern myth.

Actually, with his usual extraordinary attention to detail and consistency, he even implied this point within *The Lord of the Rings*. For already in Frodo's day, "[g]one was the *mythological* time when Valinor (or Valimar), the Land of the Valar (gods if you will) existed physically in the Uttermost West, or the Eldaic (Elvish) immortal Isle of Eressëa; or the Great Isle of Westernesse (Númenor-Atlantis)." The gods, whose judgement was (effectively) perfect and final, were no longer available; the seas were now bent, and anyone setting sail in search of the "ancient or True West" will simply return to their starting-point. The old "straight way" was gone, and with it all "straight sight".

V

With that, I have come to the edge of the "third sphere" in Tolkien's world (if one can speak so of something so vast and open-ended). There are of course endless loose ends. (Is Tom Shippey, for example, soft on Orcs?) But what really remains is to emphasise the overlap, or rather synthesis, of the three nested considerations – culture, nature and spirit – that I have identified. That synthesis, I believe, is what guided Tolkien himself, and still embodies the modern meaning of his work.

Out of the mirror of Englishness, for example, Tolkien picked not only the obviously appropriate – a love of nature in general and flora in particular – but native traditions of frugality, self-sufficiency and community. And it could be argued that the strongly implicit and tacit sense of the sacred that Tolkien conveys is peculiarly English.

But the interaction of "nature" and "spirit" is particularly potent. As Sam says deep in Mordor, recalling Galadriel's seemingly fantastic offers earlier: "If only the Lady could see us or hear us, I'd say to her: 'Your ladyship, all we want is light and water: just clean water and plain daylight, better than any jewels, begging your pardon.'" What haunts his thoughts is "the memory of water; and every brook or stream or fount that he had ever seen, under green willow-shades or twinkling in the sun." Meanwhile, the growing ravages of the Ring on Frodo are having precisely the reverse effect: "No taste of food, no feel of water, no sound of wind, no memory of tree or grass or flower, no image of moon or star are left to me. I am naked in the dark, Sam, and there is no veil between me and the wheel of fire." So much for the supposed other-worldliness (and tweeness) of *The Lord of the Rings*. It is in fact a work in which a deeply sensual appreciation of this world is interfused with an equally powerful sense of its ineffability. This is actually a movement within the story of *The Lord of the Rings*: from the simple, sensual appreciation of Pippin's bath song – "Oh! Water hot is a noble thing!" – to a deeper and truer appreciation of these things, in which their aesthetic, spiritual and (literally) vital dimensions are indissolubly one.

The vision at the heart of *The Lord of the Rings* is therefore indeed one of "[t]he cosmos as a whole [...] an organism at once *real, living* and *sacred*" (Mircea

Eliade). But it goes farther, because *while* we live, the sacred – although it extends "beyond the limits of the world," via death – is meaningless without its natural embodiment. (Or worse! since Tolkien identified the obscenity of "endless serial living" as one such attempt.)

Finally, this world-view is not simply opposed to "a positivist, mechanist, urbanized, and rationalist culture," but grafted onto some native cultural traditions whose survival-value has been (sorely) tried and tested. Without that, *The Lord of the Rings* would have remained a fantasy indeed. But just as Frodo and (in the end) Sam are no ordinary hobbits, so Tolkien envisages not a passive acceptance of English society as it is, but rather its radical transformation. (And note too that the efforts of the aristocratic and artistic Elves to merely preserve are explicitly doomed to failure.)

In short, Tolkien's work urges *a new ethic, based on the resacralisation of life, and the lineaments of life* – good earth, clean water, plain daylight – *that is deeply rooted in the local culture.* Nothing less will enable us to destroy the power of the Ring.

Such an ethic is no substitute, of course, for a political programme and determined local action; but then again, without it they will certainly fail. Nor is it all as ambitious as it perhaps sounds; all that is needed is for the "resacralisation" to become sufficiently widespread and powerful – *whatever* its class (or other) origins – for its effects to make a difference. A new church is not required.

Richard Mabey has seen this point clearly. In response to the crises of industrial society, he writes:

> increasingly the shape of the most promising alternatives is emerging out of what we loosely call "the rural tradition". That [...] may begin to succeed as a movement in the real world if we recognise that the experience of nature is not exclusive to a particular place or moment, a way of life or position of privilege, but is an aspect of all our individual lives and of our collective history.

And "collective" here means just that: everybody, even (potentially) your city-dwellers whose direct experience of nature is minimal, and whose "yearning for a relationship with nature and the land [is] based, not on ownership or labour, but on simple delight and sensual and spiritual renewal." For they too – despite their hopelessly middle-class, inchoately nostalgic, inauthentically "suburban and half-educated" character – are in search not only "for a modern role for the countryside," but for themselves. As Fraser Harrison puts it, recalling a remark of Hazlitt's that Nature is a kind of universal Home, "what must be conserved before anything else is the desire in ourselves for Home – for harmony, peace and love, for growth in nature and in our imaginative powers – because unless we keep this alive, we shall lose everything."

Just so, and that brings us (finally) back to *The Hobbit* and *The Lord of the Rings* as the literary artefacts with which we started out. For here is the answer to the charge that Tolkien was writing for or on behalf of a cosy elite; that his work was ideological in a strict and pejorative sense. The "desire for Home" may cut out many, but it certainly does so in no simple way that follows from class, race or gender. True, those principally feeling and actually acting on behalf of such a desire may be middle-class in origin; but the same may be said of those leading virtually every modern revolutionary movement (including those identified as Marxist). It does not follow that the benefits will be confined to people like themselves – or do others not need, let alone appreciate, clean water, good air and healthy food? And that applies to more "frivolous" things too. It is those who sneer at the middle-classness of ecologism who most patronise the masses.

In fact, as we have seen, any bias built into Tolkien's books works against a highly educated or literate, and to that extent privileged, readership; if they have an "average" or "typical" reader, it is just such an object of critical scorn as the humble city-dweller I have just described. So what is he or she getting from these books, and how, while the loremasters are engaged on weightier matters?

Let us recall Tolkien's belief that fairy-stories offer "in a peculiar degree or mode, these things: Fantasy, Recovery, Escape, Consolation [...]." When I first read *The Lord of the Rings* at the age of sixteen, after an unwitting preparation thanks to *The Hobbit*, seven years earlier, I was overcome with the unmistakable sense of having encountered a world that was more real than the one I lived in; or one, at least, whose reality was much more concentrated. Accompanying this feeling was the equally odd one of inexplicable familiarity with that world. And finally, there was a definite sense of loss when I had finished, which (combined with delight and curiosity) impelled me to immediately recommence reading it.

None of this was a unique experience on my part; to a greater or lesser degree, *The Lord of the Rings* has affected many readers in just this way, and it deserves some attempt at understanding.

Let's look at the "sense of loss" first. It is actually well described within the book itself, at the point where the Company is setting off in their boats on the Silverlode, when it seemed to them that "Lórien was slipping backward, like a bright ship masted with enchanted trees, sailing on to forgotten shores, while they sat helpless upon the margin of the grey and leafless world." This deprivation, with its unwilling return to a "grey and leafless world", can actually be hard to bear. Or again – and it is no coincidence that this incident also involves Lothlórien, "the heart of Elvendom on earth" – when Frodo was walking up Cerin Amroth, he felt that "[w]hen he had gone and passed again into the outer world, still Frodo the wanderer from the Shire would walk there […]."

That passage ought to remind us of another one, from the glory days of Edwardian children's literature: "wherever they go, and whatever happens to them on the way, in that enchanted place on the top of the Forest a little boy and his bear will always be playing." If, Dear Reader, that sort of thing makes you want (like Dorothy Parker) to throw up, Tolkien's is less likely to for a number of reasons. First, it is less important in the context of the book as a whole. Second, it is embedded in a much more sombre (and distinctly adult) view of life, with the monsters very nearly if not quite dead-centre. Third, it is important to notice that at the end of his tale, and various hints about other worlds notwithstanding, Tolkien returns us firmly to this one: at the Grey Havens, after the departure of Frodo and Gandalf, Sam "stood far into the night, hearing only the sigh and murmur of the waves on the shores of Middle-earth, and the sound of them sank deep into his heart." We stand with him. As his own definition of Recovery implies, Tolkien's "*evangelium*" permits only a "fleeting glimpse of Joy" in *this* world, not permanent transportation to the next. The nostalgia he engenders, therefore, is finally redirected back into our own lives here.

In my view, Tolkien's work awakes precisely that longing for Home, in which "pain and delight flow together and tears are the very wine of blessedness." And being a boy (or girl) is not a necessary prerequisite.

What about the sense of hyper-reality? And how could one feel it to be almost intimately familiar, upon the first reading of a book supposedly about a very different place and/or time? Here I think the word "mythology", so over-used in connection with Tolkien, is actually useful. Carl Kerenyi (1951) defined the stuff of mythology as:

> an immemorial and traditional body of material contained in tales about gods and god-like beings, heroic battles and journeys to the Underworld – tales already well-known but not unamenable to further reshaping. Myth is the *movement* of this material [...]

Furthermore, "Myth gives a ground, lays a foundation. It does not answer the question 'why?' but 'whence?'"All this fits Tolkien like a fine glove, and he could have supplied a clear answer to Kerenyi's rhetorical (and slightly plain-tive) question, "is an immediate experience and enjoyment of mythology still in any sense possible?"

His incorporation into *The Lord of the Rings* of English and "Northern" cultural traditions, including the mythological, was not just a calculated strategy; it was unavoidable for a man so thoroughly steeped in them. But they give his work a tremendous advantage over that of others, possibly otherwise similar, because those traditions still live. Thus, if I had been able to articulate my early experience of familiarity adequately at the time, I would have said it felt not so much like a discovery as a re-discovery, a reconnection with some-thing that I now see is a *living* tradition. It does not just embrace the myths attached to England as somehow a preternaturally "green and pleasant land" (although that counts too).

The result, it seems to me, is the same sense of wonder that Keats experienced upon encountering Chapman's *Homer*, for the same kind of reason in relation to our Greek cultural heritage; only Tolkien has performed this service (with infinitely less thanks), in relation to that of "North-west Europe", for later, larger and less "literary" generations. And again, none the less or worse for that! Amanda Craig once quoted *Private Eye* to the effect that *The Lord of the Rings* appeals only to "computer programmers, hippies and most Americans" (1992). She nicely puts this to work, observing that "[t]he fact that Tolkien's world appeals to computer programmers is possibly less a sign that it is infantile than that he developed a hypnotic style and narrative which quickens the reluctantly literate as well as the devoutly bookish. Few writers in any century can claim the same."

As for the hyper-reality of Middle-earth, one would have to be a pretty unreconstructed positivist to say that such things as mythologies, let alone cultural traditions, are somehow less real than say, the proverbial table; or even to say that they did not contain, however coded, a great deal of *emotion* in the form of accumulated human experience: hopes, wishes, fears ... Tolkien's books present a highly distilled and concentrated (albeit also highly selective) version of just that.

This analysis accords with Tolkien's own experience of writing *The Lord of the Rings*, in which it "grew", he "was drawn irresistibly" toward certain things, and "discovery" felt much more the case than "invention". If one reacts as reader in the manner I have described, it is impossible to feel that this was mere rhetoric designed to enhance his creation. And Middle-earth was emphatically not "created": certainly not, at least, in the fashionable modern sense of creation *ex nihilo*. It was a *co-creation*, in partnership with some very old and durable cultural materials. It would be unduly extravagant – or worse, fundamentalist – to say that he literally discovered Middle-earth. But neither did he simply invent it.

Whether his books are defined as quest or fairy-story or "myth" and "low mimesis" and "irony" all embedded deeply in romance, they are certainly storytelling of a kind long unfashionable as an adult genre. But giving "mythic" its full cultural and historical due allows us to see Tolkien's uniqueness more clearly. Within the baggy genre of "fantasy", for example, it is what raises *The Lord of the Rings* above even well-written books that however embody a more purely personal mythology, like David Lindsay's *Voyage to Arcturus* and Mervyn Peake's Gothic "Gormenghast" trilogy, and Freudian-fantastic fables by Angela Carter (1985); let alone meretricious fiction like Lindsay Clarke's *The Chymical Wedding*, a kind of literary "Twin Peaks".

The only books I can think of that seem strictly comparable to *The Lord of the Rings*, in the terms in which 1 have analysed it here, are Herman Melville's *Moby-Dick*, Mikhail Bulgakov's *The Master and Margarita*, and Russell Hoban's

Riddley Walker. They too draw their power from a profound and startlingly fresh connection with mythic aspects of the Judaeo-Christian cultural tradition (though not, of course, Tolkien's unique "Northern" contribution). And they have also presented literary critics with intractable problems, who are usually obliged to treat them, in the end, as *sui generis.* Except maybe for Hoban's, they could also all be described as life-works.

This is Tolkien's true company of peers. He is saved by his deep and tough roots in a particular cultural soil from the extraordinarily deracinated (and therefore shallow) universalism of *Star Wars*, with its bargain-basement Jungian archetypes, eulogised by Joseph Campbell; and by his brilliant re-creation of myth from the ghastly death-in-life of Disney's imitation, with its plastic grass and "genuine replica" fairy castles.

His books, and along with it his many readers, are fully deserving of critical respect – even a little passionate attention. They are not only a cry (as Marx said of religion) from "the heart of a heartless world, the soul of soulless conditions," but a plea for what I have called the resacralisation of life. That plea gleams with an ancient hope: peace within and among people, and between people and nature. Indeed, Tolkien's own personal epitaph might be the parting words to Aragorn or *Estel* from his mother: "I gave Hope to the Dúnedain, 1 have kept no hope for myself."

Bibliography

CARTER, Angela. 1985. *Black Venus*. London: Chatto and Windus.

CRAIG, Amanda. 1992. "Lord of all he conveyed, despite his fans." *The Independent*, 25 January 1992.

HARRISON, Fraser. 1984. "England, Home and Beauty." In Richard MABEY with Susan CLIFFORD and Angela KIND (eds.). 1984. *Second Nature*. London: Jonathan Cape, 162-172.

HARRISON, Robert Pogue. 1992. *Forests: The Shadow of Civilization*. Chicago IL: University of Chicago Press.

HARVEY, David. 1985. *The Song of Middle- earth*. London: George Allen & Unwin.

JORDANOVA, Ludmilla. 1987. "The Interpretation of Nature: A Review Article." *Comparative Studies in Society and Nature*, 29.1 (January 1987): 195-200.

KAVENEY, Roz. 1992. "The Ring Recycled." *New Statesman and Society* (20/27 December 1992), 47.

KERENYI, Carl. 1951. "Prolegomena", in C. G. JUNG and C. KERENYI, *Introduction to a Science of Mythology: The Myth of the Divine Child and the Mysteries of Eleusis*, pp. 1-32. London: Routledge and Kegan Paul.

KILBY, Clyde. 1977. *Tolkien and The Silmarillion*. Berkhamstead: Lion Publishing.

MABEY, Richard. 1984. "Introduction: Entitled to a View?" In Richard MABEY with Susan CLIFFORD and Angela KIND (eds.). 1984. *Second Nature*. London: Jonathan Cape, ix-xix.

ORWELL, George. 1940. "The Lion and the Unicorn: Socialism and the English Genius".

PURTILL, Richard L. 1984. *J.R.R. Tolkien: Myth, Morality, and Religion*. San Francisco CA: Harper & Row.

SHIPPEY, T. A. 1982. *The Road to Middle-Earth*. London: George Allen & Unwin.

STIMPSON, Catherine R. 1969. *J.R.R. Tolkien*. (Columbia Essays on Modern Writers 41). New York: Columbia University Press.

THOMAS, Keith. 1983. *Man and the Natural World: Changing Attitudes in England 1500-1800*. London: Allen Lane.

TOLKIEN, John Ronald Reuel. 1936. *Beowulf: The Monsters and the Critics*. London: The British Academy.

1978. *The Hobbit*. Fourth edition. London: George Allen & Unwin.

1981. *Letters of J.R.R. Tolkien*. Edited by Humphrey CARPENTER, with the assistance of Christopher TOLKIEN. London: George Allen & Unwin.

1988. "On Fairy-Stories." In *Tree and Leaf*. London: Unwin Hyman. (The original essay was first delivered as a lecture in 1939, and first published, somewhat enlarged, in 1947.)

1991. *The Lord of the Rings*. First edition 1954-55. London: Grafton/HarperCollins.

WEINER, Martin J. 1985. *English Culture and the Decline of the Industrial Spirit 1850-1980*. Harmondsworth: Penguin.

WILLIAMS, Raymond. 1985. *The Country and the City*. London: Hogarth Press.

ZIPES, Jack. 1979. *Breaking the Magic Spell*. London: Heinemann.

Modernity in Middle-earth

T*he Lord of the Rings* is a book that can be appreciated, and celebrated, in many different ways. In my study of it, *Defending Middle-earth: Tolkien, Myth and Modernity*, I concentrated on its contemporary meaning – what Tolkien called its "applicability" ("Foreword" to the second edition of *The Lord of the Rings*) – in cultural, social and political terms. This is not to deny its other strengths: as a remarkable feat of narrative, as an extraordinary work of philology and linguistics, or as a deeply felt meditation on the meaning of human life when faced with inevitable death. But neither should these aspects obscure the first set of meanings, which Tolkien's hostility to literal-minded allegory, certainly correct in itself, has tended to obscure. In any case, it is highly simplistic to see his book in just one way, to the exclusion of others. If, for example, it is "about Death and the desire for deathlessness" (in Tolkien's own words), can it not also be concerned with the drive for worldly "Power and Domination" (*Letters* 246)? Indeed, does this not suggest that the former may be the very motor of the latter?

To this extent, as I have argued, Tolkien's work that has had the greatest public impact is an account of resistance to the contemporary threat to three great goods, nested one inside another. First there is community: the hobbits, social to the ends of their well-brushed toes, and firmly rooted in their place, the Shire. Next there is nature: Middle-earth itself in all its wonders, from talking trees (emphatically not tree-like humans) to malevolent mountains, encompassing not only the Shire but every other place and its related race. Then there are spiritual values: the Sea, which alone escapes the compass of Middle-earth, over which lies the *fons et origo* of its history and healing from its travails, something which the Ringbearers are finally granted. Where these dimensions overlap is the heart of Tolkien's tale. Finally, in stark contrast, the

First published in Joseph Pearce (ed.). 1999. *Tolkien: A Celebration*. London: HarperCollins, 34-39.

single-visioned, imperialist perfection of power that threatens the survival of these three – after whom *The Lord of the Rings* is named, and the text of which emphasises is the strongest in Middle-earth – is, of course, embodied in Sauron and Mordor.

It is also very much to the point that Tolkien's tale is set in an imaginary (distant) time, but its place is the "mother-earth" (*Letters* 283) that we all share. And our Middle-earth, as Tolkien clearly perceived, is also in grave danger: communities steadily replaced by congeries of consumers; the natural support-systems of our own and other species (those that remain: the big mammals, like the great forests, are going fast) destroyed at an unprecedented and utterly unsustainable rate; and any ultimate values denied beyond bread and circuses: instrumental knowledge, material consumption and sensational entertainment. This is the culmination of a process that began to show itself in the seventeenth century, achieved self-consciousness in the eighteenth, developed new forms and strength in the nineteenth, and continues ever more powerfully (if still unevenly) in our own, under the banner of economic globalisation. My shorthand term for it is "modernity", but it has at least three main strands which can be distinguished (but not separated), all of which Tolkien's work calls into fundamental question: the nation-state, science and technology, and financial capital. Thus, insofar as *The Lord of the Rings* is about this world, we find ourselves reading an account of how, beyond foretelling, it was saved from the final triumph of this power.

The overwhelming reception of such an otherwise utterly unlikely book – around fifty million copies sold world-wide, to date, in at least thirty languages – is evidence, I think, that Tolkien's insights, fears and hopes in relation to modernity strike a profound chord with the reading public. Indeed, in addition to its affinities with "human nature", what has made his book, with its local, even parochial roots, an effectively universal literary phenomenon, is precisely the global extent of the crisis it addresses.

Of course, the other aspect of that phenomenon is the incomprehension and/or visceral hostility of most of its professional literary critics. But this simply confirms my explanation. Of course, just as *The Lord of the Rings* has more than one aspect or dimension, it is quite possible to dislike it for different reasons: on grounds of literary taste, for example, or religious or philosophical disagreement. But the dominant charge against Tolkien has been that of escapism and/or reaction; and the overwhelming majority of these critics, as is evident from their other writings, subscribe to the very same values of modernity – statism, scientism, economism and secularism – which are implicated in the pathological dynamic that so alarmed Tolkien, and still deeply worries his readers today. However inchoately, they perceive the cultural nihilism, social upheaval and ecological destruction that the ideology of Progress tries to disguise; and however mixed their feelings about it, they are not fooled. But the educated elite of *clercs*, by and large, is, because they have conveniently fooled themselves. As Tolkien memorably put it, they confuse, "not always by sincere error, the Escape of the Prisoner with the Flight of the Deserter" (OFS 56). And for whom is "escapism" such a crime? For the jailers, naturally, of whatever kind.

The term commonly associated with "escapism" is, of course, "fantasy". But the irony here becomes apparent when we ask, who exactly is indulging in fantasy: those who, like Tolkien, find community, nature and the spirit worth fighting for (and as do the protagonists in *The Lord of the Rings*, literally); or those who claim that science is the only legitimate kind of knowledge, that economic growth can continue forever, that nature can sustain whatever we do to her – and that we have a right to do to her whatever we want?

Tolkien deserves credit for having perceived the destructive consequences of modernity long before the great majority of his peers, and his fears have been strikingly confirmed; while the panglossian promises of the modernists, humanists and technocrats – including their literary apologists – are repeatedly deferred, never to be realised. Perhaps his prescience is not altogether surprising. As a conservative Anglo-Catholic medievalist, he was sufficiently marginal to the mainstream to see the modern world relatively objectively, yet sufficiently erudite to contextualise and articulate his perceptions (and creative, to embody them artistically). Yet he also deserves acclaim for his courage in swimming against such a powerful tide.

What is the situation now? Tolkien once remarked (in 1959) that "I look East, West, North, South, and I do not see Sauron; but I see that Saruman has many descendants" (van Rossenberg 1995: 308; *Letters* 235). Let us pay him the compliment of taking him at his word. After the main events of the War of the Ring, Saruman still managed to inflict great damage on the Shire: a kind of damage we are indeed all too familiar with today as "development". It is an institutionalisation of the relentless drive for short-term profit for a powerful few. And like the activities of Sharkey, its effects are socially divisive and fragmenting, ecologically destructive, and in all senses unsustainable. True, it is not Mordor triumphant, not the more direct infliction of evil (or the infliction of more open evil) of this century, such as in the heydays of Nazism, Stalinism and Maoism. But in the not-so-long term, if unchecked, the results will converge. As various references in *The Lord of the Rings* point out, Saruman was still doing Mordor's work, even after the passing of Sauron.

It is hard to see how global modernisation could be checked, let alone halted – without, at least, a cure at least as terrible as the disease. Yet Tolkien's moral legacy is not despair, but hope; as Gandalf rightly says, "despair is only for those who see the end beyond all doubt. We do not" (FR.II.ii). Like Frodo, Sam and the rest of the Company, our duty is plain: not to give up, but do what we each can for the things, places and people (non-human as well) that we know and love. And although Tolkien was careful to specify that such hope is "without guarantees" (*Letters* 237) – including, I would add, religious or even specifically Christian ones – the success of the Ringbearer's mission does, I think, give people hope that we too may win through, and live to wake up in a world of relative security, peace and dignity. Far from encouraging quietism, such hope enables and encourages people to act. It forms a virtuous circle, I think, with two other aspects of Tolkien's work: the love of, and power of, place; and the value of sheer wonder.[1] Taken together, for those who are not already too far gone, his mythopoeic fiction can fulfil one of the chief virtues of the myths and fairytales which are its literary forebears: recovery.[2]

This would be remarkable enough. But *The Lord of the Rings* is still, in a profound way, about inevitable loss, and the passing away – simply with time, but specifically with the passing of the three Elven rings – of many fair things. So

---

1 See my *Defending Middle-earth*, chapter 6.
2 See OFS 53-54.

not anthropomorphic, i.e. honorary humans, but sentient trees. They share the sentience with us, and exist in relationship with us, but they are also profoundly other; and in that important sense, independent of us.

Such a world is one that has not yet become disenchanted and commodified; given that so much of our world has, Tolkien's work amounts to a re-enchantment. It restores to his readers a glimpse of a long-lost world that, as in all tales told of once-upon-a-time, could equally well be in the future: a good instance of what Fraser Harrison has termed "radical nostalgia". That is why so many readers turn to it for renewal and hope.

It is, appropriately, a world of both nature and religion, except that what the modern concepts have sundered into the "material" and the "spiritual" or "supernatural" are experienced as inseparable . This was where our Paleolithic and Mesolithic ancestors lived, and it still survives – fragmented, and under severe stress – among surviving indigenous peoples today. That survival depends upon narratives: the collective, ritualized stories that are usually called "myth". And ultimately, as Sean Kane writes, "[t]he proper subject of myth is the ideas and emotions of the earth" (1994: 34). Tolkien, who drew so heavily on myth, fashioned its literary re-creation, in which narrative, place and personality are, as in aboriginal Dreamtime, all entwined. This is no insignificant cultural contribution to meeting the challenge of rediscovering geophanic wisdom, without which the present onslaught of secular and instrumental economic reason threatens to become irresistible.

For Tolkien himself, this aspect of his work presented certain problems; it existed in complex tension with his commitments to Catholicism. On the one hand, the latter (unlike Protestantism) is traditionally roomy enough to accommodate all manner of spiritual entities; on the other, its theism demands that one stop well short of allowing them full independence of God. Nor is the Earth permitted a final say, so to speak. So Frodo's experience of a tree in Lórien is one of its intrinsic value: "He felt a delight in wood and the touch of it, neither as forester nor as carpenter; it was the delight of the living tree itself" (FR.II.vi). But at other times, there is a definite ethic of Christian stewardship, as in Sam's responsibility for renewing (with Galadriel's help) the post-war Shire.

There are also conflicts in Tolkien's literary mythology; "the One" is almost entirely nominal, but the Valar (gods) are already human in form if not in power. Whereas humans are blessed or cursed (it is not finally clear which) with final transcendence, the immortal Elves are profoundly ambiguous: simultaneously humanoid and chthonic, always returning to the Earth even after death, if killed. And in his initial attempt at foundational myth in *The Silmarillion*, the Two Trees bore the Sun and Moon as fruit; but Tolkien found this ancient cosmogony increasingly uncomfortable, and subsequently spent many years trying (unsuccessfully) to replace it with a more astronomically and theologically acceptable account.

Few of his readers have felt constrained by such doubts, however. Rather they have responded to his work in their own way, framed by their own time. And for most of them – certainly from the 1970s on – that has been a time of global ecological crisis, with all its attendant suffering, fear and uncertainty. As Fangorn, the chief Ent, puts it from a tree's point-of-view: "I am not altogether on anybody's side, because nobody is altogether on my side, if you understand me: nobody cares for the woods as I care for them [...]. But it seems that the wind is setting East, and the withering of all woods may be drawing near" (TT. III.iv). And at the centre of that storm is the Ring of Power, whose modern incarnation is what Lewis Mumford aptly termed "the megamachine".

Thus it not surprising that *The Lord of the Rings* – a book about the unforeseen defeat, against all the odds, of that power – was an inspirational text for the late David McTaggart, founder of Greenpeace; and in *samizdat* form among the underground resistance (environmental as well as political) in the USSR and communist Central Europe; and for those "eco-warriors" nonviolently resisting the imposition of senseless new roads in Britain (at Twyford Down, Newbury, Bath and elsewhere), whose courage and ingenuity set the standard for environmental activism throughout the 1990s and beyond – to say nothing of millions of people trying to live constructively in smaller but no less significant ways. Tolkien's Middle-earth has never been more relevant, and new generations of appreciative readers will continue to find themselves there.

Bibliography

ABRAM, David. 1996. *The Spell of the Sensuous: Perception and Language in a More-Than-Human World.* New York: Vintage Books.

CURRY, Patrick. 2004. *Defending Middle-earth: Tolkien, Myth and Modernity.* Second edition. First edition 1997. Boston: Houghton Mifflin.

HARRISON, Fraser. 1984. "England, Home and Beauty." In Richard MABEY, Susan CLIFFORD and Angela KING (eds.). 1984. *Second Nature.* London: Jonathan Cape, 162-172 .

KANE, Sean. 1994. *Wisdom of the Mythtellers.* Peterborough: Broadview Press.

RESNIK, Henry. 1967. "An Interview with Tolkien (March 2, 1966)." *Niekas* 18: 37-43.

VELDMAN, Meredith. 1994. *Fantasy, the Bomb, and the Greening of Britain: Romantic Protests 1945-1980.* Cambridge: Cambridge University Press.

Review of *Ents, Elves, and Eriador: The Environmental Vision of J.R.R. Tolkien*, by Matthew Dickerson and Jonathan Evans. Lexington: University of Kentucky Press, 2006

This book is a major new contribution to the subject of Tolkien's work in relation to the natural world and environmentalism. Whether it is a good one, however, is much less clear.

Let me start by sketching out some of the context necessary to understand and evaluate it. Much of that context comprises what is now called "green studies" or, more narrowly but increasingly, "ecocriticism". Inspired by the environmental and ecological movements, this new field in the humanities is concerned with the relationships between human culture and non-human nature in all possible respects, including the political, social, religious, aesthetic and ethical. It can thus be seen as a major new addition to the slightly earlier critical perspectives of socialism (class), feminism (gender) and post-colonialism (race).

Ecocriticism as a discipline began in the late 1980s in the USA and slightly later in the UK. Its leading American scholars include Cheryll Glotfelty, William Howarth, Karl Kroeber and Laurence Buell; in Britain the work of Jonathan Bate has been especially influential. The principal academic organization is ASLE: the Association for the Study of Literature and the Environment.

Traditions of ecologically-oriented literature, of course, are much older. Major figures include William Wordsworth, John Ruskin, William Morris, Edward Thomas and D.H. Lawrence. In America, Ralph Waldo Emerson and Henry David Thoreau are central. And, to bring matters somewhat closer to home, in a collection edited by Laurence Coupe entitled *The Green Studies Reader* (2000), I argued that J.R.R. Tolkien deserves a place in such a context and company.

First published in *Tolkien Studies* 4 (2007) pp. 238-244.

Turning to the volume under review, then, what is indisputably good? The authors have devised an ingenious and useful distinction between agriculture for food (the domain of Hobbits), horticulture for aesthetic beauty (that of Elves), and feraculture – from Latin *ferus/fera*, wild – for wilderness preservation (Ents). Also original is the application of certain concepts from the interface of ecology and literary studies: liminality, ecotones and thick margins. More generally, the thorough discussion of Christian stewardship as an environmental ethic, and especially its central role in Tolkien's thought and writings, including his lesser work, is lovingly detailed and well-supported by a good grasp of Catholic theology.

However, the central hope of the authors is to provide "a good introduction [...] to the whole environment of Middle-earth." Here there are serious problems about which readers must be warned, lest they are tempted to accept the book in such terms. To begin with, the novice (who will probably form the majority of readers) is given almost no idea of just such a context as I have outlined. Further serious problems follow from the authors' three subsidiary and closely-linked positions: (1) that a Christian environmental ethic is the best one; (2) that Tolkien's attitude to nature as found in his books is fundamentally Christian; and (3) that no non-Christian work on the subject is worth discussing. I shall take these in order.

"In our view," the authors write, "the best foundation for an environmental consciousness is a Christian one identical with, or at least comparable to, Tolkien's" (26). In practice, however, "best" translates in this case as something quite different, namely "only". (Later on they aver that "Christianity is by no means the only religion that recognizes the spiritual significance of nature" (253) but this is a purely token gesture.) In a book with ambitions to join the ranks of contemporary ecocriticism (as mentioned in John Elder's Foreword), such exclusivity is unacceptable.

No one judging by this book would realize that Christian stewardship is but one of several kinds of environmental ethics, the others being very different and at least equally important and influential. The reader of this review is referred to my introduction to the subject (Curry 2006); suffice it to say that these authors omit any mention whatsoever of Deep Ecology or its variants (e.g., Transpersonal Ecology, Deep Green Theory, Left Biocentrism), ecofemi-nism, Gaia Theory or the Land Ethic. By the same token, Arne Naess, George Sessions, Richard Sylvan, Edward Abbey, James Lovelock and Val Plumwood make no appearance. (The Land Ethic is mentioned once (47) but associated solely with Gandalf; Aldo Leopold's name also shows up elsewhere in a list of contemporary environmental writers (259) which borders on the eccentrically selective.)

"Pagan animism" is also mentioned only once (53), and that in context of a quotation from Lynn White. There is no suggestion that pagan animism might offer a powerful, still surviving (despite violent suppression by monotheists) and much older alternative – not necessarily as a fringe religion but also as an articulation and refinement of common feelings about, and experiences of, nature.

The authors' unbalanced discussion of White's famous essay "The Historical Roots of Our Ecological Crisis" is of a piece with their approach as a whole. Despite the obvious implication of Christianity, as a matter of historical record, in environmental despoliation – if not as a direct cause, then as useful ideologi-cal justification – they are unwilling to concede him any significant degree of truth. So too with their discussion of the notorious injunctions of Genesis 1:26 and 1:28, giving humans "dominion" over the Earth and ordering them to "subdue" and "rule over" all other inhabitants. The authors' interpretation is as idealistic (in both senses) as the common understanding of those passages, which they skate over, has been otherwise. Consequently, when they assert that exploitation of nature is "radically at odds with Christian faith," it is comparable to maintaining that Islam is a religion of peace and Marxism is a philosophy of liberation. They may be, metaphysically; and perhaps they should be, in earthly reality; but *in effect, on the ground* – where, I would say, it matters most – the truth of all three assertions should be radically doubted.

The authors extol "the special place humans have in creation" (52), since ap-parently "humankind is not *merely* part of the natural order" (65): all part of the all-too-familiar story of humans deciding they are special (read, as it has been read: superior):

To an animal – a squirrel, for example – a tree is *nothing more* than a source of nuts, a place to escape from predators, and a nesting site. But if humans are more than *mere* animals, if their being transcends *mere* physical existence in some way, they can see a tree as something more (63) [my emphases].

Such dispiriting contempt for nature (not to mention presumption: how do they know this about squirrels, I wonder?) hardly seems part of a promising environmental ethic; and it is not improved by religious legitimation.

Great stress is laid on the "transcendent" character of Christian stewardship, beginning with the principle that "[t]he universe is the work of a divine creator" (24). But this may be the heart of the problem; the natural world does not have any intrinsic value but is valued only as an *instance* of something else greater, that is, as the handiwork of God. To make matters still worse, it is profoundly anthropocentric: "Arda is brought into being for the Children of Ilúvatar – for Elves and Men" (51). Hence it has no value or purpose *in itself.*

Contrast that with Sean Kane's (1998: 255) point: "all the work that various peoples have done – all the work that peoples must do – to live with the Earth on the Earth's terms is pre-empted by the dream of transcendence." Or Ronald Hepburn's (1984: 181-82): values and experiences

are essentially the result of a cooperation of man and non-human nature: the universe would not contain them, were it not for our perceptual-creative efforts, and were it not equally for the contribution of the non-human world that both sustains and sets limits to our lives. To realize that [shows] our earth-rootedness even in our aspirations. There is no wholly-other paradise from which we are excluded; the only transcendence that can be real to us is an "immanent" one.

I don't cite this alternative view to show that the authors are necessarily mistaken. The point is that there is no such discussion in *Ents, Elves, and Eriador.* Rather, Christian stewardship is misleadingly presented as constituting the whole of environmental ethics. (On other religions – which themselves do not exhaust that subject – see the excellent series published by Harvard University Press on "Religions of the World and Ecology".)

Turning to Tolkien's work, the same problem persists. It is taken as self-evident that since "Tolkien's environmental ethic was firmly rooted in a deeply Christian, Catholic understanding of the world and its creator" (xxii), it follows that his "environmental vision is a profoundly meaningful outgrowth of his Catholicism and is therefore, at bottom, Christian" (24). The trouble is two-fold.

(1) Tolkien certainly wrote as a Christian, but not *only* as a Christian. (They apparently recognize this – "*The Lord of the Rings* is a philological novel inspired by philological principles" (129) and "Tolkien wanted above all to tell a good story" (139) – but once again, these are gestures with no weight.) And in keeping with the authors' narrowly Christian programme, the fact that Tolkien also had a passionate interest in pagan Northern European mythology is ignored, along with its significant environmental implications.

(2) It does not actually follow that because Tolkien was Christian, his work is. No more does it follow that "[i]n a book whose subject is Tolkien's environmental ethic [...] stewardship is the appropriate term [because] it is the term Tolkien used in his writing [...] with full awareness of its implications for Christian belief" (40). Here the authors manage to combine both genetic and intentional fallacies. Nor will it do to invoke transcendent principles "in the sense that they are based on something beyond the personal preference of the author or of any one character or group of characters inside or outside the story in any particular time or culture" (25). This is essentialism with a vengeance, placing any "transcendent" assertions beyond meaningful criticism.

I would add that the attempt to fit Bombadil and Beorn into the box of Christian stewardship is also, significantly, highly unconvincing. Even in Tolkien's own assessment, Bombadil is a nature spirit (not something Christianity has been all that keen about, on the whole) whose ethos, as described by Goldberry to Frodo – "The trees and the grasses and all things growing or living in the land belong each to themselves" – is an encapsulation not of theistic stewardship (which is, after all, a kind of ownership, even if in someone else's stead) but of precisely animistic and, to that extent, pagan intrinsic value, as well as a pointer to the other presences in Tolkien's complex work which these authors have chosen to ignore. As for Beorn, he is first and foremost a shamanistic shape-shifter (!) and if a steward, decidedly a ruthless Machiavellian not a forgiving Christian one.

Crucially, in addition to the fallacies and errors just noted, the authors show no awareness that the meaning of a book is a highly complex amalgam of what the author has put into it *plus* what readers are finding in it – a very different matter. (This lacuna corresponds exactly to their determination that since a religion "is" only what it was purportedly intended to be, there is no need to take into account what it has been *taken* to be.)

In short, the authors' exegesis of Tolkien's environmentalism is both uncritical and unself-critical. In relation to ecocriticism generally and Tolkien studies in particular, it is therefore decidedly regressive.

Finally (3), the authors of this book are equally selective, not to say sectarian, about which prior work they choose to acknowledge and discuss. Setting aside the lack of discussion of ecocriticism as a whole, perhaps the most egregious example concerns my own. I write this in no spirit of proprietorship nor pique; what is at stake is scholarly standards. Thus, several scholars, including myself, are politely dismissed as having "addressed in a more specific, even narrowly academic manner, [what] we address on a broader and more thorough popular level" (xviii). This is highly misleading. *Defending Middle-earth: Tolkien, Myth and Modernity* was (so far as I know) not only the first full-length work to concentrate on Tolkien's environmental vision but one written precisely for the general reader rather than the academic specialist. (It has received some sharp criticism, even dismissal, on both accounts!)

So, for example, there is a section here, entitled "Myth and Wonder", in which the authors discuss how, by bringing "readers into contact with the mythical dimension of reality, and by showing the transcendent, even sacred, spiritual dimensions of nature in everyday life, Tolkien's story engenders a similar appreciation of the real world among his readers" (233). Yet unmentioned is the fact that a decade ago, in the same book about the meaning of *The Lord of the Rings* in this world – to which, I argued, it returns us – and which includes chapters specifically on myth and wonder, I defined Tolkien's literary project as "the resacralization (or re-enchantment) of experienced and living nature, including human nature, in the local cultural idiom" (29).

Why this lack of common academic courtesy or, for that matter, charity? The answer is surely plain: because my book was not written from a Christian perspective. But is that sufficient reason not to even mention previous work (in a field where there is little enough of it), and in such an obviously related context (even if only to go on to disagree with it)? No, it is not; this is simply poor practice. (I would also like to reassure readers that despite this book's bibliography, Joseph Pearce did not write my essay "Tolkien and his Critics: A Critique.")

This has been a severe review, and some may be tempted to reach for an easy explanation. But I have been equally sharp about dogmatic secular Tolkien criticism (in the same essay). Dogmatic religious criticism, however – of any kind – is no better. Let me be quite clear: if the authors of *Ents, Elves, and Eriador* had described their subject as Christian stewardship, Tolkien's commitment to that ideal and its presence in his work, without pretending that there is no other significant kind of environmental ethics, that Tolkien had no other significant commitments which affected his work in this respect (never mind how that work has been taken up), and that no earlier work on this subject is worth considering, then it would be a very different matter, and this would be a very different review. Regrettably, they chose otherwise. The result is both disingenuous and tendentious.

Works Cited

COUPE, Laurence (ed.). 2000. *The Green Studies Reader: From Romanticism to Ecocriticism*. London, Routledge.

CURRY, Patrick. 2004. *Defending Middle-earth: Tolkien, Myth and Modernity*. Second edition. First edition 1997. Boston: Houghton Mifflin.

2005. "Tolkien and his Critics: A Critique." In Thomas HONEGGER (ed.). 2005. *Root and Branch: Approaches Towards Understanding Tolkien*. Second edition. First edition 1999. Zurich and Berne: Walking Tree Publishers, 75-146.[1]

2006. *Ecological Ethics: An Introduction*. Cambridge: Polity Press.

---

1 Reprinted on pages 125-90 of the present volume.

KANE, Sean. 1998. *Wisdom of the Mythtellers*. Second edition. Peterborough: Broadview Press.

HEPBURN, Ronald. 1984. *"Wonder" and Other Essays*. Edinburgh: Edinburgh University Press.

As a matter of philosophical, practical and historical fact, these two share extensive common ground – much more than what divides them. The principal goal of both is to engineer changes in the Primary world, and both try to amass knowledge in order to predict and control that world; both adhere to the idea of laws of nature which can be manipulated for human gain. That those laws are spiritual or occult in the case of magic and material in the case of science is a point of ultimately secondary importance. Nothing in Aleister Crowley's idea of magic (quoted in *Pagan Dawn* 124, Lammas 1997)– "the art of bringing about changes in conformity with will" – would greatly upset a contemporary scientist, except perhaps for calling it an art instead of a science.

Historically speaking, a great deal of "natural magic" went into the making of modern science in the late seventeenth century, when the latter absorbed, adapted and renamed much of the former. This is especially true of the Baconian programme, Newton's work, and the Royal Society, one of whose founder members, Elias Ashmole (1652: 445), defined magic as "the Connexion of naturall Agents and Patients, answerable each to other, wrought by a wise Man to the bringing forth of such effects as are wonderfull to those that know not their causes." Specifying what kind of "natural Agents" were involved was, and continues to be, a turf war internal to Magic. Nor has the popular incomprehension of science, which continues to render its effects "wonderfull" to the public, changed much; how many people really understand telephones, let alone computers, or quantum physics?

Sometimes the magical nature of modern science is openly admitted, and even exploited: as with General Electric's corporate research laboratory, the first in the USA, which was touted as a "house of magic", staffed by white-coated "wizards".[4] More often, however, it is strenuously denied in a way that highlights the tendentiousness of the magic/science opposition. For that is to accept the dubious and self-interested claims of scientific spokespersons to have transcended states of magical enchantment – a.k.a. "superstition", "ideology", or "false consciousness" – and by virtue of a state of disinterested and disenchanted reason, to have seen and described the world "as it actually is." Thus we pass

---

4 *New Scientist*, October 11th 1997, p. 50. (Thanks to C.J. Moore for this reference.)

all too easily from rationality to rationalism, and from science to scientism, the cult of scientific reason (see Feyerabend 1987).

Tolkien's distinction between Magic and Enchantment undermines this convenient intellectual deception. It enables us to see that the tension between these two different ways of knowing and of valuing[5] exists within probably every major human discourse: in science, for example, between instrumentalist-utilitarian knowledge of the natural world enabling its exploitation, and deep appreciation of its extraordinary wonders. True, the former dominates; but there are sufficient exemplars of scientific wonder for its own sake (David Attenborough and Loren Eisley spring to mind) to show that it doesn't do so absolutely. Within magic too – whether the occult arts, New Ageism or neo-paganism – there is an ineradicable tension between the attempted manipulation of spiritual forces for power on the one hand and the worship of ultimate spiritual mysteries on the other. And by the same token, none of these domains can claim to be free of metaphysical, cultural or practical assumptions, or to have an exclusive franchise on the truth (see e.g. Smith 1997).

However, Tolkien's definition of Enchantment needs some further unpacking. If it was simply cognate with art, the result would be to replace one stereotypical cultural assumption – magic vs. science – with another, namely C.P. Snow's "two cultures" of science (as Magic) and art. But I don't think this is the case. It is true that Enchantment "is artistic in desire and purpose" (OFS 49) and usually involves the creation of a Secondary World; but its prerequisite is "the realization, independent of the conceiving mind, of imagined wonder" (OFS 18). In other words (or so I take it), Enchantment must indispensably include an experience of wonder as a reality that, so far as the person(s) involved are concerned, could otherwise or hitherto only ever have been imagined. (Note that it need not have actually been imagined – i.e. by the conceiving mind.)

Such an experience, which most of us have probably tasted at least once or twice in our lives, is indeed an essential goal of art, but it is not confined to art. Furthermore, art in this respect draws its provenance – perhaps even its meaning – from such experiences in and of the "real" world, which it seeks to

---

5 Formally speaking, epistemologies and axiologies.

re-create; a Secondary World can only use the materials, psychological as well as artistic, of the Primary. Enchantment therefore cannot be confined to art; and this actually accords well with Tolkien's otherwise somewhat baffling equation of Enchantment with "Faërian Drama", the usual effect of which "(upon a man) is to go beyond Secondary Belief. If you are present at a Faërian drama you yourself are, or think that you are, bodily inside its Secondary World [...]. To experience directly a Secondary World: the potion is too strong, and you give to it Primary belief, however marvellous the events" (OFS 49).

In any case, Tolkien is certainly right that Enchantment does not consist of a willed suspension of disbelief: you "believe it, while you are, as it were, inside. The moment disbelief arises, the spell is broken; the magic, or rather the art, has failed. You are then out in the Primary World again, looking at the little abortive Secondary World from the outside" (OFS 36-37). This too is not an experience confined to art; think of the attitude of enthralled participants in sexual congress, compared to the disenchanted view of Lord Chesterfield (Winokur 1987: 250): "The pleasure is momentary, the position ridiculous, and the expense damnable." The same gulf separates those who are "inside" from those on the "outside" of mystical experience, or even, say, a football game. True, it is possible to suspend disbelief, but that "is a substitute for the real thing, a subterfuge we use when condescending to games or make-believe, or when trying (more or less willingly) to find what virtue we can in the work of an art that has for us failed" (OFS 37). And unlike Magic, whatever Enchantment may involve it is not the will (as such). *It just happens*

Complications

I am not suggesting that the divide between Magic and Enchantment is absolute; nor, by any means, that the former is necessarily bad while the latter is good. Indeed, it may well be that both modes are a necessary part of human life, in a way reminiscent of *yang* and *yin* in Chinese philosophy, or, relatedly, maleness and femaleness (in a way that includes but transcends biological gender). But I am also not positing unchanging metaphysical principles; indeed, I am going to suggest that the way they have been constituted by and in context is why they now matter.

Magic and Enchantment overlap in complex, even paradoxical ways, as can be seen in various test-cases which clarify both their differences and their interplay. Take divination, for example; the new awareness that flows from an act of divination may – and paradigmatically, I believe, does – partake of (re-)enchantment, rather than a utilitarian usefulness as such (see Curry 1992, chapter 1). However, one may well have a new approach to acting in the "real" world afterwards, and thus an altered situation *vis-à-vis* power-knowledge. In other words, while Enchantment is not in itself an act of will intended to produce certain effects in the primary world, it may well have such effects indirectly.

Exactly the same applies to fiction – which is why both Shelley's boast about poets as the "unacknowledged legislators of the world" (Tripp 1970, sections 702-792) and Auden's lament that "Poetry changes nothing" (Tripp 1970, section 702) are so unsatisfactory. Poetry, and fiction generally, cannot, by its nature, successfully set out to change things, because that is to leave Enchantment for Magic, and thus fail as the former; the *raison d'être* of imaginative literature, as opposed to a tract, is precisely to enchant. But that does not mean that it cannot make things happen in the Primary world, albeit not always in accord with what its author would have wished. The sad case of *The Satanic Verses* illustrates this point very clearly. It is one that Yeats understood well: "Did that play of mine send out / Certain men the English shot?"[6]

It also serves to demonstrate that Enchantment is indeed, in Tolkien's term, potentially "perilous" (OFS 50). Although I'm sure it's not the sort of thing he had in mind, another example of its pathological possibilities – in a domain normally one of life's most delightful and life-affirming – is the (true) story of sexual Enchantment portrayed in Nagisa Oshima's film *Ai No Corrida*, which ends in mutual obsession, insanity for one partner and a violent death for the other. Contrariwise, there is something fundamentally psychologically and socially healthy about the spark of human (relative) initiative and (qualified) independence – without which Magic would be impossible – nurtured in the pre-modern humanism of Machiavelli, Montaigne and Erasmus. And at a more mundane though no less important level, when I go to my dentist I

---

6 William Butler Yeats, "The Man and the Echo".

prefer a competent exercise of power-knowledge, rather than an experience of spiritual transport.

Other instances can further refine our distinction. Briefly, humour: if something strikes you as funny (a form of Enchantment), well and good; but if it doesn't, no amount of willing it to be so, or explanation of why it is (a branch of power-knowledge, albeit obscure), will make it so. Or take something as simple as going for a walk in the woods, or any other natural setting. As most of us know, an over-determination to arrange everything, externally and internally, so that nothing interferes with our enjoyment, can very effectively destroy the very Enchantment that was our motive in the first place. Which is to say, perhaps, that Enchantment rarely survives becoming a goal; and that although its conditions can – indeed, arguably must – be established by will and knowledge, it cannot be forced to occur.

Facile assumptions can be misleading here. As I have mentioned, science is not necessarily the domain of Magic alone. Goethean science, predicated on phenomenological participation in nature rather than its control and prediction – and therefore marginal to the Baconian-Galilean-Cartesian mainstream – is evidence to the contrary (see Bortoft 1996; Naylor 1996). Some people think that quantum physics has the same potential. Or take another example: intercessory prayer, for the benefit of others, especially those in distress. There are certainly cases where this "works" in the experience of those involved, and as it is intended to produce certain specific primary changes, such prayer qualifies as a kind of (spiritual) Magic. But it is a kind that happens to escape the modernist/humanist ambit.[7]

The Triumph of Magic

This brings us to a crucial point – and to something of a change of mode here, as we turn to the status and operation of these phenomena in the current world situation. Very briefly, at the close of the twentieth century – for socio-historical reasons that are none the less compelling for being ultimately contingent (rather,

---

7 On humanism (of the kind I mean), see David Ehrenfeld, *The Arrogance of Humanism*; on modernism (as the self-consciousness of modernity, not a particular cultural movement), see Stephen Toulmin, *Cosmopolis: The Hidden Agenda of Modernity*.

that is, than being essential or intrinsic to their natures) – Magic has achieved a global dominance to the extent that Enchantment seems to be seriously under threat. And if you further accept, as I do (and by no means without a great deal of evidence, although in a paper like this its production is not feasible) that this dominance is responsible for rapidly escalating and in some cases irreversible degradation in human, ecological and spiritual terms, then it follows that Enchantment has become uniquely precious and important as a resource for resistance, and for the realization of better alternatives.

The modernist project is analyzable (as I have argued elsewhere) in terms of three interlocking domains: international capital, science and technology, and the nation-state.[8] In action, these three are now inseparable; and Magic lies at their heart. Indeed, the power of modernist Magic is such that via the media generally (and advertising in particular), it has given rise to what I would like to propose as a new, third category to supplement Tolkien's original two: namely, Glamour. Glamour is Enchantment in the service of Magic; Enchantment, one might almost say, enslaved.

Of course, since the wonder of Glamour is, with the greatest of pains, will and knowledge, engineered to particular and preset ends, it cannot, by definition, be genuine Enchantment. But if it is the only kind that most people are exposed to, in relentless quantities and with ever greater sophistication, how can the self-fulfilling disappearance of the real thing (as opposed, we might say, to "the Real Thing!") come as a surprise? This is not a frivolous comparison; not only does it capture the typical corporate displacement of what is (subject to the usual epistemological constraints) real by the blatantly artificial and interest-driven, but the Coca-Cola logo is now the most widely-recognized icon in the world, not excluding religious symbols. To be sure, the pseudo-Enchantment of Glamour is not necessarily driven by the profit-motive – recall how powerful was the spell of hero-worship engineered by Stalin, Hitler and Mao – but in these supposedly post-ideological days, it nearly always is. It was neatly if unintentionally summed up by a top fashion executive: "selling the dream." It is the conjunction of those two terms that constitutes Glamour.

---

8 In Curry, *Defending Middle-earth*, this three-fold analysis of modernity has been borrowed from Paul Ekins, *A New World Order: Grassroots Movements for Global Change*.

Dis- and Re-Enchantment

In recent years, the subject of modernity has generated a vast amount of discussion, especially in terms of "postmodernity". I want to avoid that here, in the same way that Kolakowski does, quite legitimately, when he writes that "the question so many of us have been trying to cope with is not so much when modernity started, but what is the core – whether or not explicitly expressed – of our contemporary widespread *Unbehagen in der Kultur* [cultural discontent] [...]. And the first answer that naturally comes to mind is summed up, of course, in the Weberian *Entzauberung* – disenchantment – or in any similar word roughly covering the same phenomenon" (Kolakowski 1990: 7). Zygmunt Bauman (1992: x-xi) points to this when he invokes postmodernity as

> restoring to the world what modernity, presumptuously, had taken away; as a re-enchantment of the world that modernity had tried hard to disenchant [...]. The war against mystery and magic was for modernity the war of liberation leading to the declaration of reason's independence [...]. [The] world had to be de-spiritualized, de-animated: denied the capacity of subject [...]. It is against such a disenchanted world that the postmodern re-enchantment is aimed.[9]

These authors, like Weber, are surely right about instrumentalist, utilitarian, bureaucratic disenchantment as the authentic hallmark of modernity.[10] That said, however, the Weberian thesis is seriously flawed – the version, at least, accepted by both modernists themselves and anti-modernists, in which disenchantment is (substantively as well as semantically) the opposite condition to enchantment, and is furthermore part of an inexorable and universal process. That is simply modernist ideology or, if you prefer, myth – not wrong on that account, by any means, but itself an integral part of the global modernization that needs resisting. Barbara Herrnstein Smith has aptly described it as "the effort to identify the presumptively universally compelling Truth and Way and to compel it universally" (Smith 1997: 179). That is why it is important to understand the modernist programme as not really disenchanted (and by implication, somehow objective, disinterested, realistic and so on), but as saturated and driven by the ideology and metaphysics of Magic – notwithstanding that it strenuously denounces magic. And there is nothing necessary, complete or

---

9 See also Hassan 1992.
10 For a fascinating analysis, see Alkis Kontos (1994).

irreversible about its contemporary victory; here and there, if often, of necessity, secretly, Enchantment survives.[11]

It follows that if "disenchantment" cannot be accepted at face-value, then neither can "re-enchantment". Re-enchantment is not about re-introducing a former condition where it no longer exists; it must rather be a matter of recognizing, articulating and encouraging Enchantment – or more exactly, the conditions for Enchantment that exist now. But it is most definitely not about making it happen or enforcing it; for the potentially terrible irony is that a programme of willed power-knowledge to create (re-)Enchantment necessarily becomes Magic, the very thing it set out to oppose. The terminus can then only be some kind of theocratic religious police – no merely hypothetical possibility, as the appalling case of contemporary Iran shows.[12] So if it be asked, "Can you fight Magic with Enchantment?" the answer is, *pace* Weber's utter pessimism, yes: but not directly.

Wonder

I would now like to examine Enchantment more closely, first in relation to wonder, then to nature. Tolkien emphasized the centrality of the former in his definition, "the realization [...] of imagined wonder." "Realization" here hovers ambiguously but fruitfully between wonder at the world – that it is, what it is, and what is in it – or what Ronald Hepburn (1984: 140) calls "existential wonder," and what makes it possible to realize that it is wondrous, or "art". In a perceptive and sensitive essay,[13] Hepburn (1984: 140, 145f, 151) has analyzed wonder in a way which strengthens the contrast with Magic that I have borrowed from Tolkien (without, I am sure, any direct influence) while refining the idea of Enchantment. He shows wonder to be a "kind of knowing" which, although it overlaps with religious or metaphysical as well as aesthetic experience, is reducible to neither; nor is it merely "a prelude to fuller knowledge." Wonder "is notably and essentially other-acknowledging" there

---

11 For two very different books arguing (in their own ways) this point, see Bruno Latour, *We Have Never Been Modern* and Roberto Calasso, *The Marriage of Cadmus and Harmony*.
12 And as Raymond Tallis mentions, in attacking re-enchantment in his *Enemies of Hope* (page 159); but Tallis conflates enchantment with religion, and specifically theism.
13 R.W. Hepburn, "Wonder". See also his essay "Nature Humanised: Nature Respected".

is "a close affinity between the attitude of wonder itself – non-exploitative, non-utilitarian – and attitudes that seek to affirm and respect other-being." Thus, the "moral correlates" of wonder include respect, compassion and humility. These all involve "openness to new forms of value" as opposed to the attitude of "We've seen it all" – as in, for example, "When you've seen one Redwood Tree, you've seen them all."

Here is another overlap with Weberian disenchantment, for the important thing about that is its monism and universalism: given a single reference point – whether spiritual (God) or material (scientific truth) – "one can, in principle, master all things by calculation" (Weber quoted in Kontos (1994: 242)). Thus there is nothing new under the sun, for everything can, at least in theory, be fitted into the ultimate schema somewhere. In contrast, enchantment for Weber was marked by a plurality of ultimately incommensurable spirits, values and/or principles, in response to which wonder is a constant and appropriate possibility. As he realized, its enemies include both science and monotheistic religion. (This was strikingly confirmed only recently in Britain, when the arch-Darwinist Richard Dawkins and an Anglican bishop buried their differences for long enough to agree publicly on one thing: the iniquity of one of the most widespread forms of popular (re-)enchantment, namely astrology.)[14] Taken together with the paradox I have already noted, that programmatic Enchantment becomes Magical, the implication is unavoidable: any attempted return to theism would only add further to the contemporary triumph of Magic.

There are echoes in this post-Weberian argument of both the late Paul Feyerabend's epistemological anarchism (since ably developed by Barbara Herrnstein Smith) and Isaiah Berlin's value-pluralism. They are highly pertinent ones – again, not in terms of direct intellectual influence but as coherently related strands of argument. In all three cases, the values of Enchantment are seen as seriously jeopardized by a totalizing monist and universalist reason, the shorthand for which is sometimes "the Enlightenment", but which I have called Magic.[15]

---

14 BBC Radio 4 "The Moral Maze", November 14th, 1996.
15 One of the best guides to this territory is John Gray, in *Enlightenment's Wake: Politics and Culture at the Close of the Modern Age* and *Endgames: Questions in Late Modern Political Thought*.

Hepburn (1984: 140) also argues that the "transformation of the merely threatening and daunting into what is aesthetically manageable, even contemplated with joy [...] is achieved through the agency of wonder." This resonates strikingly (although again, I think, coincidentally) with G.K. Chesterton's (1996: 3-4) rhetorical question, more than a century ago: "How can we contrive to be at once astonished at the world and yet at home in it? [...]. We need to be happy in this wonderland without once being merely comfortable."

Hepburn (1984: 144) also shows convincingly that although wonder by no means rules it out, it does not depend on theism: "To be evocative of wonder, an object need not be seen as filtering the perfections of deity."[16] The irony is that the only other indispensable guide to wonder I have found is Chesterton, in his splendid chapter on "The Ethics of Elfland" in that classic of Christian apologetics, *Orthodoxy*. He is worth quoting at some length:

> The man of science says, "Cut the stalk, and the apple will fall"; but he says it calmly, as if the one idea really led up to the other. The witch in the fairy tale says, "Blow the horn, and the castle will fall"; but she does not say it as if it were something in which the effect obviously arose out of the cause. Doubtless she has given the advice to many champions, and seen many castles fall, but she does not muddle her head until it imagines a necessary connection between a horn and a falling tower. But the scientific men do muddle their heads, until they imagine a necessary mental connection between an apple leaving the tree and an apple reaching the ground [...]. They feel that because one incomprehensible thing constantly follows another incomprehensible thing the two together somehow make up a comprehensible thing [...].
>
> The only words that ever satisfied me as describing Nature are the terms used in the fairy books, "charm", "spell", "enchantment". They express the arbitrariness of the fact and its mystery. A tree grows fruit because it is a magic tree. Water runs downhill because it is bewitched. The sun shines because it is bewitched [...]. I deny altogether that this is fantastic or even mystical [...]. It is the man who talks about "a law" that he has never seen who is the mystic. (Chesterton 1995: 274-76)

Despite appearances, perhaps, Chesterton is not actually guilty of hyperbole here. As I believe any true scientist would admit, no-one knows what gravity, electromagnetism or any such phenomenon actually is, and even physical laws can only be inferred in a way that leaves them permanently vulnerable

---

16 Cf. Shunryu Suzuki "The world is its own magic" (1970: 61). It is worth noting, however, that Tolkien would not have agreed.

to future revision. Furthermore, he vividly brings out "the sense of absolute contingency" (Hepburn 1984: 140) that generates existential wonder. But we have already seen that science cannot be necessarily identified with Magic nor art with Enchantment. The point is that whatever form they take, Magic and Enchantment both lay claim to a special relationship to nature. The nature of that claim, however, couldn't be more different. The former brings all of nature under one rule, the rule of a set of universal laws to which there can be neither exception nor appeal; whereas the latter sees nature as endlessly plural, particular and unique. (That is why real Enchantment, from the scientific Magician's point of view, is literally useless.)

Nature

Tolkien too emphasized Enchantment as wonder at nature, including specifically its perception, celebration and healing. Such a connection – or rather, identity – could be approached analytically in various ways. Perhaps Enchantment-as-art *is* nature in the way that Hepburn suggests when he writes that our values and experiences

> are essentially the result of a cooperation of man and non-human nature: the universe would not contain them, were it not for our perceptual-creative efforts, and were it not equally for the contribution of the non-human world that both sustains and sets limits to our lives. To realize that there is this cooperative interdependence of man and his natural environment checks the extremes of pessimism by showing our earth-rootedness even in our aspirations. There is no wholly-other paradise from which we are excluded; the only transcendence that can be real to us is an "immanent" one. (Hepburn 1984: 181-82)

If this seems rather general, recall that Hepburn also adduces humility as a moral correlate of wonder. Putting these points together makes sense of much: where Magic involves a "tragic" (temporary, conditional, partial) defiance of limits, Enchantment evokes a profoundly "comic" appreciation of our earth-rooted dependency.[17]

It may also be the case that, as William Blake bluntly put it, "Nature is Imagination itself." One way to grasp this is the idea of nature as cosmic art; for while art

---

17 See Don D. Elgin, *The Comedy of the Fantastic*.

is "conscious" and nature is supposedly not, I think modernity has encouraged us to overestimate the degree and importance of the former in art, while destructively denying (as Bauman has pointed out) nature's capacity as animate subject – except, in an ultimately patronizing way, within the limited ambit of aesthetic Romanticism.[18] A related suggestion is that of Gregory Bateson – another voice of sanity, and an admirer of Blake – who fruitfully analyzed mind and nature as "a necessary unity." Where I think Bateson's formulation falls down, however, is its dependence on the mystical idea (as Chesterton would have put it) of logical or transcendental necessity.[19] If there is to be any such unity, it must be forged in our experience, which is where it matters. But as I also mentioned, the juggernaut of modernist Magic has ever more strongly linked Enchantment and nature – equally imperilled as never before in human experience – or else impelled us to recognize their union; no hard-and-fast distinction between reality and our experience of it is possible here.

One interesting implication is that the (literally) dead art of Damien Hirst and his ilk, where this link has been severed, is not just unenchanted but actually an arm of Magic – and, as such, no longer art. It might be replied that death and putrefaction is part of nature. True; but Hirst's art, like that of his mentor, Bacon, restricts nature to just that, in a nihilistic denial of animation, subjectivity and ineffability that is the acme of modernist sensibility. Nor is the patronage of a wealthy and decadent art establishment, knowing (and setting) the price of everything and the value of nothing, a coincidence; nature as dead, fully knowable and manipulable is a precondition for its full commerical exploitation.

By the same token, modernist/humanist Magic rejects natural limits. Applied to their ultimate instance – death – the result is exemplified by cryogenics. Both individually and collectively, we are to do "whatever it takes" to get whatever we want. A recent advertisement I saw stated the following proposition: "To be truly free requires a life without boundaries. The passport to that future is technology." But a life without boundaries, as any first-year psychology student should know, is not freedom but psychosis – and in the ambition of such companies, not merely individual but global psychosis; not mastery, but mass slavery.

---

18 Thanks to Nicola Bown for the point about Romanticism.
19 See Barbara Herrnstein Smith, *Belief and Resistance: Dynamics of Contemporary Intellectual Controversy.*

At the same time, however, the new awareness of art-as-nature (and vice-versa) radically extends the possibilities of Enchantment, including "re-enchantment". It has now become possible to value the Earth in new ways – which are nearly always also very old ways that have been re-discovered and adapted from indigenous peoples, whether of the past or elsewhere – that are simultaneously, spiritual, practical, and artistic (though they need not involve traditional artistic media). Indeed, it seems to have become possible to the exact extent that it has now become necessary. Although practically everywhere has its grassroots equivalents, in Britain there is no better example than the integrity, skill and humour of those resisting that exemplar of modernist madness, the road expansion program; and its heart is the realization of nature's wonder. (The huge motorway punched through the ancient hills at Twyford Down in Hampshire, where this movement began, is modern Magic. It's not a pretty sight.)

Signs of Wonder

What are the signs that might help us to recognize genuine contemporary re-Enchantment? It seems to me they are these:

(1) Wonder in and at the natural world, its places and its non-human people but actual ones, and not merely in the abstract (even as "Gaia") – accompanied with a recognition and appreciation of their integrity and variety, independently of any use they may have to human beings. (This is the central insight of deep ecology, usually termed "ecocentrism".)

(2) As against the monism and rationalism of modernist Magic, a consistent pluralism in at least three respects: epistemologically as relativism, axiologically as value-pluralism, and politically as a project of radical and plural democracy.[20]

(3) An end to humanist/modernist (and postmodernist) secularism and its war on wonder, with the frank admission of a spiritual dimension of human experience that is not exhausted by institutionalised religion. In terms of (re-)

---

20 On epistemological pluralism, see Smith, *Belief and Resistance*; on axiological, the work of Isaiah Berlin; on political, Ernesto Laclau and Chantal Mouffe, *Hegemony and Socialist Strategy: Toward a Radical and Plural Democracy*.

Enchantment, its closest affinities are with popular animism, even more than with other sympathetic approaches: polytheism, pantheism or panentheism, and Buddhist non-theism. (It has to be said – and I am speaking here of discourses, not of individuals – that in this context, monotheism starts with some severe handicaps.)[21]

Actually, Enchantment is a result of the right relationship with the Earth just as much as the reverse; more so, indeed, in the sense that we need the Earth, whereas it does not need us. This is a vital point to remember, if we are to resist its incorporation into a program of religious power-knowledge, or its corruption into the virtual enchantment of Glamour. But it is possible – and urgent – to encourage and sustain Enchantment. What does so is living life as nature's art; and the art of living in and with nature. This requires forswearing the modernist dream of mastery. But slavery is not, as alarmists cry, the only alternative. The person "who allows himself to be 'free with' Nature" – but within nature – can, as Tolkien noted, "be her lover not her slave" (OFS 55).

Bibliography

ASHMOLE, Elias. 1652. *Theatricum Chemicum Britannicum*. London.

BATESON, Gregory. 1979. *Mind and Nature: A Necessary Unity*. New York: E.P. Dutton.

BAUMAN, Zygmunt. 1992. *Intimations of Postmodernity*. London: Routledge.

BORTOFT, Henri. 1996. *The Wholeness of Nature: Goethe's Way of Science*. Edinburgh: Floris Books.

CALASSO, Roberto. 1993. *The Marriage of Cadmus and Harmony*. London: Jonathan Cape.

---

21 On the subject of religious discourses, I am fully aware that particular individuals are capable of finding and drawing upon resources for ecologism in any of the major religious traditions; see J. Baird Callicott, *Earth's Insights*. I am also (obviously, I hope) not using the word "animism" in its classical anthropological sense of a teleologically primitive stage of religion.

CALLICOTT, J. Baird. 1994. *Earth's Insights*. Berkeley CA: University of California Press.

CHESTERTON, Gilbert Keith. 1995. *A Motley Wisdom: The Best of G.K. Chesterton.* Edited by Nigel FORDE. London: Hodder & Stoughton.

1996. *Orthodoxy*. First edition 1908. London: Hodder & Stoughton.

CURRY, Patrick. 1992. *A Confusion of Prophets: Victorian and Edwardian Astrology.* London: Collins and Brown.

2004. *Defending Middle-earth: Tolkien, Myth and Modernity*. Second edition. First edition 1997. Boston MA: Houghton Mifflin.

EHRENFELD, David. 1978. *The Arrogance of Humanism*. Oxford: Oxford University Press.

EKINS, Paul. 1992. *A New World Order. Grassroots Movements for Global Change.* London: Routledge.

ELGIN, Don D. 1985. *The Comedy of the Fantastic: Ecological Perspectives on the Fantasy Novel.* Westport CT: Greenwood Press.

FEYERABEND, Paul. 1987. *Farewell to Reason*. London: Verso.

FRAZER, James George. 1922. *The Golden Bough*. London: Macmillan.

GRAY, John. 1995. *Enlightenment's Wake: Politics and Culture at the Close of the Modern Age.* London: Routledge.

1997. *Endgames: Questions in Late Modern Political Thought*. Cambridge: Polity Press.

HASSAN, Ihab. 1992. "Pluralism in Postmodern Perspective." In Charles JENCKS (ed.). 1992. *The Postmodern Reader*. London: Academy Editions, 196-207.

HEPBURN, Ronald W. 1984. *"Wonder" and Other Essays*. Edinburgh: Edinburgh University Press.

1998. "Nature Humanised: Nature Respected." *Environmental Values* 7.3: 267-279.

KOLAKOWSKI, Leszek. 1990. *Modernity on Endless Trial*. Chicago IL: University of Chicago Press.

KONTOS, Alkis. 1994. "The World Disenchanted, and the Return of Gods and Demons." In Asher HOROWITZ and Terry MALEY (eds.). 1994. *The Barbarism of Reason: Max Weber and the Twilight of Reason*. Toronto: University of Toronto Press, 223-247.

LACLAU, Ernesto and Chantal MOUFFE. 1985. *Hegemony and Socialist Strategy: Toward a Radical and Plural Democracy.* London: Verso.

LATOUR, Bruno.1993. *We Have Never Been Modern*. Hemel Hempstead: Harvester Wheatsheaf.

NAYLOR, Jeremy. 1996. *Goethe on Science*. Edinburgh: Floris Books.

SMITH, Barbara Herrnstein. 1988. *Contingencies of Value: Alternative Perspectives for Critical Theory*. Cambridge MA: Harvard University Press.

1997. *Belief and Resistance: Dynamics of Contemporary Intellectual Controversy*. Cambridge MA: Harvard University Press.

SUZUKI, Shunryu. 1970. *Zen Mind, Beginner's Mind*. New York: Weatherhill.

TALLIS, Raymond. 1997. *Enemies of Hope. A Critique of Contemporary Pessimism: Irrationalism, Humanism and Counter-Enlightenment*. Basingstoke: Macmillan.

TOLKIEN, J.R.R. 1988. "On Fairy-Stories." In J.R.R. TOLKIEN. 1988. *Tree and Leaf*. London: Unwin Hyman, 9-73.

TOULMIN, Stephen. 1990. *Cosmopolis: The Hidden Agenda of Modernity*. Chicago IL: University of Chicago Press.

TRIPP, Rhoda Thomas. (ed.). 1970. *The International Thesaurus of Quotations*. Harmondsworth: Penguin.

WEBSTER, Charles. 1982. *From Paracelsus to Newton: Magic and the Making of Modern Science*. Cambridge: Cambridge University Press.

WINOKUR, Jon (ed.). 1987. *The Portable Curmudgeon*. New York: Portable American Library.

Enchantment in Tolkien and Middle-earth

Abstract

This paper begins with a few general remarks about enchantment as a human experience before turning to its importance both in Tolkien's creative life and in his principal public work, *The Lord of the Rings*. I turn for elucidation to the work of Verlyn Flieger and that of two philosophers, Ronald Hepburn and Jan Zwicky. My intention here is to trace the effects of enchantment – largely as understood and defined by Tolkien himself – in both his creative life and the world of Middle-earth which resulted from it. I shall start by introducing the idea of enchantment itself.

I

As is well-known, Tolkien set out his own literary programme, at least in broad outline, in "On Fairy-Stories".[1] Not the least valuable aspect of this essay is its attempt to articulate the nature of enchantment – something which is remarkably rare, even in fat tomes with the words "Enchantment" or "Re-Enchantment" in their titles.[2] In contrast, intellectuals have been happy to discuss the subject of disenchantment at length. (It is central, for example, to the concerns and publications of the Frankfurt School and related critical theory.)[3] Even Max Weber, who was responsible for introducing the idea of "the disenchantment of the world" into modern discourse, had little to say about what enchantment is, or perhaps was.[4] But that little, when added to Tolkien's speculations and those of a very few others, allows us to formulate a reasonably coherent and accurate idea.[5]

First published in Stratford Caldecott and Thomas Honegger (eds.). 2008. *Tolkien's* The Lord of the Rings. *Sources of Inspiration*. Zurich and Jena: Walking Tree Publishers, 99-112.

1 See also Curry (1999). This essay is reprinted on pages 65-82 of the present volume.
2 To pick just two recent examples: David Ray Griffin (2000) and Alex Owen (2004). These could be multiplied many times.
3 Principally the work of Theodor W. Adorno, Max Horkheimer and Herbert Marcuse.
4 The original phrase was Schiller's.
5 Especially Hepburn (1984).

That idea has three parts. One is that "Enchantment produces a Secondary World into which both designer and spectator can enter, to the satisfaction of their senses while they are inside; but in its purity it is artistic in desire and purpose" (Tolkien 1988: 49). (The relevant contrast, which we shall not pursue here, is with magic – including modern magic, i.e. techno-science.)[6] The second part, Tolkien's definition of "the primal desire at the heart of Faërie," is fundamental: "the realization, independent of the conceiving mind, of imagined wonder" (Tolkien 1988: 18).

To this we can add Weber's crucial insight that "[t]he unity of the primitive image of the world, in which everything was *concrete magic*, has tended to split" – as a result of the process of disenchantment – "into rational cognition and mastery of nature, on the one hand, and into 'mystic' experiences, on the other" (quoted in Gerth and Wright 1991: 282; my emphasis). In other words, enchantment ignores the split, deepened by Descartes but inherited by him from Platonic philosophy and thence Christian theology, between spiritual and/or mental subjectivity on the one hand and material objectivity on the other; it partakes of both.

Thus an intensive delineation of enchantment includes these characteristics:
- indispensably, existential wonder – which, as such, is useless in instrumental or utilitarian terms, but by no means therefore without effects; furthermore, enchantment is
- both ineffable and mysterious, on the one hand, and embodied, even carnal, and very precisely situated on the other;
- participatory, recalling the etymological meaning of "enchantment": to be or to find oneself in a song (the song which one is singing or to which one is listening); and finally, it is
- pluralist, in the sense that although an experience of enchantment may partake intensely of unity, completeness and infinity while it lasts, being also "concrete" it always comes to an end. Viewed from "outside", therefore, it is ongoing, incomplete, and potentially multiple.

---

6 See Curry (1999) and Curry (2004, chapter 3). The former essay is reprinted on pages 65-82 of the present volume.

An extensive delineation would include experiences of enchantment, as just described, arising out of situations such as these:

- nature (decidedly not in the abstract but particular and "real" places, things, animals, etc.);
- love (paradigmatically erotic love, but also maternal/paternal, as well as friendship);
- ritual (especially but not only religious);
- art (all the arts, related to all the senses and faculties – including humour);
- sports (as in, feeling oneself to be in the game which one is watching …);
- food (as in, slow- as opposed to fast-food); and
- learning (in the sense of lore for its own sake).

The way this list cuts across most coherent categories to which we are accustomed signals that we are dealing here with a particular, even peculiar beast, whose distinctiveness – significant commonalities with other kinds of experience notwithstanding – should be respected.

II

Now enchantment was far from being a purely theoretical or programmatic concept for Tolkien. Two intensely personal experiences of enchantment took place in his life (to put it somewhat redundantly: enchantment by its nature is personal, *as well as* more-than-personal). Both of them massively influenced that life, including his life-work. I have taken the following accounts from Humphrey Carpenter's biography.[7]

The first – characteristically linguistic for someone who was, in C.S. Lewis's words, "inside language" – took place in 1913, when Tolkien was reading the *Crist* of Cynewulf, a group of Anglo-Saxon religious poems.

Two lines from it struck him forcibly:

> Eala Earendil engla beorhtast
> Ofer middangeard monnum sended.

---

7 But see Shippey (1982: 183-85) and Flieger (1997: 148-49).

"Hail Earendel, brightest of angels / above the middle-earth sent unto men."
Earendel is glossed by the Anglo-Saxon dictionary as "a shining light, ray",
but here it clearly has some special meaning. Tolkien himself interpreted it
as referring to John the Baptist, but he believed that "Earendel" had originally been the name for the star presaging the dawn, that is, Venus. He was
strangely moved by its appearance in the Cynewulf lines. "I felt a curious
thrill," he wrote long afterwards, "as if something had stirred in me, half
wakened from sleep. There was something very remote and strange and beautiful behind those words, if I could grasp it, far beyond ancient English."
(Carpenter 1977: 64)

The second experience occurred sometime in 1917-18:

On days when he could get leave, he and Edith went for walks in the countryside. Near Roos they found a small wood with an undergrowth of hemlock,
and there they wandered. Ronald recalled of Edith as she was at this time:
"Her hair was raven, her skin clear, her eyes bright, and she could sing – and
dance." She sang and danced for him in the wood, and from this came the
story that was to be the centre of *The Silmarillion*: the tale of the mortal man
Beren who loves the immortal elven-maid Lúthien Tinúviel, whom he first
sees dancing among the hemlock in a wood. [...] Of all his legends, the tale
of Beren and Lúthien was the one most loved by Tolkien, not least because
at one level he identified the character of Lúthien with his own wife.
(Carpenter 1977: 97)

There is no need to belabour the importance of these experiences for Tolkien,
and therefore for understanding his work. But it is permissible to speculate on
that significance not only in a germinal, formative capacity but in relation to
certain tensions – themselves perhaps creative ones; at least, betimes – which, I
think, must have resulted from their juxtaposition with Tolkien's Christianity. As
we have seen, enchantments, both theoretically and in Tolkien's own experience
of them, include an inalienably "concrete" dimension which could, at the very
least, cast doubt on their validity from the point of view of a theological commitment to a single and universal spiritual truth. More: a counter-commitment
to experiences of enchantment could throw doubt in the other direction! Now
I don't say these tensions are, in principle, unresolvable psychologically or even
theologically; but it would be very surprising if they were not present and/or
were inconsequential.

The context for such a discussion, not necessarily helpfully but probably unavoidably, is the presence of Catholic Christianity and/or paganism in Tolkien's

work.[8] In my view, notwithstanding a predilection for exclusivity stemming from the universalism just mentioned, this question can only be resolved satisfactorily by starting from the position of "both and" rather than "either or". Then things can be noticed and said about which aspects of his fiction are more one or the other and, even more interesting, how the two passions interacted.

To return to Tolkien's two enchantments I have just reviewed, they relate principally and obviously, in the first case, to the "star" of Venus, whose intimate association with the female pagan deity of love and beauty – but of no less religious significance for that – long predates Christianity (which Tolkien was perfectly well aware of);[9] and in the second instance, to a passionate, including implicitly erotic, relationship – but no less spiritual for that – between two lovers. And without for a moment denying other perspectives, Beren and Lúthien were also, *qua* lovers, under the aegis of Venus.

So how did this sort of thing, integral to both Tolkien's life and his work, relate – almost certainly in both directions – with his Catholicism? I do not intend to try to work out the details here, because there are other things I want to concentrate on, but any attempt should certainly consider his carefully complex response in 1954 to a reader's criticism of Elvish reincarnation:

> "Reincarnation" may be bad *theology* [...] But I do not see how even in the Primary World any theologian or philosopher, unless very much better informed about the relation of spirit and body than I believe anyone to be, could deny the *possibility* of re-incarnation as a mode of existence, prescribed for certain kinds of rational incarnate creatures. (Tolkien 1981: 189)

There is also the nice distinction which Tolkien draws in his remark to Auden in 1965 that "I don't feel under any obligation to make my story fit with formalized Christian theology, though I actually intended it to be consonant with Christian thought and belief [...]" (Tolkien 1981: 355).

---

8 For two good papers with contrasting emphases, see Ronald Hutton's contributions to Paul E. Kerry's *The Ring and the Cross* (2011), especially "The Pagan Tolkien" (paper originally given at the "Tolkien 2005: The Ring Goes Ever On" conference at Aston University, Birmingham, 11-15 August 2005), and Stratford Caldecott, "Christianity and Literary Culture: The Case of J.R.R. Tolkien", unpublished paper from a talk given at Regent's Park College, November 15th 2005. (See also Hutton's chapter 7, "The Inklings and the Gods", in Hutton 2003.)

9 See Tolkien (1981: 385).

III

Let us turn now to enchantment *inside* his literary creation. Much of what we can learn from doing so has already been discussed, but some key points become much clearer viewed from within Middle-earth.

The most important of these is the firm identification of enchantment – consistent with "On Fairy-Stories" – as the paradigmatic experience, property and concern of the Elves. That idea is extensively introduced, in *The Lord of the Rings*, when Frodo is listening to the singing in the Hall of Fire in Rivendell (FR.II.i). But it is driven home in connection with Lothlórien, "the heart of Elvendom on earth". This is the place, by no means coincidentally, for the most explicit discussion of enchantment within the book:

> Frodo stood awhile still lost in wonder. It seemed to him that he had stepped through a high window that looked on a vanished world. A light was upon it for which his language had no name. [...] He saw no colour but those he knew, gold and white and blue and green, but they were fresh and poignant, as if he had at that moment first perceived them. [...] On the land of Lórien there was no stain.

> He turned and saw that Sam was now standing beside him, looking round with a puzzled expression, and rubbing his eyes as if he was not sure that he was awake. "It's sunlight and bright day, right enough," he said. "I thought the Elves were all for moon and stars: but this is more Elvish than anything I ever heard tell of. I feel as if I was *inside* a song, if you take my meaning." (FR.II.vi)

This experience constitutes just the healing reconnection with reality which Tolkien – contesting the charge of "escapism" – describes in his essay (1988: 52-54) as "recovery" or "the regaining of a clear view."[10]

Another important point about enchantment is made by Aragorn in his rebuke to Boromir: "'Speak no evil of the Lady Galadriel! [...] There is in her and in this land no evil, unless a man bring it hither himself. Then let him beware!'" (FR.II.vi) This is arguably the source of the danger Tolkien had in mind when he described Faërie as "a perilous land" (1988: 9). The clear implication is that any danger to mortals from enchantment lies principally not in the latter itself but in the relationship one has with it.

---

10 See also Spirito (2008).

The description of the Fellowship leaving Lórien – or rather, as they experienced it, Lórien withdrawing from them – brilliantly evokes the desolation of disenchantment, the unbearable end (forever, it may seem) of just what gives one's life its meaning:

> For so it seemed to them: Lórien was slipping backward, like a bright ship masted with enchanted trees, sailing on to forgotten shores, while they sat helpless upon the margin of the grey and leafless world. (FR.II.viii)

I am reminded here of the same thing happening at the end of another book in which enchantment figures importantly and poignantly, Karen Blixen's *Out of Africa* (1970: 381): "It was not I who was going away, I did not have it in my power to leave Africa, but it was the country that was slowly and gravely withdrawing from me, like the sea in ebb-tide." This coincidence seems to point to a truth about enchantment.

Returning to the point about what we bring to enchantment, this condition points to the chief danger, I think, inherent in any significant involvement with enchantment: attachment, dependency, and ultimately addiction. (And the resonance here with the discourse of drugs – especially those which offer an intense version of enchantment, the ever-rising price of which often emerges later – is by no means coincidental.)[11] That, above all, is what can poison the purity, beauty and intrinsic value of enchantment. For enchantment, as Tolkien wrote, "represents love: that is, a love and respect for all things, 'Inanimate' [*sic*] and 'animate', an unpossessive love of them as 'other'."[12]

So the corollary – which I make bold to assert would have obtained Tolkien's assent – is this: a healthy relationship with enchantment requires a *strong* ego, so to speak, with the ability to *do without it*.[13] And what is this but one aspect of the grit that Tolkien (and several of his characters) so admired: Northern courage, to use Tolkien's phrase? (If one seeks connections between "On Fairy-Stories" and his other great essay on *Beowulf*, this is surely one.)

---

11 See Aldous Huxley's still superb essay "The Doors of Enchantment".
12 From MS. 9, Tolkien Collection, Bodleian Library, Oxford, quoted by Flieger (1997: 247).
13 Cf. Tolkien's related assertion that "[t]he keener and the clearer is the reason, the better fantasy will it make" (1988: 51).

My point is also discernible in the history of Middle-earth. As Théoden observes rhetorically, "'however the fortune of war shall go, may it not so end that much that was fair and wonderful shall pass for ever out of Middle-earth?'" (TT.III. viii). The seal of this poignant fate is (or at least is symbolized by) the mysterious link between the One Ring – Tolkien's master trope of power- and will-driven Magic and malevolence – and the Three Rings, one of which (Galadriel's) is the guarantor of the heart of Elvendom in Middle-earth, and thence its wonder and beneficence. Sauron's hand never touched the Three. Why is it, then, that with the passing of the One, their power too wanes?

This question preoccupied me for quite a while.[14] I found what I think is the answer, however, in a passage of Verlyn Flieger's *A Question of Time*. Flieger argues convincingly that the apparent perfection of Elvish enchantment is misleading – and doubly so, given the ambivalence resulting from Tolkien's own attachment to it – insofar as human beings, unlike Elves, cannot live in, as it were, a permanent state of enchantment; and any attempt to do so is doomed. Thus,

> there is a concealed sting in Lórien's beauty. Its timelessness is not the unspoiled perfection it seems. Rather, that very perfection is its flaw. It is a cautionary picture, closer in kind to the Ring than we'd like to think, shown to us in all its beauty to test if we can let it go.
>
> *The Lord of the Rings* is, among other things, a story about the ability to let go. The Ring is the obvious example. [...] The timeless beauty of Lórien is the deeper example. (Flieger 1997: 112)

I believe this is the theme underlying and uniting the One Ring, the Three, and us. It is a theme that includes but extends far beyond Tolkien's work, the province of all religions and of none alone. Here, for example, are the reported words of the Buddha on his deathbed to his grieving friend and attendant (from the perspective of one who has transcended such suffering but spoken nonetheless, one feels, a little wearily):[15]

---

14 It was posed to me, with his usual uncomfortable perspicuity, by Michael P. Winship.
15 Quoted in Rupert Gethin (1998: 26). I once gave a short talk to the Tolkien Society in which I suggested, tongue in cheek, of course, that Tolkien was actually a Buddhist (Curry 2001); nonetheless, there is a serious point here, which I have tried to make above.

"Enough, Ananda, do not sorrow, do not lament. Have I not formerly explained that it is the nature of things that we must be divided, separated and parted from all that is beloved and dear? How could it be, Ananda, that what has been born and come into being, that what is compounded and subject to decay, should not decay? It is not possible."

IV

I also recently "discovered" a book by a Canadian philosopher, Jan Zwicky, which throws valuable light on the subject of enchantment generally, as well as specifically in relation to the work of Tolkien. (It also corroborates some of my own thinking on both counts: always welcome, in the absence of unshakeable self-confidence.)

Zwicky counterposes "the lyric" – which is more or less cognate with "enchantment" – with the technological. Thus,

> Lyric coherence is not like the unity of systematic structures: its foundation is a heightened experience of detail, rather than the transcendence (excision) of detail. (Zwicky 1992: 120)

> Lyric springs from love, love that attends to the most minute details of difference; and in this attention experiences connection rather than isolation. (Zwicky 1992: 126)

> It is poignant, and musical. (Zwicky 1992: 134)

> Lyric value is a species of teleological value: it perceives things exclusively as ends. In this, it is genetically distinct from utility. (Zwicky 1992: 158)

In contrast, the technological is instrumentalist. It sanctions exploitation, which "occurs when a thing becomes identified with a particular role in 'the story of (Western European) (human) progress'; roughly, when it becomes a commodity; when it is used in the absence of a perception of what it is" (Zwicky 1992: 222).

Recall, in this connection, Frodo's lyric experience of a tree while entering Lórien: "He felt a delight in wood and the touch of it, neither as forester nor as carpenter; it was the delight of the living tree itself" (FR.II.vi). As Zwicky says, "The experience of 'presence' precludes exploitation." But then she adds – introducing a critically important third term – "Though it does not preclude use. There is a sense of 'use' which is, we might say, *domestic*, and of a significantly different character from exploitation" (Zwicky 1992: 222; emphasis in original). To continue with the example of trees and humans, the industrial clear-cutting of whole forests, many of them ancient, is exploitation – (one is reminded of the felling of whole groves to feed the insatiable fires of Orthanc) – whereas coppicing, pollarding and selective cutting, such as surely is practised by hobbits, is domestic use.[16]

Now life utterly without enchantment or lyric would hardly feel worth living, or even, perhaps, be livable. As Zwicky puts it,

> Lyric springs from the desire to recapture the intuited wholeness of the non-linguistic world, to heal the slash in the mind that is the capacity for language.

> But as language-using creatures, it is of our essence that that gap cannot be permanently healed. The recognition that it cannot is the source of lyric's poignancy.

> Poignancy comes after yearning. It is the essential emotional colouring of lyric thought. (Zwicky 1992: 230)

And, beyond a doubt, that of Tolkien's work. "It is a fair tale, though it is sad, as are all the tales of Middle-earth" (FR.I.xi). However, we humans are not Elves, so we cannot *live* in Lothlórien. As Flieger notes, "An important impetus for [Tolkien's] subcreation was his uneasiness with the twentieth century, his desire to escape it, and his knowledge that such escape was only partly (and then only imaginatively) possible" (1997: 257). Or, as Zwicky puts the matter:

> Lyric strives for the whole in a single gesture, yearns for a wholeness with the world that, as language-users, we cannot sustain. (1992: 284)

> It is both the sadness and strength of thought that it can see beyond what drives it, the sadness and the beauty of human being that it can comprehend the in-compatibility of its essence with its most fundamental desire. (1992: 534)

That does not, of course, mean that we must therefore be Orcs, left only with technological exploitation! This is where the concept of the domestic comes into its own:

> The domestic accepts the essential tension between lyric desire and the capacity for technology. In this acceptance, it mediates. (Zwicky 1992: 258)

And, she adds,

---

16 I am grateful to Tom Shippey for pointing out the relevance of this contrast.

Domesticity lives without absolutes – including absolute clarity. (Zwicky 1992: 524)

In relation to Tolkien's great work, however, all this seems relatively clear, at least. For what are the hobbits – and thus, by Tolkien's own admission, humans[17] – if not *domestic*? And what else does the book as a whole end with – quite deliberately, we may be sure – when Sam returns home to his wife and child, evening meal and fire?[18]

As usual, Tolkien *gestures*, without the least didacticism (or in his terms, allegory),[19] to the deepest existential realities of human life, with its challenges and what we have to face them with: chiefly, courage, hope, and an appreciation of what is small and apparently insignificant; and above all, the bitter-sweet poignancy that is our peculiar gift.

Bibliography

BLIXEN, Karen. 1970. *Out of Africa*. (Originally published 1937). New York: Random House.

CALDECOTT, Stratford. 2005. "Christianity and Literary Culture: The Case of J.R.R. Tolkien." Unpublished paper from a talk given at Regent's Park College, 15th November 2005.

CARPENTER, Humphrey. 1977. *J.R.R. Tolkien: A Biography*. London: George Allen & Unwin.

CURRY, Patrick. 1999. "Magic vs. Enchantment." *Journal of Contemporary Religion* 14.3: 401-412.[20]

2001. "On Hobbits and Elves: or, Took and Baggins Again." In Helen ARMSTRONG (ed.). 2001. *Digging Potatoes, Growing Trees*. Telford: The Tolkien Society, 48-51.[21]

---

17 "The hobbits are, of course, meant to be a branch of the specifically *human* race (not Elves or Dwarves) [...]" (Tolkien 1981: 158, n.).
18 I am grateful to Sue Bridgwater for pointing out this obvious and important point which I had somehow managed to miss.
19 See his "Foreword to the Second Edition" in *The Lord of the Rings*.
20 Reprinted on pages 65-82 of the present volume
21 Reprinted on pages 245-49 of the present volume

2004. *Defending Middle-Earth: Tolkien, Myth and Modernity.* Second edition. Boston MA: Houghton Mifflin.

FLIEGER, Verlyn. 1997. *A Question of Time: J.R.R. Tolkien's Road to Faërie.* Kent OH: Kent State University Press.

GERTH, Hans H. and C. WRIGHT MILLS (eds.). 1991. *From Max Weber: Essays in Sociology.* London: Routledge.

GETHIN, Rupert. 1998. *The Foundations of Buddhism.* Oxford: Oxford University Press.

GRIFFIN, David Ray. 2000. *Re-Enchantment without Supernaturalism.* Ithaca NY: Cornell University Press.

HEPBURN, Ronald W. 1984. *"Wonder"' and Other Essays.* Edinburgh: Edinburgh University Press.

HUTTON, Ronald. 2003. *Witches, Druids and King Arthur.* London: Hambledon.

"The Pagan Tolkien." In Paul E. KERRY (ed.). 2011. *The Ring and the Cross: Christianity and The Lord of the Rings.* Madison WI: Fairleigh Dickinson University Press, 57-70.

OWEN, Alex. 2004. *The Place of Enchantment: British Occultism and the Culture of the Modern.* Chicago IL: University of Chicago Press.

SHIPPEY, Tom A. 1982. *The Road to Middle-earth.* London: George Allen & Unwin.

SPIRITO, Guglielmo. 2008. "The Influence of Holiness: The Healing Power of Tolkien's Narrative." In Stratford CALEDECOTT and Thomas HONEGGER (eds.). 2008. *Tolkien's The Lord of the Rings. Sources of Inspiration.* Zurich and Jena: Walking Tree Publishers, 199-210.

TOLKIEN, John Ronald Reuel. 1981. *The Letters of J.R.R. Tolkien.* Edited by Humphrey CARPENTER, with the assistance of Christopher TOLKIEN. London: George Allen & Unwin.

1988. "On Fairy-Stories." In *Tree and Leaf.* Edited by Christopher TOLKIEN. London: Unwin Hyman, 11-73.

2004. *The Lord of the Rings.* Originally published 1954-55. One-volume 50th anniversary edition. Boston MA: Houghton Mifflin.

ZWICKY, Jan. 1992. *Lyric Philosophy.* Toronto: University of Toronto Press.

Iron Crown, Iron Cage: Tolkien and Weber on Modernity and Enchantment

Abstract

This paper uses both a conceptual and a symbolic-mythological hermeneutic analysis of their very different work to compare the attitudes and understandings of J.R.R. Tolkien and Max Weber towards modernity. It points to fundamental commonalities and suggests that both men also counterposed modernity with enchantment. It therefore includes a closer consideration of the nature of such enchantment and the meta-politics of its relationship with modernist magic.

J.R.R. Tolkien (1892-1973) almost certainly never read the social philosopher Max Weber (1864-1920), yet their diagnoses of modernity, as well as its opposite and perhaps its remedy, were tantalizingly similar. Combining their insights results in a powerful and, in some respects, new perspective which I would like to introduce here. And my starting point is their strangely shared choice of symbolism which my title encapsulates.

I am aware, of course, that Tolkien's fiction cannot be reduced to his views. Nonetheless it is idle to pretend that those views are not in his fiction and cannot be inferred from it, together with his letters and essays. With that in mind, let us recall that the most powerful evil figure in the entire history of Middle-earth is Morgoth, the fallen Vala, of whom even Sauron the Great was originally only a servant. I further take it as significant that the ultimate token of the legitimacy and authority of Morgoth's rule was his iron crown, containing the three stolen Silmarils. (And note that the iron holds the Silmarils, not the other way around.) Finally, respecting this part of the story, and leaving aside Morgoth's eventual defeat by the remaining Valar, the only occasion when that crown ever slipped was when Lúthien Tinúviel danced its wearer into a trance

First published in Eduardo Segura and Thomas Honegger (eds.). 2007. *Myth and Magic: Art According to the Inklings*. Zurich and Jena: Walking Tree Publishers, 99-108.

and then sleep: in short – and the word is both unavoidable and, as we shall see, important – when she enchanted him.

Next we must turn to Tolkien's essay "On Fairy-Stories", where he introduces a seminal distinction between magic and enchantment.[1] Made aware of the confusing uses of the first term, he suggested that "magic" should be reserved for the exercise of power and domination, using the will, in order to bring about changes in the "Primary World". Whether the means employed are material or spiritual is ultimately a secondary consideration. Sauron is "the Lord of magic *and* machines" (*Letters* 146; my emphasis). The ultimate symbol of magic within Tolkien's literary world is, of course, the One Ring; again, as we shall see, the "one" is important.

Enchantment, in contrast, "produces a Secondary World into which both designer and spectator can enter" (OFS 49). It is "artistic in desire and purpose" (OFS 49) and its purpose is "the realisation, independent of the conceiving mind, of imagined wonder" (OFS 18). I take "realisation" here to be doubly meaningful: both to make wonder real and, I suggest, its ultimate meaning: to realise that whatever is experienced as wonderful *is* really so. So, oversimplifying but not egregiously so, the hallmark of magic is *will*, whereas that of enchantment is *wonder*.

Let us turn to Weber. In the world of social and political philosophy, Weber is perhaps best-known for his statement that "[t]he fate of our times is characterised by rationalisation and intellectualisation and, above all, by the 'disenchantment [*Entzauberung*] of the world'" (in Gerth and Mills 1991: 155). And what brings about such disenchantment? Is it knowledge of the truth about ourselves and the world? No, it is the "belief" – note, the belief suffices –

> that if one but wished one *could* learn it at any time. Hence, it means that principally there are no mysterious incalculable forces that come into play, but rather that one can, in principle, master all things by calculation. This means that the world is disenchanted. One need no longer have recourse to magical means to master or implore the spirits, as did the savage, for whom such mys-

---

1 Henceforth OFS; the original essay was first delivered as a lecture in 1939, and first published, somewhat enlarged, in 1947. The text used here is that in Tolkien (1988). See also my "Magic vs. Enchantment" in this volume. See also Verlyn Flieger's important explorations of *faërie* in Tolkien's work in *Splintered Light: Logos and Language in Tolkien's World* (Flieger 2002) and *A Question of Time: J.R.R. Tolkien's Road to Faërie* (Flieger 1997).

terious powers existed. Technical means and calculations perform the service. (Gerth and Mills 1991: 139)

Weber's use of the word "magic" here is loose and therefore ambiguous.

Here it is important to note that to master all things by calculation requires a master calculus, or more generally principle, truth and/or value from which to derive and by which to legitimate such a calculus. If there is more than one then the possibility of incommensurability between different phenomena arises – this one amenable to this calculus but that one only to that other – and thence ultimate incalculability. In other words, in the exercise of power-knowledge, or what Tolkien called "*Magic*", there can only be *one* Ring of Power, and only one hand (as Gandalf reminds Saruman) can wear it.

When sufficiently institutionalised and thence pervasive, the result of rationalisation – and this is as close as Weber ever actually got to defining enchantment positively – is that "[t]he unity of the primitive image of the world, in which everything was *concrete magic*, has tended to split into rational cognition and mastery of nature, on the one hand, and into 'mystic' experiences, on the other. The inexpressible contents of such experiences remain the only possible 'beyond,' added to the mechanism of a world robbed of gods" (in Gerth and Mills 1991: 282).

Now although Tolkien's analysis of enchantment is richer than Weber's, we can use the latter's point about wonder as both concrete and magic (that is, enchanting) to refine Tolkien's point about its "realisation": enchantment is making it possible (by art) to realise that the world we experience, and/or some part thereof, is *already* wondrous. Wonder is not something we do, create or add to the world; that would be magic. And it is not a wholly ineffable or otherworldly "mystic" experience; whatever that may be, it is not enchantment.

This means, for example, that the way (whether "back" or not) to enchantment cannot proceed through a return, collective or individual, to theism; not, that is, as long as its practice conforms to the theological exigencies of a one true God. Indeed, according to Weber, the imperative to calculate, organise and rationalise was originally a religious impulse with its roots in monotheism and especially, in the modern Western world, Protestantism. Whereas the Puritan wanted to work in such a calling, however,

> we are forced to do so. For when asceticism was carried out of monastic cells into everyday life, and began to dominate worldly morality, it did its part in building the tremendous cosmos of the modern economic order. This order is now bound to the technical and economic conditions of machine production which today determine the lives of all the individuals who are born into this mechanism, not only those directly concerned with economic acquisition, with irresistible force. Perhaps it will so determine them until the last ton of fossilized coal is burnt. (Weber 2001: 182)

Here again, the resonance with Tolkien's romantic antimodernism, with its hatred (the word is not too strong) of industrialism and fear for the future of the natural world, is entirely apt (see Curry 2004).

In the view of the Puritan divine, Weber (2001: 182) continued, "care for external goods should only lie on the shoulders of the 'saint like a light cloak, which can be thrown aside at any moment'. But fate decreed that the cloak should become an iron cage." This has become the dominant metaphor for Weber's analysis of modernity.[2]

He concluded:

> No-one knows who will live in this cage in the future, or whether at the end of this tremendous development, entirely new prophets will arise, or there will be a great rebirth of old ideas and ideals, or, if neither, mechanized petrification, embellished with a sort of convulsive self-importance. For of the last stage of this cultural development, it might well be truly said: 'Specialists without spirit, sensualists without heart; this nullity imagines that it has attained a level of civilization never before achieved'. (Weber 2001:182)

We can almost hear Tolkien cheering in the background.

Without going into any detail, I should add that Weber's account proved very influential on subsequent social theory. It was taken up by the founders of Critical Theory, Max Horkheimer, Theodor Adorno and Herbert Marcuse of the Frankfurt School, and in particular by the first two in their book *The Dialectic of Enlightenment* (1944): a brilliant and unsettling account of modernity – "the fully

---

2 Although it may well be that a better translation is "iron shell" [*stahlhartes Gehäuse*]; see Pels (2003: 26-27).

enlightened earth radiates disaster" – whose chief weakness is that if everything is really so hopeless then what did its authors hope to accomplish?

More recently, the spirit of Critical Theory passed into the work of Michel Foucault.[3] It has also surfaced in more orthodox branches of the academy such as World System Theory, whose proponents give substantial empirical as well as theoretical flesh to the bones of Weber's suggestion that although modern science has powerfully accelerated the pace of rationalisation, it is only "the most important fraction, of the process of intellectualisation which we have been undergoing for thousands of years [...]" (in Gerth and Mills 1991: 138). Frank and Gills (1993) find the origins of this process in 1500 BCE.

Now at this point I propose to do something guaranteed to make even the most hardened postmodernist blanch, and turn to the symbolism of iron.[4] Of course most of them haven't ever tried to come to grips with Tolkien's "perfectly sincere, perfectly impossible narrative" (Attebery 1992: 46), so I have the edge there. And why would I do so? Because it is just possible that Weber's and Tolkien's choice of metaphors may not be entirely random but rather meaningful in a way that a few thousand years of cultural reflection might throw some light on. Also, of course, subaltern discourses marginalised by modernity can by their alterity reveal the *aporias* of a dominant ideology. (There, that should hold them.)

Hesiod suggested that the ages of humanity have descended in quality from Golden to Silver to Bronze and finally Iron, an unpleasant and brutish period in which we are obviously still living. Persian religious literature apparently concurs. The Bible describes God's instrument of punishment as a "rod of iron" (Psalms 2:9 and Revelation 2:27). And the nails in Christ's cross were, of course, made of iron. (They were purportedly used in the early medieval crown of Lombardy, but note the difference between Charlemagne's and Morgoth's crowns: the latter made of iron but the Emperor's of gold containing, in a narrow band, the iron.)

Another characteristic of iron is more positive; it has long been held to protect against the hostile magical powers of witches, necromancers and vampires. (Hence

---

3 And not its putative heir, the neo-rationalist Jürgen Habermas.
4 I gratefully acknowledge key suggestions for this section by Liz Greene.

an iron horseshoe over the threshold.) This not only points to the importance of context, to which I shall return in a moment. It also serves as a reminder to be wary of accepting the claims of our iron age secularism at face value, for the same reason that we should beware the claims of scientism (a closely related phenomenon) to be without prejudices, assumptions or untested and untestable ultimate values. That is, modernity is indeed programmatically disenchanted and disenchanting, but it is nonetheless, as Horkheimer and Adorno perceived, thoroughly magical: "In the enlightened world, mythology has entered into the profane. In its blank purity, the reality which has been cleansed of demons and their conceptual descendents assumes the numinous character which the ancient world attributed to demons" (Horkheimer and Adorno 1994: 28).

Probably the fundamental mythic association with iron, underlying these attributes, is Mars, long held to be a "malefic" planet which is co-extensive in cultural astronomy with the Graeco-Roman god of war and all that that entails: will-power and its correlates the martial virtues: courage, personal power, the ability and willingness to push something through by main force. The shadow-side of these attributes are not far away, of course: savagery, brutality, callousness.[5]

The centrality of the will here, in either case, emphasises the appropriateness of the choice of iron to invoke the modern empire. The contextual nature of Martian virtues/vices, however, warns us not to see iron as essentially or necessarily negative. Following up this hint suggests that the modernist monism of the iron cage/iron crown is a result of its attempt to usurp the authority of the other deities and replace their messy agonistic plurality with a single, well-ordered – or rather, "properly managed" – empire: "Knowledge, Order, Rule," to quote Sauron's stooge Saruman, but actually ruled, of course, by One Ring.

This point is susceptible to more precise elaboration: Mars-Ares takes much of his nature (in the best fashion of discursive definition through mutually defining terms of opposition) from the planetary deity he forms a pair with: Venus-Aphrodite. Here surely is mythopoetic confirmation of the wisdom of both Tolkien's and Weber's decision to counterpose the iron "Magic" of moder-

---

5 Reflecting differing cultural values, Mars was more positively portrayed and highly valued by the Romans than was Ares by classical Greeks, for whom the latter god's blind fury could inspire contempt as well as fear.

nity with enchantment. For where do the roots of the latter lie if not with the ancient (pre-Olympian) goddess of love and beauty, whose power to enchant was respected and feared by even the most powerful of the other gods?[6] Is not her power precisely that of enchantment, and is not her love "concrete magic", in which the most precise and tiny physical details of the beloved acquire the most mysterious moment? And note that the Graces, patronesses of the arts, were Aphrodite's attendants (see Friedrich 1978). How appropriate, then, that Morgoth's crown only slipped, and he thereby lost a Silmaril, under the spell of Lúthien Tinúviel as she danced. (In this considerable sense, if in no other, Tolkien was arguably a feminist.)

In conclusion, then, we can say that the contemporary triumph of modernist magic – the world system, driven by will and ruled by iron – cannot be doubted, but it is not unqualified. In the interstices of the grid, among places and people (especially "small" people) overlooked by power, and even, I daresay, in the hearts of many of its servants, enchantment still lives. It is a precarious existence, of course, and cannot (as I have said) compete directly with Magic using the latter's weapons without thereby becoming the Enemy itself. As Weber too pointed out, an intellectually driven pursuit of romantic irrationalism, being programmatically willed, simply extends the bounds of disenchantment.[7]

All that can effectively be done is to protect enchantment where it already exists; to make it possible to perceive it, and encourage people to do so, where it exists but has not yet been noticed, which is the duty and privilege of art, but also education;[8] and to refuse and expose the great modern lie in which Enchantment is tacitly replaced with its power-driven simulacrum, Glamour.[9]

Beyond that, the only hope we have is that "evil will oft evil mars." We are now fast approaching the day when the last ton of fossilised coal is burnt and nature – the *fons et origo*, deified/personified as Venus-Aphrodite, of autonomous enchantment – will reassert herself against Nature plc, an insensible set

---

6 Only Athena, Artemis and Hestia were immune to Aphrodite's spells.
7 See Nicholas Gane's excellent *Max Weber and Postmodern Theory*.
8 Brian Rosebury (2003: 177-78) finds my account of enchantment too directly involved with the Primary World. But a successful, i.e. enchanted Secondary World results in seeing the Primary World in a fresh and different way, which is just what Tolkien called "recovery" (OFS 53).
9 See Curry "Magic vs. Enchantment" (in this volume).

of external manageable resources to be manipulated by power-knowledge.[10] The former nature is the one we directly experience: a sensuous, "wild and multiplicitous otherness" in which we find ourselves and which we find within ourselves.[11]

Despite other more obvious Earth deities such as Gaia, I am emphasizing the importance of Venus-Aphrodite here on the grounds of the integral connection between erotic love and nature, as well as between aesthetics and nature.[12] It is also worth recalling that Tolkien defined the principal goal of enchantment, as practised by its exemplars the Elves, as "the adornment of [E]arth, and the healing of its hurts" (*Letters* 151-52). Adornment is, of course, precisely the *métier* of Aphrodite.

The more we cling to the latter "nature", however, the more terrible that reassertion will prove. But one may hope that before then, there might be a more general disillusionment with modernist magic and the power of iron, thus opening the door, at least, to a more widespread rediscovery of what is useless but makes life worth living – and perhaps even, in the end, possible.

Abbreviations

Letters: see CARPENTER 1981

OFS: "On Fairy-Stories" in TOLKIEN (1988: 9-73)

Bibliography

ABRAM, David. 1996. *The Spell of the Sensuous: Perception and Language in a More-Than-Human World.* New York: Vintage Books.

ATTEBERY, Brian. 1992. *Strategies of Fantasy.* Bloomington IN: Indiana University Press.

---

10 See Curry (2004).
11 See David Abram's superb *The Spell of the Sensuous.*
12 On which see Hepburn (1984).

CARPENTER, Humphrey (ed., with the assistance of Christopher TOLKIEN). 1981. *The Letters of J.R.R. Tolkien.* London: Allen & Unwin.

CURRY, Patrick. 1999. "Magic vs. Enchantment." *Journal of Contemporary Religion* 14.3: 401-412.[13]

2004. *Defending Middle-earth.* Second edition; first edition 1997. Boston MA: Houghton Mifflin.

FLIEGER, Verlyn. 1997. *A Question of Time: J.R.R. Tolkien's Road to Faërie.* Kent OH: Kent State University Press.

2002. *Splintered Light: Logos and Language in Tolkien's World.* Second edition. First edition 1983. Kent OH: Kent State University Press.

FRANK, Andre Gunder and Barry K. GILLS. 1993. *The World System: Five Hundred Years or Five Thousand?* London: Routledge.

FRIEDRICH, Paul. 1978. *The Meaning of Aphrodite.* Chicago IL: University of Chicago Press.

GANE, Nicholas. 2004. *Max Weber and Postmodern Theory.* Basingstoke: Palgrave Macmillan.

GERTH, H. H. and C. Wright MILLS (eds.). 1991. *From Max Weber: Essays in Sociology.* London: Routledge.

HEPBURN, Ronald. 1984. *"Wonder" and Other Essays.* Edinburgh: Edinburgh University Press.

HORKHEIMER, Max and Theodor W. ADORNO. 1994. *The Dialectic of Enlightenment.* First edition 1944. New York: Continuum.

PELS, Peter. 2003. "Introduction: Magic and Modernity." In Birgit and Peter PELS (eds.). 2003. *Magic and Modernity: Interfaces of Revelation and Concealment.* Stanford CA: Stanford University Press, 1-38.

ROSEBURY, Brian. 2003. *Tolkien: A Cultural Phenomenon.* Basingstoke: Palgrave Macmillan.

TOLKIEN, J.R.R. 1988. *Tree and Leaf.* Edited by Christopher TOLKIEN. London: HarperCollins.

WEBER, Max. 2001. *The Protestant Ethic and the Spirit of Capitalism.* London: Routledge.

---

13 Reprinted on pages 65-82 of the present volume.

The Third Road: *Faërie* in Hypermodernity

Abstract

In this paper I borrow the idea from an old ballad of three roads, one each to Heaven, Hell and *Faërie*. I contrast the ambiguous or liminal third road with the other two, arguing that in both religious and secular versions, being parts of an official programme, they tend towards disenchantment. Then I consider the work of Tolkien and Lewis, especially how they resolved the contradiction or tension between religion (the two roads) and enchantment (the third), before turning to the strange case of Philip Pullman. I conclude by considering the fate of *Faërie* in the circumstances of the beginning of the twenty-first century.

In the eighteenth-century ballad "Thomas Rymer", the hero is abducted (without much of a struggle) by the Queen of Elfland, and their route to *Faërie* is the third road. As she says to him,

> O see not ye yon narrow road,
> So thick beset wi' thorns and briers?
> That is the path of righteousness,
> Tho' after it but few enquires.
>
> And see not ye that braid braid road,
> That lies across yon lillie leven?
> That is the path of wickedness,
> Though some call it the road to heaven.
>
> And see not ye that bonny road,
> Which winds about the fernie brae?
> That is the road to fair Elfland,
> Where you and I this night maun gae.
> (Child 1965 I: 323)

First published in Graham Harvey (ed.). 2013. *The Handbook of Animism*. Durham: Acumen, 468-478. Originally, the text was a paper for a seminar on the work of Tolkien hosted by Nick Groom at the Tremough Campus of the University of Exeter on 12 May 2009, with thanks to Professor Groom for the kind invitation. I also thank Michael Winship, Sean Kane, Ursula Le Guin, Nigel Cooper and Franco Manni for perceptive comments on previous drafts.

Let us explore (cautiously, as befits a wild and "perilous" place)[1] what is variously called Elfland, *Faërie* or enchantment – which is also, I shall suggest, an animist world. I have ventured there before in print,[2] but this time I will be guided by the metaphor of the three roads, and its significance. My main purpose is to better understand animist enchantment through its continuing presence in a field of British literature and literary culture, one where J.R.R. Tolkien, C.S. Lewis and more recently Philip Pullman have left their mark. But the literary and cultural particularities of its presence also compel attention in their own right.

The view of *Faërie* as profoundly ambiguous is an old one. Its natives, as C.S. Lewis remarked in *The Discarded Image*, "are marginal, fugitive creatures. They are perhaps the only creatures to whom the Model does not assign, as it were, an official status" (quoted in Miller 2008: 272).[3] Lewis means the medieval Christian model but it has both older antecedents and, as we shall see, subsequent heirs.

It seems to me that our personal experiences of enchantment are similarly fugitive and marginal, at least in the accounts we give of them. The third road remains the one less-travelled (or at least, reported) but simultaneously, for many if not most of us, the most enticing, fascinating and ultimately meaningful. For at the dying of the light surely a candidate, at least, for what one remembers of one's life is the moments of magic (in the sense of enchantment), whatever they may have been for each of us. That includes love, at least by Tolkien's (2005: 101) definition of *Faërie*: "it represents love: that is, a love and respect for all things, 'animate' and 'inanimate', an unpossessive love of them as 'other'."

Nonetheless, just because it is wild and unbiddable,[4] the third road remains problematised, discouraged and marginalised by every official programme, whether religious or secular. This naturally affects individuals as well as organised groups. So I would like to ask: what results when those two conflicting

---

1 "On Fairy-Stories" (in the following OFS) 9, 14. OFS was originally delivered as a lecture in 1939, and first published, somewhat enlarged, in 1947. See the recent definitive edition by Flieger and Anderson 2008.
2 Curry 2007a, 2007b, 2008 and 2012. My interest in this topic was rekindled by the discussion in Miller, *The Magician's Book*, e.g. p. 276.
3 Cf. Valerie I.J. Flint, *The Rise of Magic in Early Medieval Europe*, for a study of the process of "sorting" that the medieval Church engaged in, a process begun by the early Church fathers.
4 A term I borrow, with thanks, from Anthony Thorley.

demands, personal and formal, conflict? And when modernity has become virtually synonymous with disenchantment, what is the future of such enchantment in the twenty-first century, or what I am calling "hypermodernity"?

I

First, some pointers or field-marks to enable us to recognise enchantment when we encounter it, or *Faërie* if we find ourselves there. And let me say immediately that in order to start off on the right foot we must wholly reject any foundational distinction between "state of mind" and "world", or "inner" and "outer". Although the opposing terms in these pairs can be distinguished as a matter of emphasis, it is merely a vestigial Cartesian delusion to suppose that they can be cleanly separated, and enchantment, perhaps in particular, invariably involves both.

Tolkien – who quotes Thomas Rhymer at the start of his "On Fairy-Stories"– defines "the primal desire at the heart of *Faërie*" as "the realisation, independent of the conceiving mind, of imagined wonder" (OFS 18). Realisation, that is, in the sense both of realising that someone or something *is* wondrous, and their wonder *becoming* real. The contrast-class is given as magic, defined as "not an art but a technique; its desire is *power* in this world, domination of things and wills" (OFS 49-50). Following this lead, then, I take *wonder* to be a hallmark, and the most important one, of enchantment; and *will* its distinguishing contrary. (I have found Tolkien to be an unimpeachable guide concerning enchantment.)

Another reliable authority is Max Weber, who defines enchantment as "concrete magic". In other words, enchantment is always both material *and* spiritual, precise *and* mysterious, limited *and* unfathomable. And the contrast he draws is with the "rational cognition and mastery of nature" (Weber 1991: 282) – paradigmatically scientific and bureaucratic, but with clear religious provenance – which, Weber (1991: 155) said, results in "the 'disenchantment of the world'." This time and/or sensibility, in Tolkien's terms, is "the dominion of Men".[5]

---

5 Tolkien's description of the Fourth Age, after the events chronicled in *The Lord of the Rings*, in Appendix B of *The Lord of the Rings*.

Also instructive is the etymology of the word "enchant", coming to us from Middle English via the French, *enchanter*, itself from the Latin *incantare*, that is, *in* + *cantare*, "to sing". Emboldened by Sam Gamgee's description of Tolkien's (FR.II.vi) exemplar of enchantment, Lothórien – "I feel as if I was *inside* a song" – I interpret this to mean the experience of finding oneself *in* a song (a song one hears, or perhaps even that one is singing) and, by extension, a story of any kind.

Robert Bringhurst (2007: 248) offers a different etymology for *Faërie* from that given by the *Oxford English Dictionary*, one derived from the Greek *phêres*, meaning "creatures of the wild", and sister to the Latin *ferus*, which gave rise to "feral" and "fierce". It is thus no playground for harmlessly imaginary supernatural beings "but the mythworld itself, which is everything outside our control." This understanding resonates with others which reiterate that enchantment is wild, perilous, and natural – not supernatural, but ecological in the fullest sense of the word. As Bringhurst (1995: 15) remarks elsewhere, "[i]n North America we call this world Nature or the Wild."

The origins of the word *Faërie* take us in still another direction: Middle English from Old French *fée*, from Latin *fata*, the plural of *fatum*: "fate". And as if that isn't sufficiently tantalising, *fata* itself is the past participle of *fari*, "to speak".[6] So the path of enchantment and that of *Faërie* meet where something is fatefully spoken or sung, or (I would add) written, and fatefully heard or read. And crossroads have long been places where weird things can happen; in classical myth, they were the domain of Hermes, the bearer of messages to and from the gods. "Weird" itself comes from the Anglo-Saxon *wyrd*, meaning "fate".

The metaphor of crossroads is also relevant in a different but related respect. In a brilliant reconstruction of Amerindian animism and perspectivism, Eduardo Viveiros de Castro describes it as "a universe that is 100 percent relational," in which any apparent object "is an incompletely interpreted subject" (Viveiros de Castro 2004: 473). Transformation is then "not a process but a relation. Nothing 'happened', but everything has changed" (Viveiros de Castro 2004: 470). But

---

6 See Tolkien (2005: 143).

these relations should not be understood as idealist or (purely) spiritual; on the contrary, being radically non-modern and *a fortiori* non-Cartesian, they are, like Weber's concrete magic, both bodied and minded, ensouled and enworlded.

The upshot is that animism, *faërie* and enchantment share profound common ground. *Faërie* is the place where living perspectives meet, animism is the generic term for that dynamic, and enchantment accompanies the meeting. Nor are those perspectives restricted to human ones. Animist enchantment is strictly non-anthropocentric, so all kinds of beings, including "things", can turn out to be existentially alive, and any object a subject with agency and an agenda, with whom one finds oneself in a relationship.[7] As Tolkien (OFS 14) says

> *Faërie* contains many things besides elves and fays [...]: it holds the seas, the sun, the moon, the sky; and the earth and all the things that are in it: tree and bird, water and stone, wine and bread, and ourselves [...] when we are enchanted.

In a modernist universe, all subjects are incompletely analysed inanimate objects and therefore ethically inconsiderable potential resources to be manipulated as part of a project of the rational mastery of nature (including human nature). In a relationship, in contrast – and enchantment is nothing if not relational – by definition, neither party is in complete control; issues of ethics, negotiation, and etiquette are therefore paramount.

Of course, there are other signs of animist enchantment. (I've always thought that Kubla Khan's "flashing eyes and floating hair" were a give-away.) These markers, however – wonder, concrete magic, participation in a narrative, and nonanthropocentric relations – will do to be going on with.

II

What is the significance of the three roads, then? First, let us note that heaven and hell are co-dependent, not only defining each other but comprising routes merely to different parts of the same truth or reality, the putatively exhaustive Model of the one true God. The two roads of righteousness and wickedness are thus actually forks of a single road, and the most radical alternative to either of them is the ambiguous "third" road to *Faërie*.

---

7 Such as the stones discussed by the Ojibwe elder and Irving Hallowell; see Harvey (2006: 33-34 & ff).

This contrast also works in another way. Weber (1991: 139) makes the point that a programme of rational mastery depends upon the "belief [...] that one can, in principle, master all things by calculation." And that indispensably requires monism: a single principle in relation to which everything, at least in theory, can be grasped and ordered. In its absence, one could end up with more than one incommensurable truth with no overall *logos*, no theoretical way to adjudicate between them – which is the actual situation in animism and polytheism and their secular version, pluralism – and that is completely unacceptable for any programme with universalist aspirations. In short, in order "to rule them all [...] to find them [...] to bring them all and [...] bind them" (FR.II.ii), the One Ring is needed.

It follows ineluctably that the roots of disenchantment lie in religion – or rather, to be more precise, the Abrahamic religions (although I do not say they lie only there). Weber saw this point clearly, as did Max Horkheimer and Theodor W. Adorno (1994: 18): "Reason and religion deprecate and condemn the principle of magic enchantment." By the same token, secular modernity, religion's even more rigorous child midwifed by Protestantism, requires precisely "the extirpation of animism" (Horkheimer & Adorno 1994: 5), and "the destruction of gods and qualities alike is insisted upon" (Horkheimer & Adorno 1994: 8). Both metaphysically and historically, modernity is thus founded on a rejection decidedly not of magic, whose emphasis on power, control and manipulation is grist to its own mill, and a great deal of which was absorbed by early modern science, but of animist enchantment, particularly that of a living more-than-human nature; and that is what still haunts its troubled dreams.

It also follows that the break between theism and secular rational modernism is a relative not a radical one (see the following table).

	Christianity (spiritual)	Science (material)	Modernism (ideological)
source & goal	God	Truth	Progress
manifest in	Scripture	Laws	[Manifestos]
accessed through	revelation	scientific reason	"critical" reason, iconoclasm
authorised by	clergy (theological experts)	scientists (technical experts)	critics (theoretical experts)
heresy	superstition (heterodoxy)	superstition (ignorance)	superstition (tradition)

Truth replaces God, scientific reason replaces revelation, scientific authorities replace theologians and the nature of heresy changes, but crucial aspects of the fundamental logic do not. The origin and goal is still singular and universal;[8] there is still a royal road leading from and to it; and the enemy for both programmes remains, strikingly, "superstition" – that is, in this context, unlicensed (that is, wild) enchantment. It follows again that, as against enchantment, both religious and secular universalist programmes are different versions of the same road, with its two branches. They constitute, in effect, "two vying 'monisms'" (Jonas 1982: 16), and the noisy, tediously predictable "debate" between the so-called "New Atheists" and religious fundamentalists is largely a turf war for control over "Knowledge, Rule, Order", to use Saruman's seductive words (FR.II.ii).

That said, there remains an important difference in principle between theism and secularism. It results from the apophatic nature of God as an ultimately unfathomable spiritual mystery, which denies the final promise of analysis and control that material reality, ultimately limited even if very complex, seems to hold out to science. Theism thus denies what scientism embraces: the prospect of *ultimate* mastery, and with it *complete* disenchantment. Nonetheless, there is common ground insofar as modernist science/scientific modernism exists in continuity and contiguity with that portion of theism which is committed to programmatic control and therefore disenchantment.

---

8 I am of course aware of the doctrine of the Trinity, and it is an important qualification. Islam, in comparison, is uncompromisingly monist.

Is that a fair description? I think so, to the extent that religion wants to press enchantment into the service of God, and therefore to manage it. But enchantment cannot be managed – we might almost say, it *is* what cannot be managed – and it does not survive servitude, even to a good cause or a wholly admirable programme. Thus once again, we find that the most radical alternative to both religious and secular salvation/damnation is the third road, at once desired and feared: the way to, and of, enchantment.[9]

III

Where does this leave the work of Tolkien and Lewis, for whom both religion *and* enchantment were so very important? Briefly, I would suggest that Tolkien (OFS 99) availed himself of the metaphor of God as Creator to authorise his own act of literary sub-creation – "We make still by the law in which we're made" – and the idea of the Gospels as a fairy-tale that is, uniquely, also true in the literal sense to legitimise his own epic fairy-tale. (In their own terms, these seem quite legitimate strategies.) This strategy left quite a lot of room for uncertainty and ambiguity. Indeed, Tolkien (*Letters* 189) went so far as to reject a reader's criticism that he had "overstepped the mark" in metaphysical (meaning theological) matters by having the Elves reincarnate, arguing that no-one could deny its possibility even in the "primary" world, let alone in a fictional one.

Another point is that Catholicism, although its ultimate boundaries are strictly maintained, is distinctly more capacious than Protestantism, with its sensitivity to the charge of pagan idolatry: that is, multiple deities (or rather, theologically speaking, pseudo-deities) worshipped instead of God. On that basis, I would speculate that although there remained for both men an incompletely resolved tension between their Christianity and their love of *Faërie*, it posed a sharper problem for the Protestant Lewis than it did for Tolkien.

Of course, folk Christianity long had room for a wide range of semi-autonomous entities, from minor local spirits to grand angelic/diabolic ones, as well as saints indistinguishable in practice from deities. The Reformation and Counter-

---

9 In Curry 2008, I have explored the interdependence of power (as symbolised by the One Ring) and enchantment (as symbolised by the three Elven rings). This essay is reprinted on pages 83-94 of the present volume.

Reformation suppressed some of this, although not as effectively as mass indus-
trialisation and militarisation had by the early twentieth-century. But in British
letters, there survived a kind of patrician demotic parallel to that tolerance in the
vibrant Romantic tradition which obviously still informed and sustained Tolkien
and Lewis, among others, in attempting to reconcile religion and *Faërie*.

What concerns us more here, however, is the relationship between these two
ways of wording in the reception of their work, including what Tolkien (OFS
32) called "the effect produced now by these old things in the stories as they
are." And what strikes me is that for the reading public, any such conflict
doesn't seem to be a problem at all. At the least, is there any evidence that a
significant number of readers have found *The Lord of the Rings* objectionable
solely because of either its Christianity or its pagan/animistic enchantment? I
doubt it. Of course, there were and remain some modernist readers who reject
it in the manner of Gollum having tasted *lembas*, the nourishing Elvish waybread: "Ach! No! […] You try to choke poor Sméagol. Dust and ashes, he can't
eat that" (TT.IV.ii). We shall return to them.

As is well-known, Tolkien, although describing *The Lord of the Rings* as "a
fundamentally religious and Catholic work," deliberately excluded "all references to anything like 'religion'" (*Letters* 172) on the basis that "the Third Age
[of Middle-earth] was not a Christian world" (*Letters* 220). It seems he also
felt that their overt presence would be inappropriate, or counter-productive, in
an effectively post-Christian world. And on balance, the wisdom of his choice
has been borne out. It has enabled countless readers to enjoy his books without
having to negotiate overt ideology, and even to partake of the Christian values
(among others)[10] that requiring such negotiations might have prevented. Tolkien's
work has therefore also suffered less from the kind of distracting controversy
that has dogged Lewis's *Chronicles of Narnia*, in which Christian imagery, in
striking contrast, is often unavoidable.

As Laura Miller's book (2008) shows, however, by far most childhood readers
even of Lewis were either oblivious of or unconcerned by that imagery; and
the more determined and thoughtful of his secular and/or atheist adult readers,

---

10 See the discussion in Curry (2004: 94-109).

too, can prevent it from destroying their enjoyment of the stories, and recover something of their original enchantment.

So why isn't there necessarily a problem for us readers, so to speak – less than for the books' authors, or the critics – in the formal clash between the disenchanting power of religion and the enchanting power of *Faërie*? I think the answer is threefold. First, there is an understanding (albeit arguably a minority and somewhat unorthodox one) of God and *Faërie* as sharing some key properties, including existential wonder, unbiddability, and participation in a (divine) narrative.[11] (I say "sharing"; that doesn't mean that one follows from the other, and any attempt along those lines, being *ipso facto* programmatic, would therefore be disenchanting.)[12] Concrete magic, in the first part of the term, might seem a stumbling-block for transcendental theism; but even here the Incarnation (*kenosis*) could be adduced in favour of the argument.

Whatever their merits, however, such theological considerations are too arcane to encompass more than a tiny minority of readers. The second reason surely pulls more weight: readers don't see a problem on account of our common ability to maintain two or more formally or even empirically contradictory views at the same time. (Countless polls have confirmed that many, perhaps most voters simultaneously support lower taxes and better public services. And the entire edifice of theodicy is based upon reconciling a beneficent and all-powerful God with "an irrational world", to quote Weber (1991: 122), "of undeserved suffering, unpunished injustice, and hopeless stupidity" – apparently with considerable success.) This knack might be decried as an all-too-common inability to think. Before doing so, however, we might remember a reproof by the giant of twentieth-century physics, Niels Bohr: "You are not thinking, you are merely being logical." Note, too, the affinity with John Keats's "negative capability" – an indispensable key to allowing enchantment to happen – whereby one resists "any irritable reaching after fact and reason."[13]

To my mind, however, the third reason is (like the third road) the most compelling. There is a wonderful vignette in Laura Miller's book in which Tolkien asks

---

11 I am grateful to Nigel Cooper for raising this point in a very helpful discussion.
12 See Hepburn (1984: 140), where he argues convincingly that aesthetic wonder does not necessarily entail theism.
13 With thanks to Ursula Le Guin for pointing this out.

Lewis rhetorically: "What class of men would you expect to be most preoccupied with, and most hostile to, the idea of escape?" The answer is, of course, jailers.[14] Quite right too, but then she adds: "I, too, longed for escape, but as I saw it, *Christianity was one of the jailers*" (Miller 2008: 101; my emphasis). In other words, the power of narrative – one of the indispensable aspects of, and portals into, enchantment – is such that when the enchantment works, the wonder that it evokes, being wild and unbiddable, escapes even the intentions of its creators (in this case, as Christians) – let alone managers and administrators.

I don't make this point to denigrate Christianity but rather, among other things, to throw into radical question the claim of both those Christians and those atheists who claim to offer mutually exhaustive alternatives (and pretend to speak for religion and science respectively). There was a tiny but typical instance of this dialogue of the deaf when, on 16 April 2009, BBC1-TV broadcast "The Narnia Code". It is not the fault of Michael Ward, the author of *Planet Narnia: The Seven Heavens in the Imagination of C.S. Lewis*, that the programme's director insisted on shoehorning the subject into a mutually exclusive "choice" between either God or atheism. The third road, as usual, was rendered invisible.

IV

What of the avowed atheists, modernists, and followers of scientism? My guess, based on a survey of Tolkien's critical reception, is that they constitute a high proportion of those who react like Gollum – that is, as if they had been poisoned. Using Tolkien and his work in context as a microcosm, once again, of larger currents and dynamics, its reception among the literati has been striking. The highlights include "juvenile trash" (Edmund Wilson), "a black pit" (Jenny Turner) and, when *The Lord of the Rings* topped the Waterstone's comprehensive poll of readers in 1996 as to the most important book of the 20th century, "my nightmare" (Germaine Greer). As *The Guardian*'s literary critic Nicholas Lezard remarked more recently, "of all the means for professional suicide that are available to the writer, expressing affection for Tolkien is one of the most effective."[15] Are modernists like these allergic to enchantment, then?

---

14 Cf. OFS 56.
15 *The Guardian* (3.4.2010). See Curry 2005 and Curry 2014, both also to be found in this volume.

I would guess the answer is, yes; but they still want it. Once the most basic necessities of air, water, food and shelter are met, I don't believe it is possible to live for long without enchantment of some kind. In Tolkien's (2005: 101) words, it is "as necessary for the health and complete functioning of the Human as is sunlight for physical life." But there's the rub: what kind? I cannot avoid the conclusion that since modernism demands the consistent worship of endless, unstoppable, universal progress, its most consistent adherents must secretly seek out inadmissable, preferably unconscious, and on that account even more-than-usually dangerous enchantments. In this, of course, they closely mirror the schizophrenia of religious extremists.[16] But most of us manage to muddle along in more contextual and relative ways which keep a third road openly open, so to speak, even if we remain reluctant to discuss it in public for fear of ridicule.

Philip Pullman offers a fascinating literary study of someone caught in this dilemma. Briefly, here is a sworn atheist, and friend and supporter of Richard Dawkins, well-known for his powerful aversion to Lewis's work on account of its Christology and the reactionary views with which that is sometimes (rather one-sidedly) associated. Pullman's dislike of Tolkien is somewhat different. It stems from the latter's Catholicism, his occasionally archaic literary style and, it seems, the fact that Middle-earth is "wholly imaginary" and never "actually" existed. (I'm not making this up, not even the extraordinary literal-mindedness; I engaged in correspondence with Pullman on the subject in 2000.) A better example of what Tolkien (OFS 56) suspected as the true burden of the charge of escapism – namely, the Flight of the Deserter, from what these jailers are pleased to call "reality" – would be difficult to find, or even to imagine. Yet Pullman's own fiction is best described, indeed can only be described, as fantasy; the so-called real world is not noticeably populated with visible animal daemons, biological entities with wheels, etc.

Pullman indulges in some remarkable contortions when challenged on this striking contradiction, saying that he would much rather write realistic fiction if he only could, since he strongly dislikes fantasy (including his own?). Fortunately, the psychology of the artist is not my concern. More instructive

---

16 A headline at the time of writing from the BBC reads: "The lover of one of Europe's most influential bankers breaks down in court and admits killing him after kinky sex." It's not difficult to think of equivalent incidents of various kinds involving high-level religious figures.

is the way even the work of this ideological atheist and would-be jailer confirms the subversive power of narrative that we found in that of his Christian targets. It is confirmed positively in the excellence of his storytelling in *His Dark Materials*, which has understandably enchanted many readers; and negatively, as his programmatic dislike of religion in general, clericalism in particular and Lewis above all (even hatred – which only binds him more closely to them) gradually gains the upper hand over his desire and ability simply to tell a good story … or rather, to get out of the way as much as possible, personal opinions and all, and let the story tell itself. I am not the only reader to find a steady falling-away in quality as Pullman's three volumes progress, and the culprit, ironically, is plain. It is the same didacticism that ruined Lewis's final Narnia volume, *The Last Battle*.

How surprised should we be? When Miller was researching her book, Pullman recommended a book by John Goldthwaite (1996), a Christian writer on fantasy literature who apparently shares Pullman's loathing of Tolkien and Lewis, not least on the extraordinary grounds that "[c]reating a Secondary World, after all, is in effect a declaration that God's creation is deficient." Small wonder that Goldthwaite goes on to describe mythic fantasy – probably the most flourishing single genre in publishing – as a "dead end". He may have meant that metaphysically but in any case, as so often in this area, the critical impulse is not used to open up a world to sympathetic understanding but rather to close it off and shut it down. And whether that weapon is wielded by a dogmatic Christian or a dogmatic atheist doesn't make any significant difference.

The poet Michael Longley once observed of art that "when you capture something with precision, you also release its mysterious aura. You don't get the mystery," he added, "without the precision." (Here is "concrete magic" again.) *His Dark Materials* starts with a girl in a cupboard in a very particular room, overhearing a disturbing conversation in a richly imagined and detailed parallel Oxford. It culminates with windy denunciations of the Church and Will and Lyra's overwrought separation. Pullman seems suspiciously determined to show – as someone said of Edmund Wilson, another bitter critic of Tolkien's work – that he is the Adult in the room.

Tolkien (OFS 63) thought that great fairy stories end with a "sudden joyous 'turn'" which rends the story "and lets a gleam come through." He called what the resulting pang conveys "hope without guarantees." In the end, Pullman gives us the opposite: guarantees without hope. His decision was, I'm sure, ideologically driven, but it was not an ideological failing. It was a failure of art.

V

Concerning the second half of my title, I once argued that postmodernity – more as sensibility than historical period – had the potential to liberate us from modernity's relentless progressivism and, incidentally, enable us to appreciate the prescience of anti-modernists like Tolkien, if not necessarily their prescriptions.[17] It hasn't quite worked out like that, of course. Encapsulating absurdly, what has happened is that while it has lost a great deal of its popular legitimacy, the modernist megamachine[18] has nonetheless kept right on going, even picking up speed. In this respect nothing has changed since Weber remarked in 1899 that "[o]ne has the impression of sitting on a speeding train, while doubting whether the next switch will be correctly set" (quoted in Schaff 1989: 14). This situation has left what remains of progressive resistance in such uncomfortably paradoxical positions as hoping for an ecological collapse bad enough to halt modernist "development" (since little else seems likely to) but not, you know, *too* bad ... So where "postmodern" implies, misleadingly, that modernity is over, "hypermodernity" reminds us that it ain't so. (It's also an ugly word, which is therefore apt.)

At the same time, it is very important not to attribute even more power to the disenchanters who seem to be running the show than they actually have. To paraphrase Bruno Latour (1993), we have never been *completely* modern – which is just to say, disenchanted. In lived life and in practice, we do not and cannot (unless psychotic) live in a completely disenchanted way. So how do I read this riddle of simultaneous enchantment *and* disenchantment?

In two ways. One, very simply, is that enchantment will survive. Like the Earth – the ultimate source of enchantment, I believe – it does not need us but

---

17 As Robert Musil remarked: "Progress would be a fine thing if only it would stop."
18 Lewis Mumford's term.

we need it; so it will continue to animate, unpredictably and uncontrollably, our relationships with each other, with other animals, with nonhuman nature, with places, with art and artefacts, with food, and so on. However, inasmuch as enchantment is unbiddable, it cannot be used or exploited for any purpose or programme; so we need another term for the phenomenon, superficially very like enchantment but actually distinguishable as its wraithlike simulacrum, which is at the heart of the billion-pound hypermodern industries of advertising, PR, entertainment, political spin, fashion and so on. I have already suggested "glamour" (Curry 1999[19]). Glamour is one of the chief tools in the armoury of magic, in Tolkien's sense of power-knowledge.[20] It bears the same relationship to enchantment as the Ringwraiths of Tolkien's world, who merely continue forever because they cannot die – what he called "endless serial living" (OFS 62) – do to genuine immortality as defined by Wittgenstein (1961: 72): "If we take eternity to mean not infinite temporal duration but timelessness, then eternal life belongs to those who live in the present."

So my final conclusion is that given our susceptibility to promises, and systems of promises, to completely satisfy our endless desires (especially for security and control), disenchantment too, especially in the form of glamour, will continue. Both in weird tandem, and not only one or the other: that is our fate.

Abbreviations

Letters: see TOLKIEN 2006

OFS: "On Fairy-Stories" in TOLKIEN (1988: 9-73)

Bibliography

BRINGHURST, Robert. 1995. "Introduction." In Alice KANE. *The Dreamer Awakes*. Edited by Sean KANE. Peterborough: Broadview Press, 11-18.

2007. *Everywhere Being is Dancing. Twenty Pieces of Thinking*. Kentville NS: Gaspereau Press.

---

19 Reprinted on pages 65-82 of the present volume.
20 The echo of Foucault is deliberate and, I believe, appropriate.

CHILD, Francis James (ed.). 1965. *The English and Scottish Popular Ballads*. 5 volumes. Originally published 1882-1898. Mineola NY: Dover Publications.

CURRY, Patrick. 1999. "Magic vs. Enchantment." *Journal of Contemporary Religion* 14.3: 401-412.[21]

2004. *Defending Middle-earth*. Second edition; first edition 1997. Boston MA: Houghton Mifflin.

2005. "Tolkien and his Critics: A Critique." In Thomas HONEGGER (ed.). 2005. *Root and Branch: Approaches Towards Understanding Tolkien*. Second edition. First edition 1999. Zurich and Berne: Walking Tree Publishers, 75-146.[22]

2007a. "Enchantment." In Michael D.C. DROUT (ed.). 2007. *The J.R.R. Tolkien Encyclopedia: Scholarship and Critical Assessment*. London and New York: Routledge, 159-160.

2007b. "Iron Crown, Iron Cage: Tolkien and Weber on Modernity and Enchantment." In Eduardo SEGURA and Thomas HONEGGER (eds.). 2007. *Myth and Magic: Art according to the Inklings*. Zurich: Walking Tree Publishers, 99-108.[23]

2008. "Enchantment in Tolkien and Middle-earth." In Stratford CALDECOTT and Thomas HONEGGER (eds.). 2008. *Tolkien's The Lord of the Rings: Sources of Inspiration*. Zurich and Jena: Walking Tree Publishers, 99-112.[24]

2012. "Enchantment and Modernity." *PAN: Philosophy, Activism, Nature* 12: 76-89.

2014. "The Critical Response to Tolkien's Fiction." In Stuart D. LEE (ed.). 2014. *A Companion to Tolkien*. Oxford: Wiley Blackwell, 369-388.[25]

DICKINSON, Mark. 2011. "Review." *The Fiddlehead* 246 (Spring 2011): 106-108.

FLIEGER, Verlyn and Douglas A. ANDERSON (eds.). 2008. *Tolkien "On Fairy-stories"*. London: HarperCollins.

FLINT, Valerie I.J. 1991. *The Rise of Magic in Early Medieval Europe*. Oxford: Clarendon Press.

GOLDTHWAITE, John. 1996. *The Natural History of Make-Believe: A Guide to the Principal Works of Britain, Europe, and America*. Oxford: Oxford University Press.

---

21 Reprinted on pages 65-82 of the present volume.
22 Reprinted on pages 125-90 of the present volume.
23 Reprinted on pages 95-103 of the present volume.
24 Reprinted on pages 83-94 of the present volume.
25 Reprinted on pages 197-225 of the present volume.

HARVEY, Graham. 2006. *Animism: Respecting the Living World.* New York: Columbia University Press.

HEPBURN, Ronald. 1984. *"Wonder" and Other Essays.* Edinburgh: Edinburgh University Press.

HORKHEIMER, Max and Theodor W. ADORNO. 1994. *The Dialectic of Enlightenment.* First edition 1944. New York: Continuum.

JONAS, Hans. 1982. *The Phenomenon of Life.* Chicago IL: University of Chicago Press.

LATOUR, Bruno. 1993. *We Have Never Been Modern.* Translated by Catherine Porter. Hemel Hempstead: Harvester Wheatsheaf.

MILLER, Laura. 2008. *The Magician's Book: A Skeptic's Adventures in Narnia.* New York: Little, Brown.

SCHAFF, Lawrence A. 1989. *Fleeing the Iron Cage: Culture, Politics, and Modernity in the Thought of Max Weber.* Berkeley CA: University of California Press.

TOLKIEN, J.R.R. 1988. *Tree and Leaf.* Edited by Christopher TOLKIEN. London: Unwyn Hyman.

2005. *Smith of Wootton Major.* Extended edition, edited by Verlyn FLIEGER. London: HarperCollins.

2006. *The Letters of J.R.R. Tolkien.* Edited by Humphrey CARPENTER, with the assistance of Christopher TOLKIEN. First published 1981. London: HarperCollins.

VIVEIROS DE CASTRO, Eduardo. 2004. "Exchanging Perspectives. The Transformation of Objects into Subjects in Amerindian Cosmologies." *Common Knowledge* 10.3: 463-484.

WEBER, Max. 1991. *From Max Weber: Essays in Sociology.* Edited by H.H. GERTH and C. Wright MILLS. London: Routledge.

WITTGENSTEIN, Ludwig. 1961. *Tractatus Logico-Philosophicus.* Translated by D.F. PEARS and B.F. McGUINNESS. London: Routledge & Kegan Paul.

PART III

CRITICISM

Tolkien and his Critics: a Critique

Abstract

My paper addresses the question of why Tolkien's work is simultaneously so
enduringly popular with readers and so abhorrent to literary critics. It locates
the answer in what I define as modernity, as a project to which the latter are
heavily committed but about which the former are very worried. Both sets
of people are responding (in different ways) to the anti-modernism implicit
in Tolkien's creation, which – I argue – has been justified by subsequent
events, and in the light of which his book has assumed a new and urgent set
of "postmodern" meanings. I criticize Tolkien's modernist critics (including
literary modernist, Marxist, feminist and psychoanalytic variants) in some
detail, as well as sketching out those positive meanings.

Introduction

I want to consider the work of J.R.R. Tolkien in terms of its reception, which
combines remarkable popular success with extraordinary critical hostility.[1] What
are so many readers finding so rewarding in these books that so many professional
literary intellectuals think is so bad? The solution to this riddle, I suggest, arises
out of the meaning and values of his work as apprehended by both sets of readers,
constellated around the ideas, values and projects of modernity – something which
Tolkien's alternative, "re-enchanted" world fundamentally questions. Crucial too,
therefore, are various aspects of what has come to be called postmodernity which,
taken together, imply a passing of modernist hegemony. To put it crudely, then, I
intend to use postmodernism to defend the contemporary meaning of Tolkien's
anti-modernism against his numerous Marxist, materialist, psychoanalytic and
structuralist critics. But I shall also use the issue of re-enchantment to criticize

---

First published 1999 in Thomas Honegger (ed.). *Root and Branch: Approaches towards Understanding Tolkien*. Zurich and Berne: Walking Tree Publishers, 81-148; second edition 2005.

1 My book-length study, Curry (1997), concentrates more on the positive content of Tolkien's work as
construed by readers; this paper takes the "via negativa" of tackling his critics directly. It is also written
in a somewhat more academic vein. There is, however, some unavoidable overlap.

postmodernist secularism. I finish up with a few suggestions about both criticism and the writing of fantasy which arise out of this approach.

Without suggesting a comparable importance, a certain parallelism with Tolkien's famous lecture on *Beowulf* has emerged in the course of my own essay, except that, this time, the story is contemporary literature, and the irritatingly atavistic and intractable monster at its centre is *The Lord of the Rings* itself. I too am going to suggest that the latter's critics too have missed its point, and have done so for reasons which turn on their own relationship of complicity with modernity. For this purpose, Tolkien's most important text is his profound essay "On Fairy-Stories".

The critics' doubts are evidently not shared by the reading public. *The Lord of the Rings* (first published in 1954-55) has so far (1999) sold about fifty million copies world-wide. This makes it a candidate for the biggest-selling single work of fiction in the twentieth century. *The Hobbit* (1937) stands at about forty million. And one could add the considerable sales, now perhaps over two million, of his dark and difficult posthumously-published epic *The Silmarillion*. His books have been translated into more than thirty languages, including Japanese, Catalan, Estonian, Greek, Hebrew, Finnish and Indonesian. Furthermore, Tolkien has outlived the 60s counterculture in which he first flourished; as a now unfashionable author, he still sells steadily. In England, for example, since figures began to be kept in 1991, his books have been taken out of public libraries around 200,000 times a year; he is one of only four "classic authors" whose annual lending totals exceed 300,000 (well ahead of Austen, Dickens and Shakespeare). *The Hobbit* spent fifteen years as the biggest-selling American paperback, and *The Lord of the Rings* has been (and still is) the most valuable first-edition published in the second half of the 20th century.[2]

---

2 Relatively conservative estimates, based on figures supplied to me by HarperCollins and by Houghton Mifflin (courtesy Richard McAdoo), and on those in Ezard (1991). *Gone With the Wind* has sold about twenty-seven million copies, and according to the *Guinness Book of Records* of 1991, the single modern novel with the highest global sales is Jacqueline Susann's *Valley of the Dolls* (1966) – 28,712,000, as of March 1987. (Of course, this may have been subsequently superseded.) Translations: based on information kindly supplied by HarperCollins in 1982. Fashionability: Park (1991). In a survey of readers' "favourite novel" by the *Sunday Times* (24.09.95), with almost 1100 respondents, *The Lord of the Rings* came second (behind *Pride and Prejudice*). A survey of teenagers' reading habits showed *The Lord of the Rings* still high among fifteen- to sixteen-year-olds (*Guardian*, 16.12.95). Still sells: in England, my assertion can be confirmed by talking to the relevant buyer for any largish book-store. Libraries: Public Lending Right figures: see also *Times Literary Supplement* (14.01.94), and *Guardian* (07.01.93). Value: M. Hime, writing in *Firsts* 5.10 (October 1995): 41.

In other words, we are talking about a massively popular and successful publishing phenomenon, all the more so when one of the books in question is half-a-million words long, and neither involves any money or explicit sex – two ingredients now normally considered essential for bestsellers – let alone cannibalism, sadomasochism, serial murder or lawyers. (And how many of those will even be in print half a century after publication? The fate of Jackie Collins beckons.) Of course, without its sheer unlikeliness – an epic centred on a race of three-and-a-half-foot high creatures and a magic ring, etc. – the success of *The Lord of the Rings* would have much less literary interest; but given that unlikeliness, it should have a great deal.

This popular success was confirmed in Britain by the largest survey of readers ever conducted there, sponsored by Waterstone's books and Channel 4 television. Over 26,000 readers were asked to choose the most important books of the century. *The Lord of the Rings* came undisputed first. It was followed in second and third places by Orwell's *1984* and *Animal Farm*. Such a result was not as anomalous as it first appears: both authors, one from a conservative perspective and the other from a socialist, were deeply concerned by the direction of modernity. So too, evidently, are many readers.

As if confirmation was needed, the Waterstone's poll was followed by a survey by the Folio Society of its members (in April 1997), 10,000 of whom voted *The Lord of the Rings* their favourite book. (Interestingly, in a vote about the favourite books of under-sixteens by 11,000 bookshop customers and viewers of the TV programme *Bookworm*, *The Hobbit* came fifth but *The Lord of the Rings* did not figure at all – thus confirming, I think, that it is not essentially a children's book.)[3]

---

3 These results were carried and discussed by every major British national broadsheet on January 20th 1997. *The Daily Telegraph* apparently repeated the poll, and obtained exactly the same first three places. See also my article in the *New Statesman* of January 31st 1997. Folio Society result: *The Times* and *The Daily Telegraph*, 23.04.1997; Bookworm: *The Guardian*, 01.09.1997.

The Critics

Yet this reception has been accompanied by an equally remarkable critical disdain. Primarily, there is silence. A few examples: Margaret Drabble's *Oxford Companion to English Literature* (1985) gives Tolkien exactly thirteen lines out of 1154 pages; Drabble and Stringer's *Oxford Concise Companion to English Literature* (1996; more than 650 pages) has twelve lines; in Saunders's *Short Oxford History of English Literature* (1994; 678 pages) there is no mention at all.[4] I cannot see how this can be described as other than an unconscionable dereliction of duty on the part of people whose profession is supposedly to comprehend literature.

The other principal critical response, which comes no closer to an attempt to understand, has been vitriolic abuse. In Walter Schepp's catalogue (1975: 52), Tolkien has been accused of being "paternalistic, reactionary, anti-intellectual, racist, fascistic and, perhaps worst of all in contemporary terms, irrelevant." Goldthwaite's recent book (1996) on "Make-Believe", claiming to be "A Guide to the Principal Works", dismisses *The Lord of the Rings* – the most developed, sustained and influential of such works (even if you don't happen to like it) – as "Faerie-land's answer to *Conan the Barbarian*" (Goldthwaite 1996: 218). Otherwise good critics don't seem to be able to cope with Tolkien at all, and even his own biographer (Et tu, Brute?) has fatuously opined that "he doesn't really belong to literature or to the arts, but more to the category of people who do things with model railways in their garden sheds."[5]

There are certainly dissenters – Shippey, Elgin, Attebery, Le Guin, Swinfen, Rosebury, Flieger and Filmer to name some – but the high quality of their work must not be confused with its degree of influence in the professional literary, critical and academic world and its publishing outlets. Indeed, in Tolkien's case the two seem inversely related. This goes beyond mere unfashionability; Tolkien's name in

---

4 There is at least a reasonable entry in Stringer (1996).
5 I have never figured out whether Schepps is being ironic or not; he seems to be saying that the values in Tolkien's work are fine as long as one doesn't try to "apply" them to the so-called real world – a tortuous and unsatisfying conclusion, to say the least. See also West (1970), Johnson (1986), and Hammond (1995). Good critics: e.g., Lurie (1990). Humphrey Carpenter made the last-quoted extraordinary remark on BBC *Bookshelf*, 22.11.1991. See also Raffel (1968: 246), who concludes patronizingly that it is "magnificent but [...] not literature."

such circles is the kiss of death.[6] The extreme nature of these responses is thus as fascinating as Tolkien's popular success. Since my book concentrates on the latter, I am mainly concerned here with the critical phenomenon. So let us consider the justice of the charges, and try to determine what lies behind them.

For reasons that will, I hope, become clear, I am going to call the dominant intellectual reaction to Tolkien, and the values that drive it, "modernism". There are other possible terms; one, with considerable overlap, is "humanism". It is no coincidence that David Ehrenfeld, in his brilliant book on *The Arrogance of Humanism*, is able to read and learn from Tolkien in a way that none of his modernist/humanist critics apparently can. Unlike them, Ehrenfeld does not subscribe to the cult of reason, especially science, accepts the reality and indeed necessity of limits; and prizes what we are fast losing in the current "spectacle of global waste and destruction" (1978: 255).

It will be noticed that my examples nearly all fall politically left-of-centre. There are two reasons for this. One is that there seem to be more relevant critics of that political persuasion than right-wing or conservative ones; Tolkien failed the "PC" test well "avant la lettre". The second is that characteristically, the latter have mostly been content to call it a matter of taste and leave it at that. Their general view was perhaps best summed up by the poet John Heath-Stubbs, with that perceptiveness and unfairness required by all the best "bons mots": "A combination of Wagner and Winnie-the-Pooh."[7] There are thus fewer arguments with which to engage.

Whatever other reasons remain, however, they do not include any right-wing agenda on my part. Indeed, a crucial part of my motivation is the way Tolkien's critics' simple-minded dogmatism actually betrays their own ideals, many of which I share. And I make no apology for writing with some animus. If it were true, as one irenic Tolkien scholar (Timmons 1996: 11) believes, that "narrow-minded and hostile views are best countered through sound analyses of the

---

6 Initially, W.H. Auden and C.S. Lewis; more recently, Shippey (1992), Elgin (1985), Attebery (1992), Le Guin (1989), Swinfen (1984), Rosebury (1992), Flieger (1983), and Filmer (1992). This list is not intended to be exhaustive. For interesting additional comments on Tolkien's rejection by the English literary establishment, see Shippey (1995). (I invite anyone who wants empirical confirmation of my last remark to try to interest a mainstream and/or leading academic publisher in producing a serious book on Tolkien.)

7 A remark to the author.

author's works, rather than by bellicose rebuttals," then given such work by the authors just mentioned, the attitude I have been describing would not still hold sway. Of course, my polemic may not succeed either; but that is no reason to refrain from disturbing a cozy and fraudulent orthodoxy.

It is also relevant that another meaning of "animus" is animating soul or feeling. The ignorant arrogance I am contesting here was never better summed up than by Roz Kaveney (1991), who concluded in an article on Tolkien's centenary that his books are "worth intelligent reading, but not passionate attention." Precisely the opposite conviction drives this paper, and the book (Curry 1997) to which it is a companion piece.

Homage

It was only after much the greater part of this paper had already been written that I discovered its full and proper theoretical context in Barbara Herrnstein Smith's superlative *Contingencies of Value* (1988).[8] Consider this: Smith dares to point out that "the entire problematic of value and evaluation" – as distinct from that of interpretation – "has been evaded and explicitly exiled by the literary academy" (1988: 17). As we shall see in what follows, in the case of Tolkien (and there must be many other possible examples) this ban has allowed an axiologically pathological intellectual culture to flourish, where "interpretation" is actually driven by a tacit evaluation which cannot be brought out into the open and properly discussed.

Second, Smith (1988: 25) calls into question the "claims and judgements of literary value made by or on behalf of what may be called *noncanonical audience*, such as all those readers who are not now students, critics, or professors of literature and perhaps never were and never will be within the academy or on its outskirts." Just such claims and judgements are second nature – indeed, are indispensible – to the shoddy work of Tolkien's critics.

Third, as she writes,

> What is being missed here is that there is a politics of personal *taste* as well as a politics of institutional evaluation and explicit evaluative criticism. This resistance

---

8 Nonetheless, obviously, Smith cannot be held to account for my uses of her work.

is displayed, moreover, not only by conservative members of the literary academy but also by those who are otherwise most concerned to indicate the political implications of these issues; and the revulsion of academics and intellectuals at the actual literary preferences, forms of aesthetic enjoyment, and general modes of cultural consumption of nonacademics and nonintellectuals – including those whose *political* emancipation they may otherwise seek to promote – has been a familiar feature of the cultural-political scene since at least the 1930s. [...] [O]ppositional cultural theory and conservative humanism have repeatedly generated strictly parallel (and, indeed, often indistinguishable) accounts to explain the tastes of other people in such a way as to justify the academic intellectual's revulsion at them. (Smith 1988: 25-26)

As unwitting witnesses I call upon two prominent critics reacting to the news of *The Lord of the Rings* topping the Waterstone's survey. Germaine Greer, in *W* [*Waterstone's Magazine*] (Winter/Spring 1997: 4) wrote that "it has been my nightmare that Tolkien would turn out to be the most influential writer of the twentieth century. The bad dream has materialized." And Auberon Waugh, in *The Times* (20.01.97), described the result as "suspicious", and suggested that Tolkien's fans may have orchestrated a campaign. (To quote Helen Armstrong, in *The Guardian* (23.01.97), of the Tolkien Society – membership: approximately 500 – "In our dreams!") As an apodictically perfect demonstration of "Marxist cultural critics join[ing] Arnoldian humanists in deploring the novel/ alien cultural productions of the late twentieth century" (Smith 1988: 75), this would take some beating!

Infantile?

The critical rubbishing of Tolkien began with Edmund Wilson's extended sneer (1956: 312) about "juvenile trash" in 1956. Younger readers today may need reminding that Wilson was a pathologically ambitious critic who championed modernism in literature (and Stalinism in politics).[9] In his pompous obsession, as a contemporary put it, "with being the Adult in the room" (Parker 1956-57: 608) – and maybe, oddly enough, his priapism too – Wilson is a good exemplar of what Ursula Le Guin (1989: 125-26) called "a deep puritanical distrust of fantasy" on the part of those who "confuse fantasy, which in the psychological sense is a universal and essential faculty of the human mind, with infantilism and pathological regression."

---

9 See Meyers (1995).

Le Guin is undoubtedly right about Wilson and others of his ilk, but in a demonstration of the durability and ubiquity of this accusation, Tolkien's "infantilism" (along with "nostalgia", to which we shall return later) was later revived by Michael Moorcock (1987). Perhaps, therefore, it is no coincidence that Moorcock has now mostly abandoned his science fiction/fantasy – part of whose real appeal was precisely their rather adolescent charm ("my, what a long sword you have!") – to write supposedly adult novels. In any case, many science fiction writers are indeed committed modernists; and not a few are poorly placed to finger infantilism – witness in both respects, for example, the toys-for-boys technological fetishism of J.G. Ballard.

As Tolkien (1988: 43) noted, the connection between children and fairy-stories is an accident of history, not something essential: "If fairy-story as a kind is worth reading at all it is worthy to be written for and read by adults." But being Grown-Up is a recurring theme in modernism, with its teleological fantasy of collectively progressing towards the truth, and its mythoclasm as a necessary destructiveness in order to get there. *The Lord of the Rings* and its readers are thus doubly stigmatized, both individually/psychologically and collectively/socially. Tolkien's enormous popularity then requires such risible explanations as Robert Giddings's (1981) "PR men", at whose behest the reading public apparently took him up solely because it was told to do so.

It is true, however, that modernist hostility to Tolkien need not be of the left. *Private Eye* sneered that Tolkien appeals only to those "with the mental age of a child – computer programmers, hippies and most Americans" (see Craig 1992). And despite his trumpeted sensitivity to elite literary contempt for the reading public, the populist Oxford professor John Carey (1977: 631) repeated the charge of childishness, and attacked Tolkien for his lack of interest in "the writers who were moulding English literature in his own day – Eliot, Joyce, Lawrence" – as if English literature, to quote Brian Rosebury, were "a single substance, appropriated for a definite period, like the only blob of Plasticine in the classroom, by an exclusive group (however gifted) [...]" (1992: 133).

Useful to Get That Learned

Catherine Stimpson raised several frequent objections in 1969; they are worth noting symptomatically as having successfully set the tone for much subsequent Tolkien criticism. "An incorrigible nationalist," she wrote of Tolkien, his epic "celebrates the English bourgeois pastoral idyll. Its characters, tranquil and well fed, live best in placid, philistine, provincial rural cosiness." Second, his characters are one-dimensional, dividing neatly into "good & evil, nice & nasty" (Stimpson 1969: 8). (She was preceded in this criticism, repeatedly, by Edwin Muir, in 1954-55.) Third, Tolkien's language reveals "class snobbery". Finally, Stimpson writes:

> Behind the moral structure is a regressive emotional pattern. For Tolkien is irritatingly, blandly, traditionally masculine. [...] He makes his women characters, no matter what their rank, the most hackneyed of stereotypes. They are either beautiful and distant, simply distant, or simply simple. (1969: 13)[10]

Taking these points in order, one could reply to the first that the hobbits (excepting Bilbo and Frodo, and perhaps Sam; well, and Merry and Pippin) would indeed have preferred to live quiet rural lives – if they could have. Unfortunately for them, and her point, there is much more to Middle-earth than the Shire. By the same token, any degree of English nationalism that the hobbits represent is highly qualified. Tolkien himself pointed out that

> hobbits are not a Utopian vision, or recommended as an ideal in their own or any age. They, as all peoples and their situations, are an historical accident – as the Elves point out to Frodo – and an impermanent one in the long view.(*Letters* 1981: 197)

It is also possible, as Jonathan Bate (1991) suggests, to draw a distinction between love of the land and love of the fatherland; and in *The Lord of the Rings*, the lovingly detailed specificities of its natural world – which include but far outrun those of the Shire – far exceed the latter. But I shall return to these questions below.

As for one-dimensional, good/bad characters, Stimpson has either ignored or missed the inner struggles, with widely varying results, of Frodo, Gollum,

---

10 See Colebatch's critique of Stimpson (1990: 61-66).

Boromir, and Denethor. As Le Guin again has noted, several major characters have a "shadow", and in Frodo's case, there are arguably two: Sam, and
Gollum – who is himself doubled as Gollum/Stinker and Sméagol/Slinker,
as Sam calls them. And each race – with the exception of orcs, and even they
violently differ from each other – is a collection of good, bad and indifferent
individuals. Le Guin (1989: 57-58) asks, "When you look at it that way, can
you call it a simple story? I suppose so. *Oedipus Rex* is a fairly simple story,
too. But it is not simplistic."[11]

Regarding class snobbery: in *The Hobbit*, perhaps; the book's other virtues
(such as its quality as a story), and its having been written more than half
a century ago, will hardly put off zealous contemporary detectors of orcism
and trollism. But with *The Lord of the Rings*, this charge does not stand up.
There is certainly class awareness; but orc speech is not all the same: there are
at least three kinds, and none are necessarily "working-class" (see Rosebury
1992: 75-76), while the idioms of the various hobbits only correspond to
their social classes in the same way as do those of contemporary humans (see
Johannesson 1997). Furthermore, the accent and idiom of Sam (arguably the real
hero of the book) and most other hobbits is that of a rural peasantry;
while those of virtually all of Tolkien's major villains – Smaug, Saruman,
the Lord of the Nazgûl (and presumably Sauron too) – are unmistakably
posh. There is also the blindingly obvious fact of *The Lord of the Rings* as a
tale of "the hour of the Shire-folk, when they arise from their quiet fields
to shake the towers and counsels of the Great" (FR.II.ii).[12] Like many of
Stimpson's accusations, however, that of pandering to social hierarchy has
proved durable.[13] But as will become increasingly apparent, card-carrying
modernists find it almost impossible to bring themselves actually to *read*
Tolkien.

---

11 Cf. Attebery (1992: 33) and Rosebury (1992: 75-76).
12 All references are to book-numbers and chapter-numbers of *The Lord of the Rings*.
13 For a more recent repetition, see Kaveney (1991) who also associates Tolkien with "a broadside
   attack on modernism and even realism" (is *nothing* sacred?), and anachronistically blames him for
   current "American commercial fantasy and science fiction".

Sexist?

Then there is the question of Tolkien's, or rather, Middle-earth's, masculinity. How irritating it is will vary wildly with individual readers (including women); but in this case it is tempting to reply, guilty as charged. As evidence to the contrary, there are the characters of Galadriel and Éowyn, without whom *The Lord of the Rings* would be seriously impoverished, and who are more complex and conflicted than Stimpson allows. Galadriel in particular is a powerful and wise woman who dominates her somewhat obtuse spouse, and refuses the Ring out of strength rather than fear or weakness (see Ewijck 1995). Still, Tolkien's paternalism is unmistakable, and *The Lord of the Rings* is indeed a male-centred text. (Incidentally, he (*Letters* 1981: 293) described the family arrangements of hobbits as "'patrilinear' rather than patriarchal. [...] [M]aster and mistress had equal status, if different functions.")

Yet Tolkien has arguably committed no crime worse than being a man of his time and place, or failing to transcend it in the way J.S. Mill, say, did his in relation to feminist issues. And it is too easy to ask a work to be something it isn't, or its author to do something he or she didn't set out to do. Indeed, maybe we should be grateful that Tolkien did not attempt a more feminine Middle-earth. Without prejudice to those male writers who have succeeded in placing believable female characters at the centre of their work, the results can be ghastly.[14] Imagine what Tolkien might have wrought!

Perhaps we should also be glad that academic and literary feminists have largely ignored Tolkien (presumably as beyond the pale), and thus spared him the fate of, say, Willa Cather. Cather's plain lack of interest in sex and gender, and the focus in her fiction on quite other matters, has not prevented the kind of gross reductionism whereby "No tree can grow, no river flow in Cather's landscapes without its being a penis or a menstrual period" (Acacella 1995: 70). I say "largely" because one essay has already shown what would be the result: Tolkien and Lewis (both devoted husbands) driven by repressed homosexuality, swords all phalli, Shelob a metaphor for female genitalia and Tolkien's fear

---

14 I am thinking of two otherwise excellent writers, John Fowles and Dennis Potter, in *The Mantissa* and *Blackeyes* respectively.

of female sexuality, and even the phial of Galadriel – one of his book's several heroines – somehow, a super-phallus (Partridge 1983).

Notwithstanding such silliness, however, I think the male centredness of Tolkien's work should be acknowledged as a real limitation. But it is undeniable that countless women have enjoyed and even loved *The Lord of the Rings*. It would be the height of arrogance to accuse them all of gender-false-consciousness. I think the reason is simply that no sane and intelligent reader allows any single issue, including gender, to completely dominate all other considerations; so intelligent/non-dogmatic women, including feminists, are getting the other things from Tolkien that are so richly present, and some of which, such as reverence for nature, arguably relate to ecofeminism. I would also point out that to insist on such a dominance presumes to dictate what women's consciousness (and, by implication, men's) can and cannot experience and participate in; in its implicit "realism", it is thus also a particularly inappropriate demand in relation to *fantasy* literature, of all things.[15]

Incidentally, a related charge is the lack of sex – or rather, since there is a good deal of progenitivity, a lack of explicit or erotic sex. (Norman Talbot once remarked, with some justice, that the most erotic character in *The Lord of the Rings* is Shelob.) In a curious and historically very recent inversion of puritanism, this absence seems to present some readers with real difficulties. Thus, Kenneth McLeish says that its absence is a serious problem for those who claim a higher status for *The Lord of the Rings* than that of a "simple tale" (1983: 27). In addition to making unnecessary concessions to the fetish of a Canon, this is surely ridiculous: is *Moby-Dick* therefore a simple tale, or *A Portrait of the Artist as a Young Man*?

Racist?

Another unpleasant accusation sometimes made, related perhaps to that of class snobbery, is racism. It is true that Tolkien's evil creatures are frequently "swart, slant-eyed" (TT.III.i), and tend to come from the south ("the cruel Haradrim") and east ("the wild Easterlings") (TT.IV.v) – both threatening directions in

---

15 I am indebted to Carolyn Burdett for discussion of this point.

what Schepps called Tolkien's "moral cartography" (1975: 44-45). It is also true that black – as in Breath, Riders, Hand, Years, Land, Speech – is often a terrible colour, especially when contrasted with Gandalf the White, the White Rider, and so on. But the primary association of black here is with night and darkness, not race. And there are counter-examples: Saruman's sign is a white hand, Aragorn's standard is mostly black, the Black Riders were not actually black, except their outer robes, and the Black Stone of Erech is connected with Isildur (see Rosebury 1992: 79). Rather strikingly, it also seems to have escaped the attention of Tolkien's critics on this point that as far as one can tell, hobbits were not white-skinned but brown.

Overall, it is true, Tolkien is drawing on centuries of such moral valuation, not unrelated to historical experience attached to his chosen setting – enemies, in North-west Europe, have overwhelmingly come from the East – in order to convey something immediately recognisable in the context of his story. As Kathleen Herbert noticed, orcs sound very like the first horrified reports in Europe of the invading Huns of the fourth and fifth centuries: "broad-shouldered, bow-legged, devilishly effective fighters, moving fast, talking a language that sounds like no human speech (probably Turkic) and practising ghastly tortures with great relish" (1993: 271).

Perhaps the worst you could say is that Tolkien makes no attempt to forestall the possibility of a racist interpretation. (I say "possibility" because it is ridiculous to assume that readers automatically transfer their feelings about orcs to all the swart or slant-eyed people they encounter in the street.) But as Brian Attebery points out, "this ethical division is rendered increasingly invalid as the story progresses, as evil emerges among the kingly Gondorians, the blond Riders of Rohan, the seemingly incorruptible wizards, and even the thoroughly English hobbit-folk of the Shire" (1992: 33). Furthermore, as the anthropologist Virginia Luling has noted, the appearance of racism is deceptive, "not only because Tolkien in his non-fictional writing several times repudiated racist ideas, but because […] in his sub-creation the whole intellectual underpinning of racism is absent" (1995: 56).[16]

---

16 However, as Luling adds, the orcs – as distinct from the Haradrim, Variags and Easterlings – "are a
   separate problem, and one that Tolkien himself never really solved" (1995: 56).

Tolkien once wrote:

> In any case if you want to write a tale of this sort you must consult your roots, and a man of the North-West of the Old World will set his heart and the action of his tale in an imaginary world of that air, and that situation: with the Shoreless Sea of his innumerable ancestors to the West, and the endless lands (out of which enemies mostly come) to the East. (*Letters* 1981: 212)

Thus, as Clyde Kilby (1977: 51-52) recounts, when Tolkien was asked what lay east and south of Middle-earth, he replied:

> "Rhûn is the Elvish word for East. Asia, China, Japan, and all the things which people in the West regard as far away. And south of Harad is Africa, the hot countries." Then Mr. Resnick asked, "That makes Middle-earth Europe, doesn't it?" To which Tolkien replied, "Yes, of course – Northwestern Europe … where my imagination comes from."

(In which case, as Tolkien also indicated, Mordor "would be roughly in the Balkans.")

He reacted sharply to reading a description of Middle-earth as "Nordic", however:

> Not *Nordic*, please! A word I personally dislike; it is associated, though of French origin, with racialist theories. [...] Auden has asserted that for me "the North is a sacred direction." That is not true. The North-west of Europe, where I (and most of my ancestors) have lived, has my affection, as a man's home should. I love its atmosphere, and know more of its histories and languages than I do of other parts; but it is not "sacred", nor does it exhaust my affections. (*Letters* 1981: 375-76)

It is also noticeable that the races in Middle-earth are most striking in their variety and autonomy. Without suggesting that a clear-cut choice exists, but rather as an example of the complexity and ambiguity of his literary myth, is this an instance of ethnocentrism, or multiculturalism? Or even – given that most of the races are closely tied to a particular geography and ecology, and manage to live there without exploiting it to the point of destruction – bioregionalism? Again, one of the subplots of *The Lord of the Rings* concerns an enduring friendship between members of races traditionally estranged (Gimli and Legolas); and the most important wedding in the book, between Aragorn and Arwen, is an interracial marriage. As usual, the picture is a great deal more complex than the critics (although not necessarily the public) seem to see.

The Marxist

A major stream of adverse Tolkien criticism can be traced back to Raymond Williams, who, in *The Country and the City* (1985), noted the

> extraordinary development of country-based fantasy, from Barrie and Kenneth Grahame through J.C. Powys and T.H. White and now to Tolkien. [...] It is then not only that the real land and its people were falsified; a traditional and surviving rural England was scribbled over and almost hidden from sight by what is really a suburban and half-educated scrawl. (Williams 1985: 258)

Williams has been a massively influential critic.[17] One could produce many other commentators he has influenced: John Lucas, for example: "This is the ultimate, deeply conservative, ambition of pastoral. It falsifies the actual relations of non-city communities just as much and for the same reason that it falsifies city communities" (1990: 118). And almost interchangeably, Barrell and Bull: "The Pastoral allows for a direct opposition to social change, a reactionary clinging to a static present, and an often desperate belief in future improvement" (1974: 5). And it fades away with "the possibility of social mobility and of economic progress" (ibid. 8). (How dated this now sounds, as we face increasingly insurmountable problems as a direct result of "economic progress"!)

Let us try to put "cultural materialism" to work in relation to Tolkien. Williams writes:

> In Britain, identifiably, there is a precarious but persistent rural-intellectual radicalism: genuinely and actively hostile to industrialism and capitalism; opposed to commercialism and the exploitation of the environment; attached to country ways and feelings, the literature and the lore. (Williams 1985: 36-37)

This sounds generous, until you get to the punch-line: "in every kind of radicalism the moment comes when any critique must choose its bearings, between past and future [...]." Furthermore: "We must begin differently: not in the idealisations of one order or another, but in the history to which they are only partial and misleading responses." By the same token, in our current crises myth and revolution must be seen as "alternative", not complementary responses. In

---

17 See O'Connor (1989; especially 109-15). Two disclaimers: I note and appreciate Williams's opening-out of critical vistas from the confines of Leavisism. And I do not mean to subsume Marxism in the work of Williams; there are others, especially Adorno and Horkheimer of the Frankfurt School, who have been deeply sceptical about Enlightenment rationalism.

other words, we must have "real history" oriented to a revolutionary future, not "myth" dreaming of the past (Williams 1985: 247).

But this set of shibboleths (itself profoundly mythical in character) entails a false set of choices – the mythical *vs.* the actual, the ideal *vs.* the real – that are as politically damaging as they are philosophically naive. It conflates material-ism with matter and idealism with ideas, thus missing the crucial and highly "material" effects of the latter. It is essentialist in holding the political character of traditions and positions to be inherent and fixed. And it ignores the massive lesson that the Left, within Williams's lifetime, should have learned from Mrs Thatcher if not Gramsci: that people do not live by factual and historical bread alone, but also by ideas, values and visions of alternatives.[18] In other words, we are looking at something that includes but goes well beyond Williams's moral "self-righteousness", "a basically utilitarian attitude to art", "the claggy dreariness of his writing", and "a terrible puritanism at the heart of the criticism written by those who still follow Williams," as Tom Paulin, in *The Independent on Sunday* (16.04.95), argues.[19] These problems are *structural*.[20]

Nostalgic?

Perhaps it is not surprising, then, that Williams's treatment of pastoralism terminates in mere abuse of Tolkien's work as, absurdly, "half-educated" and "suburban". (Tolkien actually complained to his son in 1943 that "the bigger things get the smaller and duller or flatter the globe gets. It is getting to be all one blasted little provincial suburb" (*Letters* 1981: 65).)

Nor has Williams noticed that the hobbits' pastoralism is dominated and subverted by other themes. As Gildor said to Frodo (FR.I.iii), "it is not your own Shire. [...] Others dwelt here before hobbits were; and others will dwell

---

18 To be fair, this is something that the best of Williams's former students, such as Stuart Hall, absorbed and have themselves said.
19 A good example is Williams's ex-student Terry Eagleton, who eulogized him as author of "the most profound and original collection of cultural writing in 20th-century Britain" (*New Statesman & Society*, 13.10.95). As late as 1994, Eagleton was still touchingly defining culture as "a transitional point between religion and politics" ("Discourse & Discos", *Times Literary Supplement*, 15.07.94).
20 See Felperin (1985: 206-07): "The marxist fideo-materialism, with its fundamentalist ground of History and utopian goal of socialism to support and guide its reading of texts, is rather a dogmatism, another secular theology in which the old transcendental signifieds of God and the Bourgeois Author may have been superseded or sublated by History but certainly not dispensed with."

here when hobbits are no more. The wide world is all about you: you can fence yourselves in, but you cannot for ever fence it out." And as Merry too admitted, "It is best to love first what you are fitted to love, I suppose: you must start somewhere and have some roots, and the soil of the Shire is deep. Still there are things deeper and higher; and not a gaffer could tend his garden in what he calls peace but for them, whether he knows about them or not" (RK.V.viii). *The Lord of the Rings* could thus properly be seen as an extended argument that pastoralism as such is *not* enough – doomed, even: "The Shire is not a haven, and the burden of the tale is that there are no havens in a world where evil is a reality. If you think you live in one, you are probably naive like the early Frodo, and certainly vulnerable" (Grant 1981: 99).

Perhaps the political problem is the richness and centrality of the natural world in Middle-earth (and not just pastoral nature). But if so, it only serves to confirm that the Left, qua Williams & Co., remains stuck in a modernist, economistic and incipiently Stalinist problematic. Had it accepted William Morris's generous offer to meet halfway, in E.P. Thompson's terms, this tragedy need never have happened. But the more recent examples too, of its best representatives, continue to be ignored: Thompson himself, for example – Morris's biographer, a passionate critic of economistic and class reductionism, defender of Blake's counter-hegemonic cultural "mythos", and not so coincidentally, perhaps, a passionate gardener.[21] And again, Orwell (another gardener), in "Some Thoughts on the Common Toad" (1946):

> Is it wicked to take a pleasure in spring? [...] is it politically reprehensible, while we are all groaning, or at any rate ought to be groaning, under the shackles of the capitalist system, to point out that life is frequently more worth living because of a blackbird's song, a yellow elm tree in October, or some other natural phenomenon which does not cost money and does not have what the editors of left-wing newspapers call a class angle? (Ehrenfeld 1993: 25)

Orwell and Thompson – along with Dennis Potter – are also distinctive in being at once on the Left and willing to recognize the power and validity of patriotism (as distinct from nationalism), including a specifically English kind. Unfortunately, most of the Left remains terrified of this whole area,

---

21 Thompson (1976) and (1993). For Thompson's impressive catalogue of his garden on his 50th birthday, see the *New Left Review* 102 (Sept/Oct 1993).

thus continuing to cede it to potential political manipulation by the Right of the kind which Mrs Thatcher and Reagan initiated.[22] But for our purposes here, while rejecting the knee-jerk modernist hostility to this work, note the implied intimacy of nature, "nostalgia" and place. Together with myth, these are indeed crucially related – something that Tolkien recognized, and *The Lord of the Rings* embodies.

Even in the realm of power (narrowly construed) and its effects, cultural material-ism falls down. Fraser Harrison goes straight to the heart of the matter:

> While it is easy to scoff at the whimsicality and commercialism of rural nos-talgia, it is also vital to acknowledge that this reaching-out to the countryside is an expression, however distorted, of a healthy desire to find some sense of meaning and relief in a world that seems increasingly bent on mindless an-nihilation. (Harrison 1984: 170)

Accordingly, says Harrison in a wonderful phrase, "it becomes meaningful to talk of 'radical nostalgia'." Echoing Williams, he agrees that "nostalgia recognizes no duty to history"; he asks us to recognize, however, that

> there is another dimension to nostalgia and that it should not be dismissed as simply a self-indulgent, escapist and pernicious failing. Whereas its account of history is patently untrue, and more ideological than it would pretend, it does none the less express a truth of its own, which reflects an authentic and deeply felt emotion. [...] Our addiction to it is surely a symptom of our failure to make a satisfactory mode of life in the present, but perhaps it can also be seen as evidence of our desire to repair and revitalise our broken relations. The pastoral fantasy nostalgia invented is after all an image of a world in which men and women feel at home with themselves, with each other and with nature, a world in which harmony reigns. It is an ideal [...]. (Harrison 1984: 170-71)[23]

Now Tolkien gives us to understand, as strongly as possible while still writ-ing a story and not a tract, that nostalgia pure-and-simple will not suffice. In Middle-earth, it is the Elves whose nostalgia is the strongest – both in the sense of yearning for the past and attempting to maintain that past now, in places like Lothlórien and Rivendell. But the Elves, despite their valiant resistance, plainly offer no real solution to the central problem of the Ring. Yet it is also

---

22 Hence the furious reaction to historian Samuel (1995), who dares to question this shibboleth; typical was that of the nostalgia- and patriotism-phobic Patrick Wright. As a hopeful sign to the contrary, albeit well outside mainstream political (and musical) discourse, note the success in the UK of critically patriotic "new folk" bands like The Levellers.

23 Cf. Harrison (1992: 156): "nostalgia keeps open the vision of historical alternatives [...]."

true that his work is suffused with the "pastoral fantasy" of a better world, equally memory and longing, to which Harrison refers. And such ideals have real power in the world.

The "Problem" of Evil

Tolkien has often been savaged on this question. Thus, Robert Giddings:

> The evil in the world as portrayed by Tolkien has nothing whatever to do with social or economic causes. It is evil, pure and simple. Consequently there is no need for change of socio-economic conditions, the environmental conditions of life, relations between different classes, etc., etc. – all these things which make up the very fabric of a society, *any* society, are perceived by Tolkien as totally beyond any need or possibility of change. (Giddings 1983: 12-13)[24]

Giddings exaggerates inexcusably – *The Lord of the Rings* is full of "social, economic and environmental" changes which are not exactly randomly related to the War of the Ring, and the crucial effects of which are recognised by all its participants.

In a related point, I am really not sure what Nick Otty (1983) means (although it is clearly not meant kindly) when he writes that in *The Lord of the Rings* "There are no concrete or operational assertions which make it clear why we should eschew evil." Is it any less clear why in Middle-earth Mordor should be eschewed than, say, fascism now? Or is he so disabled by a perceived absence of "concrete or operational" instructions and labels that without them he is ready to snuggle up to the first Nazgûl, or contemporary equivalent, that he meets?

However, Giddings is not altogether wrong about Tolkien's position. His characters spend a great deal of their lives, and sometimes lose their lives, combating evil as it exists in their world. They are therefore active, not quietist, and to that extent not "escapist". Nevertheless, as Gandalf repeatedly stresses, that is *all* one can do:

> it is not our part to master all the tides of the world, but to do what is in us for the succour of those years wherein we are set, uprooting the evil in the fields that we know, so that those who live after may have clean earth to till. What weather they shall have is not ours to rule. (RK.V.ix)

---

24 Cf. the similar point made by Jackson (1988: 154-55).

There is no permanent solution. Ultimately, Tolkien is of the same opinion as Primo Levi: evil "spreads like a contagion. It is foolish to think that human justice can eradicate it. It is an inexhaustible fount of evil [...]" (1987: 188). Or, only slightly less darkly, William Empson: "it is only in degree that any improvement of society could prevent wastage of human powers; the waste even in a fortunate life, the isolation even in a life rich in intimacy, cannot but be felt deeply, and is the crucial feeling of tragedy" (1979: 4-5). Le Guin, not for the first time, puts her finger on it: "Those who fault Tolkien on the Problem of Evil are usually those who have an *answer* to the Problem of Evil – which he did not" (1989: 100).

Of course, this issue is itself not the sort of question that comes with an answer in the back of the book, against which yours is "right" or "wrong". While any response to evil is inevitably problematic and incomplete, however, Tolkien's is at least as complex and tenable as that of his more meliorist opponents. And within that problematic, his characters are as activist as anyone could ask, moved by the same kind of ideals that I have just suggested have real power in the primary world. Once again, this is something Tolkien's readers have noticed where his critics have been blind.

Quietist?

To pick a local and contemporary example, there are (mainly) young people trying, as I write, to defend the remaining countryside outside Newbury, Berkshire, against yet another destructive, expensive and futile bypass. Their principal means of resistance is to put themselves, with extraordinary determination and valour as well as good humour, up trees and literally in the way of an army of security guards, bailiffs, contractors and police, not to mention bulldozers and chainsaws. And among them, I found one person out of dozens who hadn't just read *The Lord of the Rings* but knew it, so to speak, inside out. (Indeed, among its leaders, if that is the word I want, is one Balin.) It is no coincidence, then, that an early supporter of one such proposed bypass, running through Dartmoor, called his opponents "Middle-earth hobbits" (Veldman 1994: 110). Nor, for that matter that the fashionable and supposedly avant-garde writer J.G. Ballard dismisses road protesters as a "a group of weirdos that are anti-car."[25] Once again, we must ask, who are really the fantasists, the indulgers in nostalgia, the reactionaries here: Tolkien and his readers, or his modernist critics?

This is not the only example. Once I started looking, having seen through the lie that Tolkien's books are a bucolic retreat from "reality" that induce an apolitical passivity and/or right-wing quietism, others quickly appeared. Like Meredith Veldman, I too found profound common ground between the work of the left-wing historian and peace activist E.P. Thompson and that of Tolkien. What Veldman calls "the romantic protest movement" unites the CND/END campaign of resistance to nuclear weapons, the ecology movement beginning in the 1970s, and what Veldman calls "Middle-earth as moral protest." Thus, the countercultural success of this otherwise unlikely figure among 60s radicals and dissidents was no anomaly; far from it. In 1972, David Taggart sailed into the French nuclear testing area – an action which led directly to the founding of Greenpeace. His journal records that "I had been reading *The Lord of the Rings*. I could not avoid thinking of parallels between our own little fellowship and the long journey of the hobbits into the volcano-haunted land of Mordor [...]" (Veldman 1994: 108). Nor had it escaped Taggart's notice, or Tolkien's other readers unblinded by modernist promises, that Mordor's landscape is one of industrial desolation, polluted beyond renewal; and that such desecration is inseparable from its autocratic, unaccountable and unrestrained exercise of political power.

There seems no reason to shrink from adding that in addition to my having delighted in Tolkien in 1967, the late E.P. Thompson is one of my intellectual and moral exemplars, and I was an active Greenpeace supporter from the mid-1980s; and I still see no contradiction in this combination. But there is no autobiographical element to my final and most recent example. Here is Maria Kamenkovich on Tolkien in the former USSR, where *The Lord of the Rings* circulated in "samizdat" form:

> Western readers must understand that for us Tolkien was never any kind of "escape". When hobbits laughed at the absurd "distribution", we didn't laugh at all, because the same thing caused millions of deaths among the peasants in the USSR in the 1920s. When Aragorn held up the elf-stone at the parting

---

25 Quoted by John Ryle, *Guardian* (25.11.96).

with the hobbits, we felt desperate because we did not have any hope of win-
ning our battle at home [...]. (Kamenkovich 1992: 36)

Thus the Siege of the White House in Moscow found itself intertwined with
the Battle of the Green Fields in the Shire:

> Western friends of Russia know what happened in Moscow on 19-22 August
> 1991, but I doubt that they were informed that many people remembered
> Tolkien when they made barricades from trolley-buses (just like hobbits
> from country wains!). It is important to remember that the first [complete]
> translation officially published went on sale only a few days before. Moscow
> members of the Tolkien Society spent all those fearful thunderstorm and
> rainy nights near the White House holding a defence. The war-machines got
> as crazy as Oliphaunts and stamped down three young archers. And Gandalf
> stood before the King of Angmar saying: "You shall not pass" [...]. Tolkien
> never meant to describe any real events either in the past or the future. But
> he certainly added something to earthly events. It just cannot be helped.[26]
> (Kamenkovich 1992: 38)

Maybe our political problem is not too much fantasy, but *not enough of the
right kind.*

Fascist?

Raymond Williams says that

> [nostalgic] celebrations of a feudal or aristocratic order [embody values that]
> spring to the defence of certain kinds of order, certain social hierarchies and
> moral stabilities, which have a feudal ring but a more relevant and more dan-
> gerous contemporary application [...] in the defence of traditional property
> settlements, or in the offensive against democracy in the name of blood and
> soil. (Williams 1985: 35-36)

In the light of the unpleasant implications in the last passage, perhaps this is
the place to consider the politics (in the narrow sense) of both Tolkien and
Middle-earth. Tolkien noted in 1943 that

> My political opinions lean more and more to Anarchy (philosophically under-
> stood, meaning abolition of control not whiskered men with bombs) – or to
> "unconstitutional" Monarchy. I would arrest anyone who uses the word State
> (in any sense other than the inanimate realm of England and its inhabitants,
> a thing that has neither power, rights nor mind) [...]. (*Letters* 1981: 63)

---

26 See also Grushetskiy (1995) and Grigorieva (1995); and "Tolkien Fantasies Strike Russian Chord",
The Globe and Mail (28.05.94).

Actually, arguably anticipating the eco-sabotage of Earth First!, his approval stretched to the war-time "dynamiting [of] factories and power-stations; I hope that, encouraged now as 'patriotism', may remain a habit! But it won't do any good, if it is not universal" (*Letters* 1981: 64).

Some years later, Tolkien wrote:

> I am not a "socialist" in any sense – being averse to "planning" (as must be plain) most of all because the "planners", when they acquire power, become so bad – but I would not say that we had to suffer the malice of Sharkey and his Ruffians here. Though the spirit of "Isengard", if not of Mordor, is of course always cropping up. The present design of destroying Oxford in order to accomodate motor-cars is a case. But our chief adversary is a member of a "Tory" Government. (*Letters* 1981: 235)

He was referring to a narrowly-defeated proposal in 1956 to put a so-called relief road through Christ Church meadow – something with a typically contemporary ring.

So Tolkien himself can be classed as an anarchist (or libertarian) and/or a conservative – not at all in the contemporary sense of the last, which has been almost entirely arrogated by neo-liberalism, but in the sense of striving to conserve what is worth saving. Neither category can easily be assimilated to either Left or Right, which is itself usually sufficient cause to be dismissed by those who like to have these things cut-and-dried. In a consistently pre-modern way, Tolkien was neither liberal nor socialist, nor even necessarily democrat; but neither is there even a whiff of "blood and soil" fascism.[27] In this, he contrasts strongly with modernists such as T.S. Eliot, Ezra Pound, D.H. Lawrence, Wyndham Lewis and arguably Philip Larkin:[28] writers to whom Tolkien is sometimes unfavourably compared. But his absence from these ranks is no surprise; he was trying to do something completely different. Consider too that besides imperialistic nationalism, of which Tolkien was very suspicious, something common to all strands of fascism (but especially Nazism) is the worship of technological modernism, which he positively hated.[29]

---

27 For a fuller discussion of Tolkien's opposition to fascism, see Plank (1975) and Yates (1995).
28 See Harrison (1966); on Larkin, see Hitchens (1993: 161-74). W.B. Yeats would appear to be ambiguous here.
29 See Bauman (1989), Payne (1996), and Herf (1984).

That antipathy is obvious throughout his works, down to the background detail of, say, the fall of Númenor (Tolkien's Atlantis) through *"hubris"*, which consisted of both domestic political autocracy and intolerance of dissent and a foreign policy based on technological and military supremacy. Actually, German Nazism was a particular tragedy for Tolkien. In 1941, he wrote to his son Michael that

> I have in this War a burning private grudge [against Hitler, for] ruining, perverting, misapplying and making for ever accursed, that noble Northern spirit, a supreme contribution to Europe, which I have ever loved, and tried to present in its true light. (*Letters* 1981: 55-56)

It is also noteworthy that when the German publishers of *The Hobbit* wrote to Tolkien in 1938 asking if he was of "arisch" (aryan) origins, and could prove it, he refused to do so, indignantly remarking that "if I am to understand that you are enquiring whether I am of *Jewish* origin, I can only reply that I regret that I appear to have *no* ancestors of that gifted people" (*Letters* 1981: 37). He consequently advised Allen & Unwin to "let a German translation go hang" (*Letters* 1981: 37). It may be, as Tom Paulin has suggested (instancing T.S. Eliot), that anti-Semitism is historically integral to the formation of Englishness; but not in Tolkien's case.

It is true that Tolkien had been shocked by the violent anti-clericalism of the republicans in the Spanish civil war, and for that reason favoured the nationalists; the link here with his Catholicism is direct.[30] But however reactionary and repressive Franco's regime (which I do not dispute), there is no justification for conflating his reactionary conservatism with fascism; and Spain was noticeable in the Second World War, despite intense pressure from Hitler, by its neutrality.

Nor is Middle-earth fascist, let alone Nazi. The Shire, for example, functions by a sort of municipal (not representative) democracy, which Tolkien himself described as "half republic half aristocracy" (*Letters* 1981: 241). The former half has, typically, been ignored by Tolkien's critics in their eagerness to assail the latter; but even here, their case is weak. Of the three positions of authority in the Shire, two are hereditary and one elected; but their powers (and duties) are

---

30 See Tolkien (1981: 95-96).

minimal. True, by the end of *The Lord of the Rings* there is again a King; but he merely grants to the Shire (and other areas) the kind of effective independence they already had. And his accession was only with the approval of the people of his City (RK.VI.v). In other words, it is a case of local self-government (or subsidiarity) – most decisions are taken at the lowest possible level, closest to those who are most affected by them.[31]

This is the nature of the Shire as a yeoman-republic, including real connections to the tradition of civic republicanism, with its emphasis on a self-governing citizenry and its fear of corruption by clique and commerce. As Donald Davie noticed, the implication of *The Lord of the Rings* points firmly "towards the conviction that authority in public matters [...] can be and ought to be resisted and refused by anyone who wants to live humanely" (1973: 93-94). This tradition has pre-modern roots, in Aristotle, Cicero and Machiavelli, but its contemporary relevance is none the less for that; and in no respect more importantly than to remind us that modern parliamentary liberalism has no franchise on democracy and community, or on solutions to our problems.[32]

Other societies in Middle-earth function differently still, although mostly under the aegis of non-autocratic royalty. Each is distinct, even among humans: Gondorians, the Riddermark and the Bree-folk are not interchangeable. Tolkien would have agreed with that humane and sceptical humanist – in an earlier and more honourable sense than the cult of "reason", technology and Progress that it has now become – Hubert Butler: "It is as neighbours, full of ineradicable prejudices, that we must love each other, and not as fortuitously 'separated brethren'" (1986: 95). And indeed, *The Lord of the Rings* does hold out hope that very different kinds of traditions and communities can respect one another's differences and live at peace, without being subsumed into a vacuous Benneton-style multiculturalism dominated by American-led market forces: what Tom Shippey (1996) has aptly called "burbocentrism".

But none of these societies resemble Mordor: an utterly authoritarian state, with a slave-based economy centred on intensive industrialism and industrialised

---

31 See Finch (1994: 12-13), and Williams (1995: 17, 19).
32 See Curry (1995) for an introduction.

agriculture – "great slave-worked fields away south", while "in the northward regions were the mines and forges" (RK.VI.ii) – all of which is directed towards the goal of global military domination. It is worth noting, too, given the cults of Hitler, Stalin and Mao (all leaders of supposedly secular states) that Mordor is also an "evil theocracy (for Sauron is also the god of his slaves) [...]" (Tolkien 1981: 154). Once again, Tolkien has dared to offend modernist/humanist orthodoxy – or should I say, fantasy? – and name the truth.

To conflate Sauron with the pre-industrial kingships of Gondor or Rohan would thus be absurd. As Madawc Williams (1995: 17) points out, "if one king feels morally bound to respect your existing rights while the other is planning either to enslave you or feed you to his Orcs, you'd have little trouble knowing which side you ought to be on!" Furthermore, what is "The Scouring of the Shire", politically speaking, but an account of local resistance to fascist thuggery and modernization?[33]

That leaves the "approval of traditional property settlements." Well, I doubt if Tolkien's approval could have been taken for granted; it would probably have depended a great deal on what was proposed for the land in question. And as Jonathan Bate (1991: 46) points out, redistributing ownership is not going to be much use if the land in question is poisoned beyond use.

As I mentioned earlier, Bate (1991: 11) makes another important point too: a distinction between love of the land and love of the fatherland. The former, which is clear both in Tolkien's personal life and his books, involves a fierce attachment to highly specific and local places and things. As such, it offers little foothold to the inflated emotional abstractions that are so essential to nationalistic fascism. This is vividly illustrated in Sam's saving realization, when tempted by the Ring of Power, that "[t]he one small garden of a free gardener was all his need and due, not a garden swollen to a realm; his own hands to use, not the hands of others to command" (RK.VI.i).

---

33 See Plank (1975); he also points out that "Tolkien opposes fascism as a conservative rather than as a democrat" (1975: 114).

The Cultural Student

Williams was the chief founding father in this country (along with Hoggart) of what is now called cultural studies. One of its luminaries, and Williams's biographer in a work he himself describes as an act of homage, is Fred Inglis (1995, and see 1994). He wrote essays on Tolkien in 1981 and 1983. I will try to be brief, because I already addressed some of their content, but also because his work here plumbs such a nadir of mendacity.[34]

Inglis writes that Tolkien's prose "*is* moving, there is no doubt, but it moves a reader away from and never towards real life" (1981: 192). "Real life" is a purely rhetorical gesture here, of course, signifying "what us left-Leavisite Grown-Ups have, in our wisdom, decided is real". But there is worse to come, for "Tolkien's 'schmaltz-Götterdämmerung'" is such that "for once it makes sense to use that much-abused adjective, and call Tolkien a Fascist" (Inglis 1981: 197). Williams, of course, implied the same; as have others: Jonathan Miller, for example, in a characteristically glib equation of Tolkien and Wagner.[35] Now, I have already shown the utter flimsiness of such a charge. In addition, there is simply no Wagnerian "Götterdämmerung" in *The Lord of the Rings*; "Victory neither restores an earthly Paradise nor ushers in New Jerusalem" (Muirhead 1986: 20). In addition, Tolkien strongly disliked Wagner, all the more so for drawing directly on some of the same mythological material that the latter only knew second-hand, and to such very different ends (see Shippey 1992: 296). (Interestingly, Ragnarok was a relatively late aspect of Germano-Scandinavian mythology that never caught on in the pagan Anglo-Saxon England that so influenced Tolkien. Even then, it was, apparently, unEnglish in its melodrama (Branston 1957: 155).)

Inglis makes a number of other bizarre assertions to back up his specious claim: "Like all popular cultures, Middle-earth's utopia is prehistoric and classless," his prose "abjures any corporeal solidity," being "bodiless", "colourless", and

---

34 Although, to be fair, it is no worse than his editor and some of his fellow contributors to Giddings's (1983) execrable collection, thankfully already discussed by Colebatch (1990: 67-81). See, e.g., the slimy sub-cultural materialism of Nigel Walmsley, Nick Otty's confusions about deconstruction and Brenda Partridge's dysfunctional psychoanalysis.

35 This is typical of Miller in its arrogance and ignorance, as so often when he ventures out of his area of actual expertise; but personal psychology apart, it also typifies the consequences of a dogmatic belief in the tenets of scientific secularism, rationalism and modernism.

"unreally picturesque", and "none of his characters reflect on their actions for a moment." Overall, "the whole book is suffused with an intense spirituality which [...] transposes what is physical into the soaring splendours of musical experience which, having no referent, cannot *signify* but only move" (Inglis 1983: 33, 35-37). I say "bizarre" because (1) again, there is no such utopia, at least in the sense Inglis means, and what is there is saturated with historicity; (2) it is precisely the corporeal reality of Middle-earth that impresses the overwhelming majority of readers; and (3) there is hardly a major character in the book who doesn't, at some point, reflect on his or her actions. (Inglis's utilitarian contempt for music speaks for itself.)

He comments that "Such a feeling does not transcend culture, it is created by culture" (Inglis 1983: 33). Here we at least touch usefully on a fundamental flaw in cultural studies, which is to conclude that because something is learned, cultural, contingent or constructed it isn't real or true. Of course, by simply reversing the conservative valuation of instinctive, natural, necessary and revealed, the same impoverished oppositions are preserved intact, and any critical advance on them disabled. As Antony Easthope (1991: 45) puts it, the "literature-as-construction analysis relies on an erroneous either/or: either literary value is a textual essence independent of the reader; or there is no literary value at all." Above all, to quote Derrida (1988: 136), "All that ['quite simply everything'] is political, but it is not only political." Quite so. Tolkien's work cannot "transcend culture" in the way Inglis absurdly implies, because *no* discourse can. On the other hand, although "created by culture" it addresses a great deal more than that: nature, ethics, myth ...

But Inglis's chief strategy is carefully to condemn and disown a series of critical tactics before proceeding himself to turn them on Tolkien. Thus, he mocks the "old, round way of dealing with bestsellers" (Inglis 1983: 25), which viewed their readers as seeking refuge "in a fantasy world (swear word) whose emotional gratifications (ditto) compensated for (school-teacher's report judgement) the emptiness of everyday life (guerilla slogan)" (ibid. 27). Yet only a few pages later, we find a cringingly florid caricature of a "typical" Tolkien reader – a former head of art in a market-town grammar-school, sitting in a new, pine-panelled unit in a converted farm building, reading Tolkien to his two young sons – doing exactly that (ibid. 31-32).[36]

Inglis continues that "[t]o write of Tolkien's version of this tradition is not in the least to say that [...] [in] a now familiar but entirely empty putting-down, it is nostalgic [...]. *But*" – nonetheless – Tolkien's nostalgia "implies not only some distortion of vision but also a privileging of the past over the present such that the present can *only* be lived in terms of its failure to measure up to the past [...]" (1983: 28). And his final disingenuous gesture is to retract his claim that Tolkien is a fascist, before asserting that his work is: "instead of Nuremberg, Frodo's farewell" – equally a travesty of the text and the history that as Clay Ramsay remarked, "Inglis uses on Tolkien apparently to situate him, but really to engulf him."[37]

The Psychoanalyst

It is almost a relief to turn to another of Tolkien's sternest critics, Rosemary Jackson, a literary critic with strong commitments to both Marxism and psychoanalysis. She believes that Middle-earth is somehow "outside the human [...] free from the demands of historical time, or of mortality" – which is presumably why "fairy tales discourage in the importance or effectiveness of action," and why those of Tolkien (together with C.S. Lewis and a host of other offenders) function "as conservative vehicles for social and instinctual repression [...] supporting a ruling ideology" and serving only to "reinforce a blind faith in 'eternal' moral values, really those of an outworn liberal humanism." In addition to the by-now-familiar charge of "nostalgic", she attacks "the chauvinistic, totalitarian effects of [Tolkien's] vision [...]" and sympathizes with those victims of repression, the orcs, of whose hairiness (as a sign of desire) she makes much (1988: 154-56).

---

36 As he himself admits, "Once we have set the irony-stereotypewriter to work, it is easy for any bookish person who lives within the London-Bristol ellipse of thriving capital to go on remorselessly in this vein" (1983: 3). So why does he do so, and allow it to stand as substantive and fair comment?

37 Personal communication. (Typically, Inglis's determination to make his point overrides his "grateful" acceptance of Claude Rawson's correction on this point in the *Times Literary Supplement* of 26.06.82; (Inglis 1983: 41, n. 18).

Since Jackson too is fond of what she calls "reality", let us run a textual reality-check on her own claims. Tolkien's work is saturated with historicity – a claim which I submit to the judgement of any informed reader; "Death and the desire for deathlessness" was perhaps his most fundamental theme (see *Letters* 1981: 262); *The Lord of the Rings* is nothing if not packed with action, upon the outcomes of which everything subsequent hangs; and whatever the values inherent in his work – and liberal humanism is an odd description of them: Tolkien as E.M. Forster? – "outworn" would seem rather presumptuous in the light of their popular reception. As for the hairiness of Jacksons's orcs, what of hobbits' famously hairy feet? Or is that bourgeois hair?

Already by 1953, Kenneth Burke could justifiably complain that "people have gone on too long with the glib psychoanalytic assumption that an art of 'escape' promotes acquiescence. It may, as easily, assist a reader to clarify his dislike of an environment in which he is placed" (1957: 119). Three-and-a-half decades later, Jackson and most of Tolkien's other leading critics are still making the same glib assumption. And driving her Freudian anathema we find the same atavistic Enlightenment essentialism, with its faith in the power of Reason to liberate us from "repressive energies" and attain utopia: "De-mystifying the process of reading fantasies will, hopefully, point to the possibility of *undoing* many texts which work, unconsciously, upon us." Why? Because "In the *end* this may lead to *real* social transformation" (Jackson 1988: 10, my emphases). Let us pause here, note the modernist profession of faith in demystification, and ask: what is this state of freedom, equally "hors le texte" and the bonds of "savoir/pouvoir", into which such "undoing" (magically uninfluenced by any new reading) releases us? Exactly what and when is this distinctly eschatological "end"? And what is this equally absolutist "real" transformation, as opposed to the kind we know from mere history and quotidian experience? In short, who is really the utopian fantasist here: Tolkien, or Jackson?

What *shouldn't* be utopian is to find not a nonpolitical criticism, certainly, but in Joan Acacella's words "a sophisticated criticism – one that, while indebted to a certain politics, can balance that concern with a sustained attention to what the artist is saying" (1995: 71). But by now it should come as no surprise to find (as Attebery (1993: 23) has pointed out) that Jackson also cites an essay by the politically acceptable W.H. Auden as the source of some of Tolkien's ideas in his "On Fairy-Stories", when the former appeared twenty-one years after the latter. (Valentine Cunningham recently performed a similar trick when using Auden's satire on "ruralizing simple-lifers" to sneer at Tolkien's "mythic and escapist fairyland" (1989: 232). He conveniently fails to mention Auden's fulsome praise for *The Lord of the Rings*.)

Escapist?

This was a charge which recurs throughout the attacks of Tolkien's critics, and he was familiar with it early in his career. His essay "On Fairy-Stories" provides his own best defence. As an instance, Tolkien mentions the recent technological innovation (in his time) of mass-produced electric street-lamps. Any writer who ignores such developments, or prefers to discuss, say, lightning, is liable to be labelled escapist:

> out comes the big stick: "Electric lamps have come to stay," they say. [... Or:] "The march of Science, its tempo quickened by the needs of war, goes inexorably on ... making some things obsolete, and foreshadowing new developments in the utilization of electricity": an advertisement. This says the same thing only more menacingly. (1988: 56)

The prison, to encapsulate my theme, is enforced modernity, whose human casualties alone now number in many millions, while for animals and the natural world the holocaust is still continuing. And its intellectual and cultural warders are the "realists" and "rationalists" whom Tolkien has in mind when he says, for example, that "The notion that motor-cars are more 'alive' than, say, centaurs or dragons is curious; that they are more 'real' than horses is pathetically absurd" (1988: 57). In the years before Nazism, Stalinism and Maoism provided such grim confirmation, and before global consumer capitalism took over the job, Tolkien already saw this clearly. Yet his only honour among the elites is still to be accounted escapist, juvenile and irrational. This, with Tolkien, I utterly deny:

> it is after all possible for a rational man, after reflection (quite unconnected with fairy-story or romance), to arrive at the condemnation, implicit at least in the mere silence of "escapist" literature, of progressive things like factories, or the machine-guns and bombs that appear to be their most natural and inevitable, dare we say "inexorable", products. (1988: 58)

The Lord of the Rings is hardly escapist within its own context, either, centred as it is around a war, struggle, hardship and suffering. And at the end of his tale, occasional hints about other worlds notwithstanding, Tolkien returns us firmly to *this* one: at the Grey Havens, after the departure of Frodo and Gandalf, Sam "stood far into the night, hearing only the sigh and murmur of the waves on the shores of Middle-earth, and the sound of them sank deep into his heart" (RK.VI.ix). We stand with him. At best, Tolkien's "evangelium" permits only a "fleeting glimpse of Joy" in this world, not permanent transportation to the next (1988: 62). The nostalgia he engenders, therefore, is finally redirected back into our own lives here. In Geoffrey Grigson's still more compact words:

> be comforted.
> Content I did not say.

The Structuralist

Christine Brooke-Rose is an eminent structuralist, professor of literature in Paris, and author of experimental modernist novels.[38] Here again, we find the heavy guns of Theory employed not to comprehend Tolkien but to get rid of him. Gimli and Legolas serve "no functional role [...] [and are] wholly gratuitous." Any maps and appendices are mere "semiological compensation". And *The Lord of the Rings*'s histories and genealogies are "not in the least necessary to the narrative, but they have given much infantile happiness to the Tolkien clubs and societies [...]" (Brooke-Rose 1981: 237-38, 247).

The modernist dread of being thought infantile shared by Wilson and Brooke-Rose seems to be related to a widespread contempt for Tolkien's "fans" (almost always "fans", perhaps to invoke an implicit association with something like football). The editor of one book of scholarly (but mostly dull) essays on Tolkien (Isaacs and Zimbardo 1981: 2) poisonously dismisses as "fanfluff" publications by Tolkien societies that contain very little worse and not a little

---

38 The latter, persistently unpopular, were recently defended by Lorna Sage in the *Times Literary Supplement* (12.08.94), who wrote that Brooke-Rose's "voice has seemed more distant and characterless than in fact it is" – something to treasure alongside Mark Twain's observation, more deliberately ironic, that Wagner's music "is better than it sounds."

that is better.[39] Tolkien himself, as Carpenter (1992: 233) writes, once "referred to the widespread enthusiasm for his books as 'my deplorable cultus'." Yet the objects of this fastidiousness are readers for whom Tolkien's work is large and alive, and who are therefore better-placed to understand it than his narrowly scholarly dissectors. It is the latter who deserve pity and scorn.

Like Jackson, Brooke-Rose puts *The Lord of the Rings* through the structuralist text-grinder in order (she supposes) to attain freedom through disenchantment. Another practitioner, Nick Otty, similarly recommends "deconstructing" *The Lord of the Rings* "so that we may see the text as a construct produced in a certain context," and are therefore "no longer 'in thrall' to it" (1983: 155) – an ambition whose risibility I have already discussed.[40] All that distinguishes Brooke-Rose's (1980) version is its detailed and dismal emphasis on "the machinery of realism", "mechanisms inherent to the marvellous," and so on. I am forcibly reminded of Treebeard's description of Saruman: "He has a mind of metal and wheels; and he does not care for growing things [...]" (TT.III.iv). This is no mere conceit: structuralism, like Marxism and psychoanalysis, bears a heavy freight of what Howard Felperin called "a lingering nineteenth-century faith or superstition – that the study of literary texts can be, should be, or, in the case of their own work, *is* scientific" (1985: 57).[41]

No wonder, then, that Brooke-Rose cannot seem to comprehend Tolkien, or indeed, even *read* him: "orks" – "the Gollum" – "Tolkien's trilogy" – "Sam Gamjee" – "Elf-people" – "Belin" (for Balin) – "Edora" – "Minas Mogul" – "Moria Mountain" (1981: 237-38, 244-45, 247). (Edmund Wilson had already saved her some time with "Gandalph" and "dwarfs", and Stimpson with "Sarumen".) She gives the wizards their own language, states that Gandalf, "although a wizard, can only perform minor magic" (!), and has Arwen's father Elrond as her brother.[42] The sloppiness of such an astounding catalogue of errors, and

---

39 Such as the (UK) Tolkien Society's *Mallorn* and the (USA) Mythopoeic Society's *Mythlore*, *Arda* (Sweden) and *Lembas* (Netherlands). This is evidently an attitude shared even by Rosebury (1992: 129); but not, I am glad to say, by Shippey or Attebery.

40 See my remarks on Jackson, above. (It is equally amusing to find him complaining about Tolkien's "fusion and confusion of levels of reality" and narratives – unlike, say, that of Borges, O'Brien or Calvino?)

41 Note too the cultural studies mantra of "interrogating" texts, which reveals a common mentality if not indeed origin in the Baconian interrogation of nature, bound and on the rack.

42 Some of Brooke-Rose's mistakes are mentioned in Rosebury (1992: 154); and see Shippey (1992: 282-84).

the arrogance it implies, would hardly be tolerated in other areas of scholarly inquiry, and it speaks volumes about Brooke-Rose's (and her publisher's) attitude to her subject.

A Literary-Industrial Establishment

Brooke-Rose's attitude is also part of a larger critical problem in relation to the whole genre that Tolkien's success unintentionally created. Consider, for example, how mainstream literati lapped up the magic and spirituality of South and Central American and African "magic realism" because it seemed exotic, while condemning to the "fantasy" ghetto any local and native expressions of the same. Alternatively an author identified as a mainstream novelist is frequently praised for imaginative daring when he or she incorporates fantasy into a novel, but authors who have been pigeon-holed as fantasy-writers can do the same thing (only better) in vain.[43] And any fantasy-writer with a local product that threatens to succeed more widely is firmly slapped down with the usual modernist clichés: "childish", "phantastic", and partaking of an "underlying irrationality" which is "okay" in poetry and children's writing, but not "in a grown-up novel for grown-ups" (Turner 1996). This is not reviewing, it is policing.

Such an attitude was early and aptly analyzed by Walter Benjamin, in a wonderful essay entitled "The Storyteller", whose every resonance applies to Tolkien. He noted that

> the art of storytelling is coming to an end. Less and less frequently do we encounter people with an ability to tell a tale properly. More and more often there is embarrassment all around when the wish to hear a story is expressed. [...] The art of storytelling is reaching its end because the epic side of truth, wisdom, is dying out. [...] A great storyteller will always be rooted in the people, primarily in a milieu of craftsmen. [...] The fairy tale, which to this day is the first tutor of children because it was the first tutor of mankind, secretly lives on in the story. (Benjamin 1969: 83, 87, 101, 102)[44]

---

43 E.g. high praise for Mark Helprin's "literary" *Winter's Tale* (1983) but ignoring John Crowley's superior "fantasy" *Little, Big* (1982), for Deepak Chopra's New Age *The Return of Merlin* (1995) but not Robert Holdstock's genuinely chthonic *Mythago Wood* (1982), and so on.

44 Benjamin's modernist admirers, at least those who have also engaged in Tolkien criticism, seem to have missed this essay. I am very grateful to Nicola Bown for bringing it to my attention.

Benjamin described the novel as a huge step away from storytelling, with its roots in the oral tradition; the modern obsession with information is yet another huge removal. And the novels are bad enough: permitted only

> that necessary degree of irony which is the sole form of "honesty" modern prose styles or conventions readily allow. [...] Unhappy with myth, wary of emotion, harried by empty political terminologies, scornful of "character", eager, it seems, to refine, redefine and narrow down the material until the works in question are about themselves, nothing else but themselves. Affirmation, no. Consolation, certainly not. (Potter 1984: 12-13, 31)[45]

No wonder that, as Tolkien (1981: 209) believed, "the 'fairy-story' is really an adult genre, and one for which a starving audience exists."

This *trahison* of readers by the clerks is one in which critics colloborate with writers and publishers. If, as Brian Attebery (1992: 17) suggests, "the task of literary theory is to provide a framework capable of accounting for the story's success in its own terms, rather than denying that its aims are achievable or worth the attempt," then literary theory has dismally failed with Tolkien, and fantasy literature in general. Indeed, as Bill Buford (1996: 11-12) pointed out, in the 1,383 pages of the authoritative *New Princeton Encyclopedia of Poetry and Poetics*, there is no entry for "story"! In the book pages of the quality press, the situation is no better. Those calling the shots include people like Martin Amis, self-consciously clever modernist "par excellence", for *The Sunday Times*; and Robert McCrum, for *The Observer*, who seems to view Marx and America with equal reverence (and no sense of contradiction).[46]

Now that Seamus Heaney has won the Nobel prize for Literature, will it begin to dawn that as he remarked, "the movement is always from delight to wisdom and not vice versa"? I doubt it. As much as ever it remains the case, to quote Nuala O'Faolain, writing in *The Irish Times* (07.11.1992), that

---

45 The depressing degeneration of Italo Calvino's fiction is a characteristic case in point.

46 Amis's attitude to anything at odds with the modernist credo was perhaps revealed by his "review" for the *London Review of Books* of Robert Bly's *Iron John* – a book which, whatever else one might think of it, at least raised serious and interesting issues. The entire piece consisted of variations on sniggering occasioned by Bly's title denoting a gay man in Amis's boyhood English slang. Asked in an interview in the *New Statesman and Society* (03.05.1996), "Which books and authors have had the greatest influence on your political beliefs?" McCrum replied "*The Communist Manifesto* and *The Eighteenth Brumaire* by Karl Marx." Yet "Which event during your lifetime has had the greatest effect on your political beliefs?" "My first visit to America in 1976 showed me how it was possible to live in a genuinely free society."

[t]he language of highbrow criticism can only cope with a certain kind of fiction. It has no vocabulary with which to discuss a world where neither the individual nor the society is self-conscious, and the author pretends not to be either. [...] The ordinary reader is far ahead of the critics in ease with such a world.

This in turn relates to the "déformation professionelle" of modern criticism, journalism and publishing as a whole – aggressively secular, cynical, snobbish and incestuous – which is beyond my scope here.[47] But I will give Karel Capek, writing in *PEN International* (45:1, 1995), the last word on the subject:

look how often the cultural world pronounces a sentence of annihilating rejection. How old-fashioned ideas, other people's views, or those of the habitues of a different literary cafe, are arrogantly dismissed out of hand. [...] This is variously called literary criticism, ideological struggle, a matter of principle, or the generation gap. In truth it is merely prickly intellectual exclusiveness running around looking for something to turn its nose up at. If your nose is in the air, though, you cannot see properly.

Nor can you read very well.

Why?

The question remains: how could so many otherwise intelligent critics be so slapdash, unfair and just plain wrong? First, let's notice that they are so in significantly similar ways. The specific charges against Tolkien and the values in whose name they are made make up a strong family resemblance, and I have suggested we call it modernism. Indeed, Williams's Marx, Jackson's Freud, Brooke-Rose's Saussure – these are among the very avatars of modernism, whose "grand narratives" of modernity – secularised versions of divine revelation – were supposed to supply essentially complete accounts of our progress towards the realisation of the truth. But there have been too many broken promises by now, and too many terrible "successes". The human being has become a stranger not only to the cosmos and the Earth but to each other, and him- and herself. By now, "man himself has become, after God and nature, an anthropomorphism" (Schnädelbach 1992: 314).

---

47 On a "snide and aggressive" media, see Gopnik (1994: 84-102); also Nicholson-Lord (1995), and Midgeley (1997).

Modernism is not the only description possible; another strong candidate I have already mentioned is humanism, as analyzed in David Ehrenfeld's *The Arrogance of Humanism* (1978) – a book which, not coincidentally, cites or quotes Tolkien approvingly several times. On balance, however, I think the former term has the edge. But in either case, Tolkien's apostasy (or perhaps more properly, since he never subscribed to it in the first place, heresy) often seems so strongly felt by true believers as actively to interfere with being able actually to read him. As J.P. Stern once remarked, "contempt is a poor guide." The modernist missionaries arrive in Middle-earth dressed in a space-suit of Theory, protected from contamination by what they have already decided is its infantilism, escapism and reactionary politics. This is hardly good critical practice; can you imagine any of them admitting with William Empson, writing in the *London Review of Books* (04.02.1988), that "A literary critic must be prepared to say, 'This is good, though I don't know why; not yet anyhow' […]"? Or finding it in their hearts to say a good word – on any grounds whatever – about Wodehouse, Kipling or Yeats? Yet Orwell somehow managed it, without losing his socialist soul.[48]

But the modernists are right, in their own twisted way. *The Lord of the Rings* really is a text whose predominant available meanings powerfully contradict their own values;[49] and whose popular success, as a sign of widely shared doubts if not repudiation, makes it, from their point of view, all the worse. In the intention of its author an anti-modernist text, attacking industrialism, secularism, and the myth of Progress, *The Lord of the Rings* falls into the traditions of what Jonathan Bate (1991) calls "romantic ecology", Don Elgin (1985) "the ecological perspective of comedy" and Meredith Veldman (1994) "Romantic Protest". And like the works of other such authors – William Wordsworth, John Ruskin, William Morris – it has acquired powerful new meanings in a *post*-modern context.[50] When this dimension overlaps with Tolkien's enduring popularity in the same way as that of Dickens, Kipling and Hardy, you get some

---

48 See, by contrast, Raymond Williams's biographical attack on Orwell – a perfect sample of dogmatic socialist sanctimony.

49 As was noticed by Wilson (1974: 37), *The Lord of the Rings* "is at once an attack on the modern world and a credo, a manifesto."

50 Veldman's book (1994) shows connections between Tolkien's popularity and the CND/END protest movement that far outweigh E.P.Thompson's superficial use of imagery from his books to describe a Cold War mentality – something about which he was corrected (as he later acknowledged) by Jessica Yates; see her article "Tolkien the Anti-totalitarian" (Yates 1995).

idea of the potential power of his books – and of the critics' irresponsibility in so cavalierly dismissing them.

Of course, as both Shippey and Rosebury have pointed out, there are important modern elements in Tolkien's work: its stress on the anti-heroic and unmilitary hobbits and their reluctant participation (and that of others, such as Faramir and indeed Aragorn; the martial Boromir comes to a bad end) in the War of the Ring; war itself as at best a necessary evil; its Actonian view of power (in the Ring) as unavoidably corrupting; and even its absence of explicit religion.[51] But Tolkien's very syncretism offends modernist purism.

Ironically, therefore, it is his critics who belong to the past, and Tolkien to the future. It is they who are nostalgic for the past, including their role as legislators (in Zygmunt Bauman's terms) rather than the interpreters they have become. Behind their instinctive antagonism lies an uncomfortable sense that here is a coherent fictional critique and alternative, in every major respect, to the exhausted myth of modernity which has so far underwritten their own professional status; and worse still, it is a popular one. Not for the first time, those who claim to speak for universal truth and reason are lagging behind "the people" whom they often claim to represent, and whose interests to know better than the people themselves.[52]

Now, it is perfectly possible to imagine Tolkien's books "being" truly reactionary: racist, nationalist, etc. – that is, having those kinds of effects. In fact, there is one historical instance of just that, when his writings were briefly adopted by some violent right-wingers in Italy who held a "Camp Hobbit" outside Rome in June 1978.[53] What I am arguing, however, is that (1) neither in his intention nor (especially) essentially or inherently is Tolkien's work pathologically reactionary; and that (2) *as it happens* – as things have actually turned out – his implicit diagnosis of modernity was prescient; and his vision of an alternative,

---

51 See Rosebury (1992: 148) and Shippey (1992: 24).

52 Another good example: the attempt by modernists like Waldemar Januszczak and Martin Pawley to trash the doubts, fears and dislike of much modern architecture by Prince Charles in 1989-90. They invoked everything from the size of his ears, and associations with Hitler to economic "realism" and "progress". But the vast outpouring in the media from members of the public in Charles' defence demonstrated that he was, overwhelmingly, speaking for them; and to those feelings, the experts had no convincing reply.

53 See Bjorgo (1995: 234), who cites Franco Ferreresi (ed.), *La Destra Radicale*. I am grateful to Matthew Kalman for this reference.

progressive. (Of course, it also follows that his critics, despite their loud claims to being both, were neither.)

Thus, in the context of global modernisation and the resistence to it, his stories have become an animating and inspiring new myth. It is one that suggests that just as there was life before modernity, so there can be after it. They are deeply nostalgic, certainly; but it is an emotionally empowering nostalgia, not a crippling one. And it joins up with a growing contemporary sense, represented in postmodernism, of history's sheer contingency – the liberating perception that it-might-have-been-different, and therefore *could* be different now.[54]

Post/Modernity and Re-Enchantment

By modernism I mean not so much a particular literary or artistic or architectural movement as the self-conscious articulation and celebration of the chief values and goals of modernity. And by modernity I mean the co-dependent power of corporate and finance capital, the modern political state and modern science that is probably best summed up in Lewis Mumford's term, "the megamachine". These have generated, and are served by, the ideologies of economism, statism and scientism. The last, particularly relevant to us here, is the belief that only science, being dis- or unenchanted, has access to the truth; it is therefore the only legitimate kind of knowledge, to the exclusion (and if possible elimination) of all others, e.g. traditional and local forms (see Ekins 1992). A primary commitment is thus to deny and/or disguise the fact that science, as an epistemological practice, is no less a contingent and fallible human construct than any other kind; in other words, that even science is not "scientific" in the way they mean it.[55]

Modernity began to grow in the late seventeenth century, received clear and programmatic articulation in the Enlightenment of the eighteenth century, developed powerful new political and economic forms in the nineteenth,

---

54 For a brilliant essay on Middle-earth as a "Fourth World" Europe, unstained by industrialism and imperialism, see Luling (1995).
55 In addition to Paul Feyerabend's books, see recent work in the history and sociology of science – e.g. by Stephen Shapin and Simon Schaffer, to mention only two names out of many – as well as the new growth industry of attempting to debunk this work by scientific publicists.

and attained truly global dimensions of natural and social engineering in the twentieth (see Toulmin 1990). Its chief characteristics – historically formed, but nonetheless essential for that – can be defined as *monism* and *universalism*: truth, initially divine and apprehended through revelation, but then (without significant modification of its "modus operandi") secular and apprehended through reason, that is single and universal. And this truth must be certain; hence the modernist obsession with "theoria", or science, going back to Descartes, Galileo, Bacon and Hobbes. (Toulmin identifies these men as instituting a "counter-enlightenment" to the earlier pre-modern humane scepticism of Montaigne and Erasmus.)

As Kolakowski points out, the origins of this modernity can be dated back as far as the eleventh century; but

> the question so many of us have been trying to cope with is not so much when modernity started, but what is the core – whether or not explicitly expressed – of our contemporary widespread "Unbehagen in der Kultur"? [...] And the first answer that naturally comes to mind is summed up, of course, in the Weberian "Entzauberung" – disenchantment – or in any similar word roughly covering the same phenomenon. (Kolakowski 1990: 7)

The characteristic rhetorical gesture of modernism – its sacrament, one might say – is indeed unmasking, demystifying, debunking, and indeed destroying false gods, false truths, false consciousness. The trouble is, this process recognizes no limits; hence the power granted to its economic expression, neo-liberal market-forces, to tear up and make over everything – nature, communities, human nature. Without limits, however – which must therefore come from other sources – the terminus of this process is natural impoverishment, social violence and cultural nihilism (see Gray 1995).

Since my focus here is primarily cultural, let me illustrate the last by quoting art critic Sarah Kent, a big fan of the fêted corpse-artist Damien Hirst. Extolling an exhibition of life-size castrated and mutilated dummies, she wrote: "They satisfy your [*sic*] blood-lust, they seduce, and they make you sick. Brilliant."[56] This sort of thing is sometimes backed-up with aesthetic theory, e.g. Bernstein (1996: 16):

---

56 From *Time Out* (05-12.10.1994).

Art cannot avoid the progressive disenchantment of the world that has occurred outside art; if it sought to obtain authenticity and authority for itself by
summoning dead gods and dead meanings into its precincts, it would rightly
be accused of naivete or anachronism. [...] Authenticity without cruelty is no
longer possible.

And indeed, just these accusations are frequently levelled against *The Lord of
the Rings* (including an unconscionable lack of cruelty).

But who says the gods and meanings to which it refers are dead, and on what
warrant? Whether historically or metaphysically, it takes a peculiarly narrow
and teleological modernism to assign them to the grave, only to be perpetu-
ally amazed at "the return of the repressed". In Russell Hoban's words, "Why
cannot any god die? Because gods do not replace one another [...] gods are
a cumulative projection of everything in us" (1992: 138).[57] And as Tolkien
long ago noted,

the true road of escape from such weariness is not to be found in the wilfully
awkward, clumsy, or misshapen, not in making all things dark or unremit-
tingly violent; nor in the mixing of colours on through subtlety to drabness,
and the fantastical complication of shapes to the point of silliness and on
towards delirium. Before we reach such states we need recovery. We should
look at green again, and be startled anew (but not blinded) by blue and yellow
and red. (1988: 53)

And that is why, rather than a still further disenchantment that ends by eating itself, and utterly capitulating to the logic of capital and the market (art
and otherwise), re-enchantment is needed: as Ted Hughes (1992) argued, the
whole point of art is "to reopen negotiations with the mythic plane." The
implication, which I shall not try to follow up here, is that postmodernists'
militant secularism (such as that of Richard Rorty) actually disables their
own programme.

Nonetheless, the basic critique of modernity (including its articulations in
modernism) which has come to be called postmodernism is correct as far as
it goes. It has been aptly summed up by Barbara Herrnstein Smith as "in-
tellectual/political totalitarianism (the effort to identify the presumptively
universally compelling Truth and Way and to compel it universally) [...]"

---

57 He adds, "I'm not trying to reduce this to psychiatry – I mean that we worship the gods projected by
the god-force that projects us as well on the screen of its mind."

(1988: 179).[58] The essence of this programme is not rationality "per se", "but a deranged, totalizing rationalism which yields disenchantment," whose products include, as Max Weber foresaw (and some of whom I have already quoted), "[s]pecialists without spirit, sensualists without heart; this nullity imagines that it has attained a level of civilization never before achieved" (Kontos 1994: 235, 233). Modernity therefore need not, indeed cannot be countered with mere irrationality. Culturally speaking, these exemplars of nullity may now simply and without any regrets be abandoned:

> The growing sense that we are not bound to *complete* the project of modernity (Habermas' phrase) and still do not necessarily have to lapse into irrationality or into apocalyptic frenzy, the sense that art is not exclusively pursuing some telos of abstraction, non-representation, and sublimity – all of this has opened up a host of possibilities for creative endeavors today. (Huyssen 1986: 217)

Nor is postmodernity a new era marking the end of modernity or even modernism; but it does articulate a process in which hitherto largely unquestioned modernist truths look increasingly, to increasing numbers of people, like highly questionable assumptions. And people *do* have questions – more people, with more and deeper fears and worries, than perhaps ever before. By now, only a fool (or convert, or employee) would say they are groundless.

By contrast, then, the chief characteristics of postmodernism – as an articulation of postmodernity – are *pluralism*, *localism*, and *perspectivism* (or "relativism").[59] As against the quest for certainty, there is room for Keats's negative capability, that is, "capable of being in uncertainties, mysteries, doubts, without any irritable reaching after fact and reason." The postmodern question is not "is it true?" but "is it any use?"; its "modus vivendi", accordingly, is not theory but the "practical wisdom" of "phronesis". And its proper cultural project, in response to modernist nihilism (or what Michael Ende (1993) calls "the Nothing") is *re-enchantment*: what Tolkien (1988: 18) described as "the primal desire at the heart of Faërie: the realization, independent of the conceiving mind, of imagined wonder." But the "realization" here is ambiguous, and properly so; it signifies both the making of the natural world wondrous through the crea-

---

58 Cf. Laclau and Mouffe (1985: 191-92): "This point is decisive: there is no radical and plural democracy without renouncing the discourse of the universal, and its implicit assumption of a privileged point of access to 'the truth', which can only be reached by a limited number of subjects."
59 These can be summed up as "anti-essentialism".

tion of a "Secondary World [...] artistic in desire and purpose" (1988: 49), *and* the realization (through the former) that the Primary or "real" world actually is wondrous.[60] Ultimately it has to be that way, for to adopt wonder as a way to save the world merely re-admits humanist utilitarianism by the back door.

Such a project cannot succeed as an act purely or even primarily of will, because that is precisely the domain not of enchantment but of magic, which (in Tolkien's words) "is not an art but a technique; its desire is *power* in this world, domination of things and wills" (1988: 49-50). Thus "Faërie itself may perhaps most nearly be translated by Magic – but it is magic of a peculiar mood and power, at the furthest pole from the vulgar devices of the laborious, scientific, magician" (1988: 15). Tolkien's intuition here is historically borne out by modern science's continuity with, and largely unacknowledged borrowings from, magic.[61] And why it cannot save us now is that together with capital and the state, such science is what has created this crisis.

Aspects of postmodernism that are most relevant here have been voiced by Paul Feyerabend (1987: 89) – "we either call gods and quarks equally real, but tied to different sets of circumstances, or we altogether cease talking about the 'reality' of things and use more complex ordering schemes instead" – and Zygmunt Bauman (1992: x-xi):

> Above all, postmodernity can be seen as restoring to the world what modernity, presumptuously, had taken away; as a re-enchantment of the world that modernity had tried hard to disenchant. [...] The war against mystery and magic was for modernity the war of liberation leading to the declaration of reason's independence. [...] [The] world had to be de-spiritualized, de-animated: denied the capacity of subject. [...] It is against such a disenchanted world that the postmodern re-enchantment is aimed.

But note that we are not comparing a prior or later state of enchantment (what Tolkien identifies as "Faërie") with one of disenchantment; that concedes far too much to the disingenuous mythology of modernism, which pretends it is fundamentally different. Recalling Tolkien's distinction between magic and enchantment permits us to recognize what such scientists are doing, and their representatives defending, for what it is, namely, modernist magic: a powerful

---

60 The point about (re-)enchantment not being a matter of will was also asserted to me, in conversation, by Roberto Calasso.
61 Out of a vast literature, see Webster (1982).

negative or *counter*-enchantment, much of whose power stems from being a spell that denies that it is one, a secular religion – literally a bad faith, born of Descartes's dream (again, literally) of a perfect and certain knowledge that has culminated in the avowal of Edward Teller, "father" of the hydrogen bomb, that "there is no case where ignorance should be preferred to knowledge [...]." That may well be true for science; it is by no means always true for humanity. With better reason than he knows, Teller's interviewer described him as "our great master of the black art of detachment."[62]

That is why modernists cannot afford to take myth, folk-tale and fantasy seriously, and find any serious exemplars or discussion thereof offensive and even threatening. As Le Guin (1989: 36) notes of fantasy, "It isn't factual, but it's true. Children know that. Adults know it too, and that is precisely why many of them are afraid of fantasy." To admit that would come perilously close to admitting the possibility that their own "factual" truths partake of a perverted and disguised mythicity.

A note of clarification is appropriate, however. My critique of modernism and secularism should not be taken to imply advocacy of a return, somehow, to past religious certainties; and for these cogent reasons: (1) such a thing is impossible; (2) any such attempt is therefore bound to end up in the grossly distorted form of religious fundamentalism; and above all, (3) even if it were possible it would be highly undesirable. The fact is that modernist monism and universalism has its roots firmly in the universalist monotheism of the Judaeo-Christian tradition, and its logic is essentially the same. The minimal requirements for an enchanted world, in which nature is respected as alive, integral and active, are "mystery and a plurality of spirits"; whereas a single god, as Max Weber realized, establishes a monopoly which implies that everything can be subjected to a single, "rational", and therefore disenchanted ordering (Kontos 1994: 226ff).[63] "Returning to God" therefore offers no solutions to the problems of modernity; quite the contrary. The only real advance is to a pluralist, locally-rooted, and "relativist" re-enchantment that is *new*.

---

62 Hitchens (1994: 45).
63 This idea relates fundamentally to the "value pluralism" of Isaiah Berlin, itself deriving from Machiavelli.

Nor do I equate enchantment with all that is good. But I do maintain that in some form or other, it is humanly unavoidable; and that critique which rejects scientist essentialism must address itself not to which discourses are truths and which merely narratives/stories/myths, but to which of the latter are helpful and which are not. I need hardly add, I hope, that if there is no master-template of single, universal and unenchanted Truth, then it follows that you are left with various and plural truths – *not*, as some would disingenuously have it, nothing but lies.

Richard Kearney is right (1985: 78): "It is our ethical duty to use our powers of 'logos' to discriminate between the authentic and inauthentic uses to which 'mythos' is put in our culture." But the irony is that you cannot even begin to distinguish pathological myth from healthy and encourage the latter until you have admitted its reality and, when healthy, desirability. Dogmatic secularists and atheists stigmatize all forms alike and attempt to force an impossible (and undesirable) universal disenchantment; thus, failing to understand the legitimacy of the desire for (re-)enchantment as such, and wasting their fire on harmless or healthy kinds, they leave us more exposed than ever to its pathologies. Hence, in part, Tolkien's (1988: 45) insistence that "Fantasy is a rational not an irrational activity." But rational, appropriately, in the ancient (and postmodern) sense of "phronesis", not "theoria". As Milton Scarborough (1994: 110) writes,

> The ultimate assessment of myth must be of a kind suited to the nature of myth as giving expression to apprehensions of the life-world and as functioning to provide an orientation for living in that world. Within those strictures myth is neither true nor false *in a theoretical sense* but viable or not viable for the tasks (both theoretical and otherwise) which confront us. This viability is not determined in intellectual terms but in the very process of living, by whether or not one is energized, whether or not problems are being solved, whether or not life is integrated at a variety of levels, whether or not it is endowed with a significance that pulls one toward the future in hope.

Back to Fantasy

All this has very specific and significant implications for fantasy literature in general and Tolkien's books in particular, which speak powerfully to precisely our present conditions. Drawing on the power of ancient Indo-European myth, they invite the reader into a compelling and remarkably complete pre-modern world, saturated with corresponding earlier values, which therefore feels something like a lost home. They are just the values whose jeopardy we most now feel: relationships of respect with each other, and nature, and (for want of a better word) the spirit, which have not been stripped of personal integrity and responsibility and decanted into a soulless calculus of financial profit-and-loss. Wisdom in Middle-earth is not a matter of economic, scientific or technological expertise, but of practical and ethical maturity. If Middle-earth had a prophet, he was John Ruskin (1862, quoted in Wilmer 1985: 222): "THERE IS NO WEALTH BUT LIFE." And:

> To watch the corn grow, and the blossoms set; to draw hard breath over ploughshare or spade; to read, to think, to love, to hope, to pray, – these are the things that make men happy; they have always had the power of doing these, they never *will* have the power to do more. The world's prosperity or adversity depends upon our knowing and teaching these few things: but upon iron, or glass, or electricity, or steam, in no wise. (Ruskin 1856, quoted in Bate 1991: 81)

But this same world, as we begin *The Lord of the Rings*, is under severe threat from those who worship pure power, and are therefore its slaves – the technological and instrumental power embodied in Sauron (after whom the book itself is named, after all), and the epitome of modernism gone mad. Reading this story, one therefore finds oneself reading our own story. That is one reason why so many readers have taken it so to heart. Another is that just as Sauron is vanquished in *The Lord of the Rings* – albeit barely, temporarily, and at great cost – so Tolkien, crucially, offers his readers *hope* that what is precious and threatened in our world might survive, too.

Only those who cling to the modernist myth of a singular universal truth – as opposed to myth and story and indeed interpretation as such, which is somehow directly accessible to those with the "correct" understanding – only these will look at Tolkien's glorious tree and see (to use an apt image of William Blake's) only "a green thing standing in the way." To the modernist, the choice is between truth and myth (or falsehood). Whereas the postmodernist, giving up the pretense of a direct line to the Truth, sees the choice as between truths; or to put it another way, between myths (or stories) that are creative and liberating, and those that are destructive and debilitating.

So, for example, what really matters about the image of pre-Conquest England "as a free and equal rural community" benefitting from "a primitive freedom [and] the perpetual impulse and teaching of 'Nature'" (in Williams's excellent description (1985: 79)) is not the extent to which things were "actually" otherwise – though that too, itself an interpretation rather than a "fact", may become mobilised as a resource in one political direction or another – but the *use* of such an image in the present. In his own way, Tolkien (1988: 32) himself saw this clearly: "When we have done all that research [...] can do [...] there remains still a point too often forgotten: that is the effect produced *now* by these old things in the stories as they are." Indeed, Tolkien's anti-positivism is bizarrely in tune with some of the best and most refreshing aspects of postmodern philosophy:

> You call a tree a tree [...] and you think nothing more of the word. But it was not a "tree" until someone gave it that name. You call a star a star, and say it is just a ball of matter moving on a mathematical course. But that is merely how *you* see it. By so naming things and describing them you are only inventing your own terms about them. And just as speech is invention about objects and ideas, so myth is invention about truth. (Carpenter 1992: 151)

Furthermore, "[t]he incarnate mind, the tongue, and the tale are in our world coeval" (Tolkien 1988: 24), and "History often resembles 'Myth', because they are both ultimately of the same stuff" (1988: 31). As for the Derridean endless flux of discourse, fairy-stories "have a greater sense and grasp of the endlessness of the World of Story than most modern 'realistic' stories, already hemmed within the narrow confines of their own small time" (1988: 72).[64]

This resonance is less surprising if one recalls that Tolkien was strongly influenced by Owen Barfield's *Poetic Diction. A Study in Meaning* (1928).[65] In a more recent adumbration, Barfield concluded that "Literalness is a quality which some words have achieved in the course of their history; it is not a quality with which the first words were born. [...] [The word 'literal'] means something which is the end-product of a long historical process" (1977: 41). Furthermore, "[a]bandon-

---

64 Most recently, in his *Spectres of Marx* (1994), Derrida has written of the "infinite promise" of emancipation, which always risks betrayal through a vulgar and literal-minded realization. But isn't this what Tolkien meant by the hope of Escape – from modernity, from poverty and injustice, and from death itself – which runs exactly the same risk: e.g., in the last instance, the attempt at "endless serial living"? If so, how delicious an anticipation!
65 See the fascinating discussion by Hipolito (1993).

ing the specter of born literalness, we shall also abandon the whole dream of fixed entities with which literal meanings must somehow correspond."

Compare this with Laclau and Mouffe (1985: 111): "Literality is, in actual fact, the first of metaphors." Or Paul Veyne (1988: 38): "the flowering of myth and all manner of foolish tales ceases to mystify us by its gratuitousness and uselessness if we see that history itself is ceaseless invention and does not lead the reasonable life of a petty economizer." And it would be possible to quote any number of other authors to the same effect, questioning the naive reality of "the real" and demonstrating the inescapability of metaphoric interpretation. Furthermore, this is the point at which myth, as one particularly powerful kind thereof, starts to become an enormous and fascinating subject which should at this point be addressed; but cannot be, here. For now, let us just note with Tolkien (1988: 51) that

> Fantasy is a natural human activity. It certainly does not destroy or even insult Reason. [...] On the contrary. The keener and clearer is the reason, the better fantasy it will make. If men were ever in a state in which they did not want to know or could not perceive truth (facts or evidence), then Fantasy would languish [...] and become Morbid Delusion.

> For creative Fantasy is founded upon the hard recognition that things are so in the world as it appears under the sun; on a recognition of fact, but not a slavery to it.

He rightly adds that "If men really could not distinguish between frogs and men, fairy-stories about frog-kings would not have arisen." It is thus the vulgar "scientific" and "materialist" literalists who have an interest in destroying meta-phor and the creativity – in science no less than art and play – upon which, as Tolkien correctly notes, it depends.[66]

For closely related reasons, postmodernism has also restored the crucial impor-tance of narrative, the way by which we produce and find meaning.[67] Thus, Brian Attebery (1992: 40-41) has suggested that "Postmodernism is a return to storytelling in the belief that we can be sure of nothing but story." He (1992: 46) shrewdly adds not only that postmodernist criteria are much better suited to explaining Tolkien's success than are realist or modernist criteria, but

---

66 On the last point, see Bateson (1972).
67 Although not an explicitly postmodernist text, see Carr (1986).

that fantasy "makes its metafictional statements most effectively when it seems most ingenuous, as in Tolkien's perfectly sincere, perfectly impossible narrative." By contrast, the tedious authorial reminders of textual artificiality that are often identified with postmodernism are actually a ritualistic and compromisingly modernist attempt at demystification.[68]

At the very heart of their effect now, both of fantasy in general and Tolkien in particular, is that of wonder. It has been given profound new life by the postmodern cultural project of re-enchantment. Along with Brian Attebery, C.N. Manlove – otherwise no fan of Tolkien – sees this clearly: "there is a very definite and constant character to fantasy, and in nothing is it perhaps so markedly constant as its devotion to wonder at created things, and its profound sense that that wonder is above almost everything else a spiritual good not to be lost" (1983: 156).[69]

But critics like Jack Zipes and Marina Warner – despite their pre-eminence on the subject of fantasy, fairy tales and myth – sadly do not. The reason is plain: their subject-matter is less significant than their commitments to cultural materialism and political feminism respectively – projects that take place within the modernist problematic, where that of mythopoeic enchantment (including near-relations like creative "DIY" politics, eco-feminism and neo-paganism) subverts it.

Three Critics

Let me briefly flesh out this indictment. In Zipes's *Breaking the Spell* (1979), real and exciting insights successfully struggled free of Marxist dogma and turgid academic jargon. Drawing on Marcuse and Bloch, Zipes (1979: 18) argued convincingly that

> To the extent that the folk and fairy tales of old as well as the new ones form alternative configurations in a critical and imaginative reflection of the dominant social norms and ideas, they contain an emancipatory *potential* which can

---

68 Cf. Beatie (1967: 8): "The more real it seems, the more fictional it is." An instance of the last-mentioned tendency is Calvino's interminable *If on a Winter's Night a Traveller* (in contrast with his own earlier wonderful tales, such as *The Baron in the Trees*).
69 Cf. Brian Attebery (1980: 3).

never be completely controlled or depleted unless human subjectivity itself is fully computerized and rendered impotent.

And he convincingly applied this *aperçu* to Tolkien.

Sadly, his more recent *Fairy Tales as Myth, Myth as Fairy Tale* (1994) marks a retreat to dogma. He approvingly quotes Barthes on myth as really "*nothing but* a product of class division and its moral, cultural and aesthetic consequences" (1994: 6, my emphasis). His own definition of myth is any discourse with "a structure, image, metaphor, plot, and value [fixed] as sacrosanct" (Zipes 1994: 15).[70] This is one way (political and epistemological) of looking at it, to be sure; but by itself, it is too facile, abstract and (above all) amenable to a modernist appropriation whereby myth in its original meaning becomes cognate with falsehood, delusion and infantilism.[71]

His definition is therefore seriously inadequate (especially for a book nominally half-devoted to the subject). This could be done in a number of ways; in order of generality, for example, Milton Scarborough (1994) suggests convincingly that myth is an orientation for existence which is not only comprehensive of the life-world but a special "a priori" condition of all theoretical thinking.[72] Less ambitiously, there is myth as culturally collective narratives which help people answer ethical/existential questions, and whose truths therefore surpass properly factual or "scientific" justification. Or there is Roberto Calasso's suggestion, which has the virtues of historical and cultural specificity, and simplicity: "Stories of the gods and heroes as defined by the ancients."[73] Finally, isn't there a thread running through each of these views?

In any case, we can place no confidence in Zipes as a guide here – not even where the last suggested definition, surely closest in spirit to the other half of his subject-matter, fairy-tales, is concerned. For example, his free-association about Robert Bly's title *Iron John* results in twenty-four names and concepts

---

70 (Emphasis added.) Zipes's text is also marred by the worst kind of in-house academic jargon, e.g., "the evolution of the fairy tale as a literary genre is marked by a process of dialectical appropriation involving duplication and revision that set the cultural conditions for its mythicization, institutionalization, and expansion as a mass-mediated form [...]" (Zipes 1994: 10).

71 I am aware, of course, that such a definition has much older roots, notably in that great enemy of myth, Plato.

72 Cf. Dews (1995), on the unavoidability of metaphysics.

73 At a talk at the South Bank, London, on November 11th,1995.

(1994: 96). Yet extraordinarily, Mars (or Ares) never occurs to him, although through its "rulership" of iron, it is precisely the ancient mythical key – from its Mesopotamian roots and Greek and Roman versions, through its Hermetic codification and Renaissance neo-Platonic restatement, to its ubiquitous appearance in modern astrological discourse – to "Iron John" in all his aspects and symbolic associations (masculinity, hardness, war and so on). As Paracelsus wrote, "He who knows what iron is, knows the attributes of Mars. He who knows Mars, knows the qualities of iron." And he who doesn't, he might have added, knows neither.[74]

Zipes also possesses the usual modernist faith in the power of demystification. (Not that there is anything wrong with faith as such; but with this particular one, yes.) Thus, he seems to think that the chief problem with Disney is that "[t]he pictures conceal the controls and the machinery. They deprive the audience of viewing the production and manipulation, and in the end, audiences can no longer envision a fairy tale for themselves as they can when they read it" (1994: 84). The last point is right, but not for the reason he gives. Viewing Disney's production and manipulation involved in making Disney films would interest, let alone "free", very few people; indeed, it wouldn't work, so to speak, unless it was itself the (successful) result of such a process. Conversely, the pathology of Disney films lies not in production/manipulation – which, as such, is unavoidable – but in the particular *kind* they involve: the true and deliberate infantilizing of imagery, the relentless exploitation of both the medium and the stories for colonizing the imagination, and all driven by the logic of a global pop monoculture, a culture of capital itself, with all its unmatched ability "to degrade, vulgarise, constrict, or, as the argot has it, 'tabloidise'" (Cockburn 1995).

As Tolkien (1988: 50) said, the creative desire for enchantment "is only cheated by counterfeits, whether the innocent but clumsy devices of the human dramatist, or the malevolent frauds of the magicians" – and with computerized film, these two are as one. But revealing their means of production and manipulation will have negligible effect; if you want to undermine Disney, you must

---

74 If I was asked who I trust on the subject, I would include: Walter Otto, Heinrich Zimmer, Karl Kerenyi, Roberto Calasso, P.L. Travers, Ursula Le Guin and Tolkien. In other words, it is a necessary if insufficient prerequisite at least to respect myth in its own terms.

give people (or if you are parents, find) *something better*: in other words, not a disenchantment but an alternative enchantment.[75]

Turning to Marina Warner, one is struck by certain paradoxes. One is that such a prolific author, and one claiming such a wide remit, could omit so much; her recent *From the Beast to the Blonde* (1994), despite the comprehensive sub-title, does not actually concern fairy-tales at all, but "traditional nursery classics". Even then, there is no discussion of any such classics featuring boys (*Puss in Boots, Tom Thumb, Jack and the Beanstalk*, etc.), nor the stories of such authors as George MacDonald, Hans Christian Andersen, or Tolkien.[76] (And lest I be accused of merely subjective partisanship, let us recall that *The Hobbit* is easily the most popular fairy-story of this century.) The doubt unavoidably stirs that these were simply unamenable to what she wanted to conclude.

Another curious thing, if more ineffable, is the distinct odour of sanctity that clings to this avowedly secular and analytical writer's work – one that noticeably exceeds any attached to that of Tolkien, an unshakable Catholic. The reason, it seems to me, is Warner's devout adherence to the pieties of literary feminism and modernism, acclaimed and protected by the same congregation that has already canonised Angela Carter. Once again, disenchantment and demystification, through revealing the origins of fairy-tales in specific "social and material conditions," is again the secular sacrament.

Another such tenet is the cosy meliorist creed – one of Tolkien's targets in his essay on *Beowulf* – that there is no real, intractable and ultimately irrefragable evil, because (in Warner's words) "monsters are made, not given. And if monsters are made, they can be unmade, too" (*The Independent*, 03.02.94).[77] Thus, interviewed about the recent slaughter of Scottish schoolchildren, she delicately eschews "evil" for "vice"; even when confronted with the example of Nazism, she will not look it in the eye, proferring instead that "I don't think there was

---

75 Incidentally, the film *Company of Wolves*, based on Angela Carter's disenchanted version of *Red Riding Hood*, provides a perfect example; although its director, Neil Jordan, was at least as responsible as she for the extent to which it bears out Tolkien's pessimism. Films that enchant are possible, if rare.
76 The same was true of another ambitiously-entitled address, "Re-Thinking the Uses of Enchantment", on June 21st 1992, at The Society of Antiquaries of London.
77 Cf. "Children are our copy, in little [...]" (*The Independent*, 10.02.94).

enough resistance there. People were duped or taken in and the vitiation spread
[…]" (quoted in Porter 1996).

Vitiation! This is a serious failure of the moral imagination – as if, to quote Le
Guin (1989: 58-59),

> evil were a problem, something that can be solved, that has an answer, like a
> problem in fifth grade arithmetic. […] *That* is escapism, that posing evil as
> a "problem", instead of what it is: all the pain and suffering and waste and loss
> and injustice we will meet all our lives long, and must face and cope with over
> and over, and admit, and live with, in order to live human lives at all.

That, as we have seen, was Tolkien's opinion too.

Finally, a genteel but relentless concern with the single dimension of gender
excludes everything that is not grist to its mill; thus, any hint of the power
of myth, folk- and fairy-tales to induce wonder *as such* – the very heart, in a
postmodern context, of Tolkien's "On Fairy-Stories" "point too often forgotten: that is the effect produced *now* by these old things in the stories as they
are" (1988: 32) – is utterly absent. She thus misses an invaluable opportunity
to counter the stranglehold of a sclerotic modernism on literature and criticism,
one of the chief remedies for which is precisely, in Ihab Hassan's (1992: 204)
words, "to remythify the imagination, at least locally, and bring back the reign
of wonder into our lives."

Once again, unsung readers probably have the edge on literary professionals. The great Indologist Heinrich Zimmer (1948: 1-3) pointed to the heart
of the matter:

> The dilettante – Italian "dilettante" (present participle of the verb "dilet-
> tare", "to take delight in") – is one who takes delight in something. […] The
> moment we abandon this dilettante attitude toward the images of folklore
> and myth and begin to feel certain about their proper interpretation (as
> professional comprehenders, handling the tool of an infallible method), we
> deprive ourselves of the quickening contact, the demonic and inspiring as-
> sault that is the effect of their intrinsic virtue. We forfeit our proper humility
> and open-mindedness before the unknown, and refuse to be instructed. […]
> What they demand of us is not the monologue of the coroner's report, but
> the dialogue of a living conversation.

Jameson's "Magical Narratives"

There is no better example of the coroner's report than my third choice of critic Frederic Jameson's "Magical Narratives: Romance as Genre", so I am going to give it a little extra attention. It was published in 1975, and many of its premisses (notably the Marxist metaphysics) have suffered since then. But many of Jameson's generation who shared his convictions are now ensconced in positions of institutional power. And as his subsequent work shows, the fundamentals of those convictions have changed little; his subsequent "post-modernism" is really simply neo-Marxism, in which the command "Always historicize" applies to everything except itself and its own particular assumptions.

Discussing Vladimir Propp's structuralist analysis of folktales as "a process of abstraction, whereby *surface* events or elements are assimilated to emptier and ever more general categories," Jameson criticizes it as insufficiently coronistic – or in his words, "still too meaningful." He wants "a type of analysis which aims at seeing the entire narrative in terms of a single [...] *mechanism*" (Jameson 1975: 146-48; my emphases). What better statement of the modernist dream, with its chilling monist and imperialist ambitions, could be imagined?

Along the way, so-called "surface events" are not the only victims. So too is "the belief in good and evil" – apparently *any* kind of such belief. This fundamental human experience is dismissed as "a magical thought mode, that is, one which springs from a precapitalist, essentially agricultural way of life" (Jameson 1975: 141). And since the mode of production is all-powerful, the reader

> now finds himself obliged to justify the henceforth scandalous and archaic activity of fantasy, so that what we have called the replacements for the older magical function also serve as so many rational ways of explaining it away – in Stendhal by way of psychology, and in Eichendorff by the demonstration that it was not really there at all in the first place. (Jameson 1975: 145)

We must ask: really? Are there any of these modernist "replacements" in *The Lord of the Rings*? And do any of its millions of readers miss them?

Perhaps that is why Jameson (1975: 161) specifies the work of Tolkien and Lewis as "archaic nostalgia" (which, for modernists, is about the worst thing you can say). But his own theory cannot explain either their continued existence or popularity except as pure mass infantilism, which really ought (or should it be, who ought?) to be eliminated. The higher knowledge/cause that justifies this lofty purism is our old friend Marx and Engel's "base": that muscular starting point of "real men" and "real existence" which consigns to the dustbin of epiphenomena "what men say, imagine, conceive [...] men as narrated, thought of, imagined, conceived. [...] Morality, religion, metaphysics, all the rest of ideology and their corresponding forms of consciousness." Magically enough, the "base" determines all this "superstructure" without being affected in return. And Marxists like Jameson *know* this because their creed is not "simply one more critical language or method among others"; uniquely, its critical operation "requires us to correlate literary phenonema, not with [...] conceptual abstractions, but rather with the realities to which those abstractions correspond" (1975: 157, 159). That is, Marxist concepts alone, being somehow not conceptual, escape abstraction. Such an assertion has all the intellectual authority of "what I tell you three times is true".[78]

For many readers, this will be old ground, hardly worth retracing. But I disagree; we need reminding of the arrogant fatuity that has become a mentality, an entrenched habit of thought amounting to a "déformation professionelle", among many influential literary professionals. This is what anyone who wants to see understanding (as well as explanation) and value (as well as interpretation) restored to the heart of the critical enterprise is up against. Such a reader might well take heart from the rich perceptiveness – the wisdom, to give it its proper name – of Walter Benjamin, who lamented the dying out of "the epic side of truth, wisdom" (1969: 89), and with it, the art of storytelling:

> no event any longer comes to us without already being shot through with explanation. In other words, by now almost nothing that happens benefits storytelling; almost everything benefits information. Actually, it is half the art of storytelling to keep a story free from explanation as one reproduces it. [...] There is nothing that commends a story to memory more effectively than that chaste compactness which precludes psychological analysis. (Benjamin 1969: 91)

Benjamin concludes, in words that apply directly to Tolkien and celebrate the survival of what Jameson regards as an atavistic abberation, that "[t]he first true storyteller is, and *will continue to be*, the teller of fairy tales" (1969: 102).

---

78 Thompson's wonderful polemic (1978) is still relevant here.

Three Writers

The approach I have urged has interesting implications for various writers, too
– especially those who apparently share the category of "fantasy", and draw
on the same stock of myth, folk- and fairy-tales. Here, very briefly, are three
examples. The stories of Terry Pratchett, the hugely successful English comic
fantasy writer, are stuffed with trolls, dwarves, witches and wizards and magic
generally. Yet these are devices he uses to produce quintessentially humanist
tales. But not of the scientistic and universalist modernist kind – Pratchett's
idiom is unmistakably local, i.e. English (not "British"), and his humanism is
in the best pre-modern Montaignian tradition of humane, tolerant, sceptical
humanism. In Elgin's terms, Pratchett is a comic and ecological writer: accepting of nature, the body, and human limits.[79] As such, his stories partake
of postmodern localism and pluralism; and they refresh, not dessicate, the
contemporary soul.

My second example is the vivid contrast between Tolkien's work and that of the
late Angela Carter. This goes deeper than the latter's earthy feminism, and the
generation gap between her 1960s anti-authoritarianism and Tolkien's residu-
ally Edwardian love of a quiet, green world. Consider the fact that Carter's best
fiction centres on the circus and the theatre, both arenas whose magic, while
potent, falls well within the humanist and secular ambit of drama. This is an
art-form which, if Tolkien was right, is necessarily anthropocentric, unlike
literature, which can (if rarely now does) escape into the non-human world, or
nature – and thus nature, in turn, into art. And literature which harkens back
to ancient myth would have a special impetus, and ability, to let the voices of
non-human nature speak.

True, the two authors drew upon many of the same European and English folk-
and fairy-tales; and Alison Lurie (1996) thinks Carter shares a Northern air with
Karen Blixen that I had already decided linked the latter with Tolkien. But I would
contend that their projects were exactly opposite; Carter was primarily interested
in *dis*enchanting her readers – freeing them from a false glamour cast by a sexist
and racist capitalism – whereas he, despite sharing to a surprising extent the same
concerns, was trying to work an alternative *re*-enchantment.

---

79 In this as well as in narrower literary terms, the comparison with P.G. Wodehouse is not misplaced.

These represent very different strategies. Neither is necessarily more effective than the other; Carter's sophisticated and anti-mythic subversion of enchantment limits her audience in one way, just as Tolkien's contrary approach does his in another. In terms of appeal discernible through sheer numbers of readers, of course, Tolkien obviously has the edge. But I would also reject the suggestion that, Carter's left-of-centre affiliations notwithstanding, her work is inherently more "radical". Indeed, if I am right about the destructiveness of unchecked modernity, then Tolkien's is the more needed; and, ironically, the less naive. (The same could be said of Fay Weldon's fiction, for example, and Warner's criticism; but definitely not of the work of Ursula Le Guin – surely no less a feminist than they, so that cannot be the fundamental consideration.)

Nor, in my terms, is Salman Rushdie, my third example, a consistently or success-fully postmodern writer. For all its irony, pastiche and hybridity, *The Satanic Verses* was correctly recognized by its Asian Islamic readers (for all their near-illiteracy) as a serious secularist attack on their religion: a classic case of modernist debunking, in fact.[80] And it is significant that both Carter and Rushdie – the former rightly praised by the latter as "a thumber of noses, a defiler of sacred cows" – have de-clared their devotion to *The Wizard of Oz*.[81] For the fundamental point about the Wizard of Oz – Oz the Great and Terrible – is this: he was a cheat and a fraud, and as such, a comforting anti-fairy-tale for secular and modernist Grown-Ups: just "a little, old man, with a bald head and a wrinkled face." "'Hush, my dear [...] don't speak so loud, or you will be overheard – and I should be ruined. I'm supposed to be a Great Wizard.' 'And aren't you?' [...] 'Not a bit of it, my dear; I'm just a common man'" (Baum 1993: 122-23).

Now if I were ("horribile dictu") Fred Inglis, I would now play my trump card, and point out that while it would be disgraceful to use the fact against him, it should nonetheless be noted that L. Frank Baum was a violent racist who publicly advocated genocide against the (remaining) American Indians.[82] I will content myself, however, with noting that Baum doesn't exactly leave Tolkien gasping at the back of the radical sweepstakes; and since reactionary modernists abound

---

80 This should not, of course, be taken to imply that I agree in the slightest with the outrageous "fatwa" threatening his life.
81 *New York Times Book Review* (08.03.92).
82 See *Twin Light Trail: American Indian News* 2 (1992): 15.

(Wyndham Lewis, T.S. Eliot, and many Weimar intellectuals),[83] so political backwardness, too, cannot really be the problem.

The real problem Tolkien poses for modernists is that his work has committed the crime – like a felled tree he once mourned – of being "large and alive." Its success calls time on them, and underscores their own dead hand. And not before time. For wonder alone cannot save us, or a world worth living in; but without it, the outlook is very dark indeed.[84]

Bibliography

ACACELLA, Joan. 1995. "Cather and the Academy." *The New Yorker* (27.11.1995): 57-71.

ATTEBERY, Brian. 1980. *The Fantasy Tradition in American Literature.* Bloomington: Indiana University Press.

1992. *Strategies of Fantasy.* Bloomington: Indiana University Press.

BARFIELD, Owen. 1977. "The Meaning of 'Literal'." In *The Rediscovery of Meaning, and Other Essays.* Middletown CT: Wesleyan University Press, 32-43.

BARRELL, John and John BULL (eds.). 1974. *The Penguin Book of English Pastoral Verse.* Harmondsworth: Penguin.

BATE, Jonathan. 1991. *Romantic Ecology: Wordsworth and the Environmental Tradition.* London: Routledge.

BATESON, Gregory. 1972. *Steps to an Ecology of Mind.* New York: Chandler/ Ballantine Books.

BAUM, L. Frank. 1993. *The Wizard of Oz.* Ware, Herts.: Wordsworth Editions. First edition c. 1900.

BAUMAN, Zygmunt. 1989. *Modernity and the Holocaust.* Cambridge: Polity Press.

1992. *Intimations of Postmodernity.* London: Routledge.

BEATIE, Bruce A. 1967. "Folk Tale, Fiction, and Saga in J.R.R. Tolkien's *Lord of the Rings.*" *The Tolkien Papers Mankato State College Studies* II.1: 1-17.

---

83 See Herf (1984), Harrison (1966), and Carey (1992).
84 See the superb analysis by Hepburn (1984), which I have used in Curry (1999). The latter essay is reprinted on pages 65-82 of the present volume.

BENJAMIN, Walter. 1969. "The Storyteller" In *Illuminations: Essays and Reflections.* Edited by Hannah ARENDT. New York: Schocken Books, 83-109.

BERNSTEIN, Jay. 1996. "The Death of Sensuous Particulars: Adorno and Abstract Expressionism." *Radical Philosophy* 76: 7-18.

BJORGO, Tore (ed.). 1995. *Terror from the Extreme Right.* London: Frank Cass.

BRANSTON, Brian. 1957. *The Lost Gods of England.* London: Thames and Hudson.

BROOKE-ROSE, Christine. 1980. "The Evil Ring: Realism and the Marvellous." *Poetics Today* 1.4: 67-90.

1981. *A Rhetoric of the Unreal: Studies in Narrative and Structure, Especially of the Fantastic.* Cambridge: Cambridge University Press.

BUFORD, Bill. 1996. "The Seductions of Storytelling." *The New Yorker* (24.06. & 01.07.96): 11-12.

BURKE, Kenneth. 1957. *Counter-Statement.* Second edition. First edition 1953. Chicago IL: University of Chicago Press.

BUTLER, Hubert. 1986. *Escape from the Anthill.* Mullingar: Lilliput Press.

CAREY, John. 1977. "Hobbit-Forming." *The Listener* (12.05.1977): 631.

1992. *The Intellectuals and the Masses.* London: Faber.

CARPENTER, Humphrey. 1992. *Tolkien: A Biography.* First published 1977. London: Grafton.

CARR, David. 1986. *Time, Narrative and History.* Bloomington IN: Indiana University Press.

COCKBURN, Alexander. 1995. "Fatal Attraction." *The Guardian* (12.05.1995).

COLEBATCH, Hal. 1990. *Return of the Heroes. "The Lord of the Rings", "Star Wars" and Contemporary Culture.* Perth: Australian Institute for Public Policy.

CRAIG, Amanda. 1992. "Lord of All He Conveyed, Despite His Fans." *The Independent* (25.01.1992).

CUNNINGHAM Valentine. 1989. *British Writers of the Thirties.* Oxford: Oxford University Press.

CURRY, Patrick. 1995. *Machiavelli for Beginners.* Cambridge: Icon Books.

1997. *Defending Middle-Earth: Tolkien, Myth and Modernity.* Edinburgh: Floris Books. New York: St Martin's Press; paperback edition 1998, London: HarperCollins.

1999. "Magic vs. Enchantment." *Journal of Contemporary Religion* 14.3: 401-412.[85]

DAVIE, Donald. 1973. *Thomas Hardy and British Poetry*. London: Routledge and Kegan Paul.

DERRIDA, Jacques. 1988. "Afterword: Toward an Ethic of Discussion." In *Limited Inc*. Evanston IL: Northwestern University Press, 111-160.

1994. *Spectres of Marx*. London: Verso.

DEWS, Peter. 1995. *The Limits of Disenchantment*. London: Verso.

DODDS, David Llewellyn. 1993-94. "The Centrality of Sex in Middle-Earth." *Lembas Extra* (1993-94): 59-80.

DRABBLE, Margaret. 1985. *The Oxford Companion to English Literature*. Oxford: Oxford University Press.

and Jenny STRINGER. 1996. *Oxford Concise Companion to English Literature*. Oxford: Oxford University Press.

EASTHOPE, Anthony. 1991. *Literary into Cultural Studies*. London: Routledge.

EHRENFELD, David. 1978. *The Arrogance of Humanism*. Oxford: Oxford University Press.

1993. "The Roots of Prophecy: Orwell and Nature." In *Beginning Again: People and Nature in the New Millennium*. Oxford: Oxford University Press, 8-28.

EKINS, Paul. 1992. *A New World Order: Grassroots Movements for Global Change*. London: Routledge.

ELGIN, Don R. 1985. *The Comedy of the Fantastic. Ecological Perspectives on the Fantasy Novel*. Westport CT: Greenwood Press.

EMPSON, William. 1979. *Some Versions of Pastoral*. London: Chatto & Windus.

ENDE, Michael. 1993. *The Never-Ending Story*. English translation of *Die unendliche Geschichte*, originally published 1979. London: Roc/Penguin.

EWIJCK, Annemarie van. 1995. "Sex in Middle-Earth." *Lembas Extra* (1995): 23-33.

EZARD, John. 1991. "Tolkien's Shire." *The Guardian* (28-29.12.91).

FELPERIN, Howard. 1985. *Beyond Deconstruction: The Uses and Abuses of Literary Theory*. Oxford: Clarendon Press.

FEYERABEND, Paul. 1987. *Farewell to Reason*. London: Verso.

FILMER, Kath. 1992. *Scepticism and Hope in Twentieth Century Fantasy Literature*. Bowling Green OH: Bowling Green State University Popular Press.

---

85 Reprinted on pages 65-82 of the present volume.

FINCH, Jason. 1994. "Democratic Government in Middle-earth." *Amon Hen* 129: 12-13.

FLIEGER, Verlyn. 1983. *Splintered Light: Logos and Language in Tolkien's World.* Grand Rapids MI: Wm. Eerdmans.

GIDDINGS, Robert (ed.). 1983. *J.R.R. Tolkien: This Far Land.* London: Vision Press.

and Elizabeth HOLLAND. 1981. *J.R.R. Tolkien: The Shores of Middle-earth.* London: Junction Books.

GOLDTHWAITE, John. 1996. *The Natural History of Make-Believe: A Guide to the Principal Works of Britain, Europe and America.* Oxford: Oxford University Press.

GOPNIK, Adam. 1994. "Grim Fairy Tales." *The New Yorker* (12.12.94): 84-102.

GRANT, Patrick. 1981. "Tolkien: Archetype and Word." In Neil D. ISAACS and Rose A. ZIMBARDO. (eds.). 1981. *Tolkien: New Critical Perspectives.* Lexington KT: University of Kentucky Press, 87-105.

GRAY, John. 1995. *Enlightenment's Wake: Politics and Culture at the Close of the Modern Age.* London: Routledge.

GRIGORIEVA, Natalia. 1995. "Problems of Translation into Russian." In Patricia REYNOLDS and Glen H. GOODKNIGHT (eds.). 1995. *Proceedings of the J.R.R. Tolkien Centenary Conference.* Milton Keynes: The Tolkien Society/Altadena CA: The Mythopoeic Press, 200-205.

GRUSHETSKIY, Vladimir. 1995. "How Russians See Tolkien." In Patricia REYNOLDS and Glen H. GOODKNIGHT (eds.). 1995. *Proceedings of the J.R.R. Tolkien Centenary Conference.* Milton Keynes: The Tolkien Society/Altadena CA: The Mythopoeic Press, 221-225.

HAMMOND, Wayne G. 1995. "The Critical Response to Tolkien's Fiction." In Patricia REYNOLDS and Glen H. GOODKNIGHT (eds.). 1995. *Proceedings of the J.R.R. Tolkien Centenary Conference.* Milton Keynes: The Tolkien Society/ Altadena CA: The Mythopoeic Press, 226-232.

HARRISON, Fraser. 1984. "England, Home and Beauty." In Richard MABEY, with Susan CLIFFORD and Angela KING (eds.). 1984. *Second Nature.* London: Jonathan Cape, 162-172.

HARRISON, John R. 1966. *The Reactionaries.* London: Victor Gollancz.

HARRISON, Robert Pogue. 1992. *Forests: The Shadow of Civilization.* Chicago IL: University of Chicago Press.

HASSAN, Ihab. 1992 "Pluralism in Postmodern Perspective." In Charles JENCKS (ed.). 1992. *The Post-Modern Reader.* London: Academy Editions, 196-207.

HEPBURN, Ronald. 1984. *"Wonder" and other Essays*. Edinburgh: Edinburgh University Press.

HERBERT, Kathleen. 1993. *Spellcraft: Old English Heroic Legends*. Hockwold-cum-Wilton, Norfolk: Anglo-Saxon Books.

HERF, Jeffrey. 1984. *Reactionary Modernism*. Cambridge: Cambridge University Press.

HIPOLITO, T.A. 1993. "Owen Barfield's Poetic Diction." *Renascence* 46.1: 3-38.

HITCHENS, Christopher. 1993. "Something about the Poetry: Larkin and 'Sensitivity'." *New Left Review* 200: 161-174.

1994. "Dr Strangelove, I presume?" *New Statesman and Society* (30.09.94): 44-45.

HOBAN, Russell. 1992. *The Moment under the Moment*. London: Jonathan Cape.

HUGHES, Ted. 1992. *The Goddess of Complete Being*. London: Faber.

HUYSSEN, Andreas. 1986. *After the Great Divide: Modernism, Mass Culture, Postmodernism*. London: Macmillan Press.

INGLIS, Fred. 1981. *The Promise of Happiness: Value and Meaning in Children's Fiction*. Cambridge: Cambridge University Press.

1983. "Gentility and Powerlessness: Tolkien and the New Class." In Robert GIDDINGS (ed.). 1983. *J.R.R. Tolkien: This Far Land*. London: Vision Press, 25-41.

1994. *Cultural Studies*. Oxford: Basil Blackwell.

1995. *Raymond Williams*. London: Routledge.

ISAACS, Neil D. and Rose A. ZIMBARDO (eds.). 1968. *Tolkien and the Critics*. Notre Dame: University of Notre Dame Press.

and Rose A. ZIMBARDO (eds.). 1981. *Tolkien: New Critical Perspectives*. Lexington KT: University of Kentucky Press.

JACKSON, Rosemary. 1988. *Fantasy: The Literature of Subversion*. London: Routledge.

JAMESON, Frederic. 1975. "Magical Narratives: Romance as Genre." *New Literary History* 7.1: 135-163.

JOHANNESSON, Nils-Lennart. 1997. "The Speech of the Individual and of the Community in *The Lord of the Rings*." In Peter BUCHS and Thomas HONEGGER (eds.). 1997. *News from the Shire and Beyond – Studies on Tolkien*. Zurich and Berne: Walking Tree Publishers, 12-47.

JOHNSON, Judith A. 1986. *J.R.R. Tolkien: Six Decades of Criticism*. Bibliographies and Indexes in World Literature 6. Westport CT: Greenwood Press.

KAMENKOVICH, Maria. 1992. "The Secret War and the End of the First Age: Tolkien in the (former) USSR." *Mallorn* 29: 33-38.

KAVENEY, Roz. 1991. "The Ring Recycled." *New Statesman and Society* (20. & 27.12.1991).

KEARNEY, Richard. 1985. "Myth and Motherland." In Seamus DEANE et al. 1985. *Ireland's Field Day*. London: Hutchinson, 61-80.

KILBY, Clyde. 1977. *Tolkien and the Silmarillion*. Berkhamsted: Lion Publishing.

KOLAKOWSKI, Leszek. 1990. *Modernity on Endless Trial*. Chicago IL: University of Chicago Press.

KONTOS, Alkis. 1994. "The World Disenchanted, and the Return of Gods and Demons." In Asher HOROWITZ and Terry MALEY (eds.). *The Barbarism of Reason: Max Weber and the Twilight of the Enlightenment*. Toronto: University of Toronto Press, 223-247.

LACLAU, Ernesto and Chantal MOUFFE. 1985. *Hegemony and Socialist Strategy. Toward a Radical Democratic Politics*. London: Verso.

LE GUIN, Ursula K. 1989. *The Language of the Night*. Edited by Susan WOOD. London: The Woman's Press. (First edition 1979. New York: Berkeley Books.)

LEVI, Primo. 1987. *If This Is A Man and The Truce*. London: Sphere Books.

LOBDELL, Jared (ed.). 1975. *A Tolkien Compass*. La Salle IL: Open Court.

LUCAS, John. 1990. *England and Englishness*. London: Hogarth Press.

LULING, Virginia. 1995. "An Anthropologist in Middle-earth." In Patricia REYNOLDS and Glen H. GOODKNIGHT (eds.). 1995. *Proceedings of the J.R.R. Tolkien Centenary Conference*. Milton Keynes: The Tolkien Society/Altadena CA: The Mythopoeic Press, 53-57.

LURIE, Alison. 1990. *Don't Tell the Grown-Ups. Subversive Children's Literature*. London: Bloomsbury.

1996. "Winter's Tales." *The N.Y. Times Book Review* (19.05.1996).

MANLOVE, C.N. 1983. *The Impulse of Fantasy Literature*. London: Macmillan.

MCLEISH, Kenneth. 1983. "The Rippingest Yarn of All." In Robert GIDDINGS (ed.). 1983. *J.R.R. Tolkien: This Far Land*. London: Vision Press, 125-136.

MEYERS, Jeffrey. 1995. *Edmund Wilson*. London: Constable.

MIDGELEY, Mary. 1997. "Sneer Tactics." *The Guardian* (07.09.97).

MOORCOCK, Michael. 1987. *Wizardry and Wild Romance*. London: Victor Gollancz.

MUIRHEAD, Ian A. 1986. "Theology in Gandalf's Garden." *Arda* (1986): 14-24.

NICHOLSON-LORD, David. 1995. "Write Me a Novel I Can Actually Read." *The Independent on Sunday* (30.04.95).

O'CONNOR, Alan. 1989. *Raymond Williams: Writing, Culture, Politics*. Oxford: Basil Blackwell.

OTTY, Nick. 1983. "A Structuralist's Guide to Middle-Earth." In Robert GIDDINGS (ed.). 1983. *J.R.R. Tolkien: This Far Land*. London: Vision Press, 154-178.

PARK, James. 1991. *Cultural Icons*. London: Bloomsbury.

PARKER, Douglass. 1956-57. "Hwaet We Holbytla…" *The Hudson Review* 9.4: 598-609.

PARTRIDGE, Brenda. 1983. "No Sex Please – We're Hobbits: The Construction of Female Sexuality in *The Lord of the Rings*." In Robert GIDDINGS (ed.). 1983. *J.R.R. Tolkien: This Far Land*. London: Vision Press, 179-197.

PAYNE, Stanley G. 1996. *A History of Fascism, 1914-1945*. Madison WI: University of Wisconsin Press.

PLANK, Robert. 1975. "The Scouring of the Shire: Tolkien's View of Fascism." In Jared LOBDELL (ed.). 1975. *A Tolkien Compass*. La Salle IL: Open Court, 107-115.

PORTER, Henry. 1996. "Reason Eclipsed by Evil." *The Guardian* (17.03.1996).

POTTER, Dennis. 1984. *Waiting for the Boat: On Television*. London: Faber & Faber.

RAFFEL, Burton. 1968. "*The Lord of the Rings* as Literature." In Neil D. ISAACS and Rose A. ZIMBARDO (eds.). 1968. *Tolkien and the Critics*. Notre Dame: University of Notre Dame Press, 218-246.

REYNOLDS, Patricia and Glen H. GOODKNIGHT (eds.). 1995. *Proceedings of the J.R.R. Tolkien Centenary Conference*. Milton Keynes: The Tolkien Society/ Altadena CA: The Mythopoeic Press.

ROSEBURY, Brian. 1992. *Tolkien: A Critical Assessment*. London: Macmillan Press.

SAMUEL, Raphael. 1995. *Theatres of Memory*. London: Verso.

SAUNDERS, Andrew. 1994. *The Shorter Oxford History of English Literature*. Oxford: Oxford University Press.

SCARBOROUGH, Milton. 1994. *Myth and Modernity: Postcritical Reflections*. Albany NY: SUNY Press.

SCHEPPS, Walter. 1975. "The Fairy-tale Morality of *The Lord of the Rings*." In Jared LOBDELL (ed.). 1975. *A Tolkien Compass*. La Salle IL: Open Court, 43-56.

SCHNÄDELBACH, Herbert. 1992. "The Face in the Sand: Foucault and the Anthropological Slumber." In Axel HONNETH et al. (eds.). *Philosophical Interventions in the Unfinished Project of Enlightenment*. Cambridge MA: Harvard University Press, 311-340.

SHIPPEY, T.A. 1992. *The Road to Middle-Earth*. Second edition. First edition 1982. London: Grafton/HarperCollins.

1995. "Tolkien as a Post-War Writer." In Patricia REYNOLDS and Glen H. GOODKNIGHT (eds.). 1995. *Proceedings of the J.R.R. Tolkien Centenary Conference*. Milton Keynes: The Tolkien Society/Altadena CA: The Mythopoeic Press, 84-93.

1996. "Burbocentrism." *London Review of Books* (23.05.1996).

SMITH, Barbara Herrnstein. 1988. *Contingencies of Value: Alternative Perspectives for Critical Theory*. Cambridge, MA: Harvard University Press.

STIMPSON, Catherine R. 1969. *J.R.R. Tolkien*. Columbia Essays on Modern Writers 41. New York: Columbia University Press.

STRINGER, Jenny (ed.). 1996. *The Oxford Companion to Twentieth-Century Literature in English*. Oxford: Oxford University Press.

SWINFEN, Ann. 1984. *In Defence of Fantasy. A Study of the Genre in English and American Literature since 1945*. London: Routledge Kegan Paul.

THOMPSON, E.P. 1976. *William Morris*. Second edition. First edition 1955. New York: Pantheon.

1978. *The Poverty of Theory and Other Essays*. London: Merlin Press.

1993. *Witness Against the Beast: William Blake and the Moral Law*. Cambridge: Cambridge University Press.

TIMMONS, Daniel. 1996. "J.R.R. Tolkien's Genealogies: The Roots of His 'Sub-creation'." *Mallorn* 34: 7-11.

TOLKIEN, J.R.R. 1981. *The Letters of J.R.R. Tolkien*. Edited by Humphrey CARPENTER, with the assistance of Christopher TOLKIEN. London: George Allen & Unwin.

1988. "On Fairy-Stories." In *Tree and Leaf*. Edited by Christopher TOLKIEN. London: Unwin Hyman, 11-73. (The original essay was first delivered as a lecture in 1939, and first published, somewhat enlarged, in 1947.)

1991. *The Lord of the Rings*. First edition 1954-55. London: Grafton/HarperCollins.

TOULMIN, Stephen. 1990. *Cosmopolis. The Hidden Agenda of Modernity.* Chicago: University of Chicago Press.

TURNER, Jenny. 1996. "Lost in the Bush." Review of Alan Garner's *Strandloper* in *The Guardian* (24.05.1996).

VELDMAN, Meredith. 1994. *Fantasy, the Bomb, and the Greening of Britain: Romantic Protest, 1945-1980.* Cambridge: Cambridge University Press.

VEYNE, Paul. 1988. *Did the Greeks Believe Their Myths?* English translation. Originally published 1983. Chicago: University of Chicago Press.

WALMSLEY, Nigel. 1983. "Tolkien and the '60s." In Robert GIDDINGS (ed.). 1983. *J.R.R. Tolkien: This Far Land.* London: Vision Press, 73-85.

WEBSTER, Charles. 1982. *From Paracelsus to Newton.* Cambridge: Cambridge University Press.

WEST, R.C. 1970. *Tolkien Criticism: An Annotated Checklist.* Kent OH: Kent State University Press.

WILLIAMS, Madawc. 1995. "Good Government in Middle-earth." *Amon Hen* 132: 17-19.

WILLIAMS, Raymond. 1985. *The Country and the City.* London: Hogarth Press.

WILMER, Clive (ed.). 1985. *John Ruskin: Unto This Last and Other Writings.* London: Penguin Books.

WILSON, Colin. 1974. *Tree by Tolkien.* Santa Barbara CA: Capra Press.

WILSON, Edmund. 1956. "Oo, Those Awful Orcs!" *The Nation* 182.15 (14.04.1956): 312-314; reprinted in his *The Bit between My Teeth.* New York: W.H. Allen, 326-332.

WRIGHT, Patrick. 1986. *On Living in an Old Country.* London: Verso.

YATES, Jessica. 1995. "Tolkien the Anti-Totalitarian." In Patricia REYNOLDS and Glen H. GOODKNIGHT (eds.). 1995. *Proceedings of the J.R.R. Tolkien Centenary Conference.* Milton Keynes: The Tolkien Society/Altadena CA: The Mythopoeic Press, 233-245.

ZIMMER, Heinrich. 1948. *The King and the Corpse. Tales of the Soul's Conquest of Evil.* Princeton NJ: Princeton University Press.

ZIPES, Jack. 1979. *Breaking the Magic Spell: Radical Theories of Folk and Fairy Tales.* London: Heinemann.

1994. *Fairy Tale as Myth, Myth as Fairy Tale.* Lexington KT: The University Press of Kentucky.

On Reading Tolkien

Abstract

"On Reading Tolkien" explores the links between narrative, place and animism, beginning with the way Tolkien's compelling narratives are emplaced and conversely his places are storied. I maintain that that is how our minds and lives work – which can be best thought of as animism – when unconstrained by the demands of modernism, and end by suggesting that in order to do justice to his work, Tolkien scholarship needs to pay more attention to anthropology and the ecohumanities.

In *Defending Middle-earth: Tolkien, Myth & Modernity*, one of my chief concerns was to understand the depth and breadth of the appeal of his work. It still seems to me that while its literary production has been almost exhaustively examined, relatively little time and thought has been expended on its reception.[1] Dare I suggest that the latter is at least as interesting, worthy and difficult a challenge? What follows is a brief meditation on how one might take it up and go further than we yet have.

Simplifying radically, I argued that the appeal of Tolkien's work – particularly *The Lord of the Rings*, which remains his most read and loved book – grows out of its recognition of both readers' fears respecting modernity and their hopes for what might survive it, itself made recognisable and accessible through a masterfully crafted story.[2] (Please note that this is not an allegorical reading; it merely avails itself, as Tolkien explicitly allowed, of what his readers find to be the books' applicability to their own experience.)

An earlier version is available online at http://www.lotrplaza.com/forum/forum_posts.asp?TID=239887&PID=7294565&title=patrick-curry-on-reading-tolkien (January 11th, 2014).

1 An exception is Tom Shippey's excellent *J.R.R. Tolkien: Author of the Century*.

2 I should also mention in this connection Tom Shippey's important *J.R.R. Tolkien: Author of the Century*. The best single work I know on modernity is Stephen Toulmin's *Cosmopolis: The Hidden Agenda of Modernity*.

I further suggested that those fears and hopes find three broad forms in *The Lord of the Rings*, each nested within the next and all much older than modernity itself: human community, symbolised by the Shire; the living natural world, Middle-earth itself; and ultimate spiritual values, the Sea. As the book opens, all three are under severe threat from the power of Mordor, the only "modern" state in Middle-earth, with all its chief marks: a highly organised political and bureaucratic ruling apparatus, an industrial economy, and techno-scientific research – funded and directed, as is much of ours, with a view to military applications. And as the book ends, each domain has survived – albeit only just, and ambiguously. (What will "the Dominion of Men" bring? It doesn't sound promising.)

I also briefly discussed (in chapter five) the power of narrative, storytelling, and mythopoeic fiction: a set of closely-linked ways of worldmaking which have been largely expelled by the modernist-influenced literary profession to the so-called genres, leaving, as Tolkien noted, a large adult audience hungry for "fairy-stories" (and one that will understandably settle for ersatz fascimiles if that's all they can find).[3] After all, narrative is essentially how we experience our own lives, both individually and collectively; and if it comprehensively breaks down, we break down with it. Of course, a breakthrough is possible too; but that then becomes the basis of a new narrative.

Putting the elements of this analysis together, then, we might say *The Lord of the Rings* enables readers (or those readers who do not subscribe to modernist hegemony and are not cowed by its opinions) to find their own fears and hopes addressed in a compelling narrative that doesn't analyse, lecture or patronise them but shows them truths about themselves and the world. It then becomes *our* story, and its truths become personal and emotional ones.

It appears from the (lack of) critical response that this approach has filled a much-needed gap, but I persist in thinking it has much to recommend itself. I don't feel it has all the answers, however, so let me gesture towards what might

---

3 An aside: in "Tolkien and his Critics: A Critique", I wrote of "the professional literary, critical and academic world" that "Tolkien's name in such circles is the kiss-of-death" (see earlier in this volume). That remains largely true. Cf. the *Guardian's* literary critic Nicholas Lezard's recent remark: "of all the means for professional suicide that are available to the writer, expressing affection for Tolkien is one of the most effective" (April 3rd, 2010).

take it farther, or deeper. That is signalled by something that many people (including myself) have remarked upon: the extraordinary reality of *places* in *The Lord of the Rings*. Tolkien's places are simultaneously two things that modernity maintains are mutually exclusive and has tried hard to keep apart. On the one hand, they are fictional and imaginary, or rather "imaginal"[4] – thus conceding nothing to the modernists' peculiar insistence that imaginary = unreal or untrue. You cannot take easyJet to anywhere in Middle-earth. Yet its places also feel thoroughly real; each one has its own particular and unmistakeable sensuous qualities and indeed personality. (As I have long insisted, Tolkien's nature is not only nonmodern and therefore alive and agentic, but nonanthropocentric: humans are definitely not its only persons.)[5]

What hasn't yet been realised in relation to Tolkien, however, is the internal or constitutive link between place and his mythopoetic narrative. That link is obvious, really: everything that happens in the story happens in a particular place, but not in such a way that it could have happened anywhere or nowhere: in other words, the so-called objective "view from nowhere" (or everywhere) that modernity so prizes. Rather, in keeping with life in a nonmodern world, every event is constituted by and inseparable from its place, just as every place is constituted in turn by what has happened there. They are mutually mapped. (But remember that the actors are not restricted to humans or humanoids, or even to biological organisms.)

Add to this the fact that, as Bruno Latour cogently argued in his book of the same title, *We Have Never Been* [entirely] *Modern* (1993) – indeed, we have been nonmodern for tens of thousands of years longer than we have been (partially, incompletely, temporarily) modern – and it becomes legitimate to speculate that the power of place-as-story and story-as-place goes very deep in the psyche of the human animal, and is never very far from the surface. Aboriginal Australian songlines are only the most obvious example; an equivalent, however effaced, fragmented or suppressed, survives within every indigenous culture in the world. And don't forget, "Westerners" too once were – and in some important

---

4 I borrow this term (if not its neo-Platonist baggage) from Henri Corbin.
5 This understanding is central to the "the new animism" in anthropology – see Graham Harvey, *Animism* – and in philosophy – see Edward Casey, *Getting Back into Place*.

if frequently overlooked sense, still are – indigenous people. (Suspiciously frequently: it jars with the Programme.)[6]

My conjecture, then, is that *The Lord of the Rings* reawakens readers from the deadening and indeed, often deadly spell of modernism and its pathological narrative of "Knowledge, Rule, Order," in the words of the quisling Saruman. It throws open the windows and doors of our self-made prison and lets in the light and smells and sounds of embodied life, enchanting and perilous. It is a call to *live* life, as we used to, and reminds us – coming out from under the Shadow, as the book ends – that notwithstanding everything, we still can. (Hence Fraser Harrison's marvellous term which I borrowed, "radical nostalgia".)

We need reminding, most of us. That's understandable: we are such busy, forgetful, fearful creatures. So perhaps my hypothesis also makes it understandable why many of us regularly (whether the interval is one year or several) reread *The Lord of the Rings*. It's not because we don't know what's going to happen next in the story! The point of doing so is rather that it has become a *ritual*, one that renews our sense of life and of being alive. And I use the word "ritual" advisedly, because that is something else that secular modernity, in particular, has tried to eliminate, tarring it with the brush of irrationality, emotion and so on. Ritual is still central to religion, of course; but there it is controlled and managed by each religion for its own soteriological purpose.[7]

Like enchantment,[8] however, with which it is intimately associated, ritual has an older, wilder existence, again under the sign of animism: a hundred, a thousand, who knows how many different gods, inhering in each place, moment and event, and each with an appropriate ritual to enable mutual recognition, respect and negotiation. That's how you do it in *Faërie* – that is, *this* world when it is enchanted (just as Tolkien defined it in "On Fairy-Stories"). As Mark Dickinson says, "*féerique* […] nods to the old ancient universe that prevails

---

6 See at least these two excellent books: Sean Kane, *Wisdom of the Mythtellers*, and Keith H. Basso, *Wisdom Sits in Places*.
7 See my essay "Enchantment and Modernity" in this volume.
8 Several papers on enchantment in this context can be accessed on my website – www.patrickcurry. co.uk – under Papers -> Tolkien.

here on earth wherever human beings are not in control."[9] (Which, may I point out, and as the Earth often forcibly reminds us if ongoing social chaos doesn't suffice, we *aren't*.)

I hope others may feel inspired to consider Tolkien's work along these lines, and to develop it further. To do so, however, will require leaving what seems for many to be the more comfortable grounds of literary criticism, historical research and theology for the wilder shores of anthropology, philosophy, and the ecohumanities. Adventures are nasty disturbing things, of course, but there is the promise of treasure. (Even if destroying the Ring is another matter altogether.)

Bibliography

Basso, Keith H. 1996. *Wisdom Sits in Places*. Albuquerque NM: University of New Mexico Press.

Casey, Edward. 2009. *Getting Back into Place*. Second edition. Bloomington IN: Indiana University Press.

Curry, Patrick. 2005. "Tolkien and his Critics: A Critique." In Thomas Honegger (ed.). 2005. *Root and Branch: Approaches Towards Understanding Tolkien*. Second edition. First edition 1999. Zurich and Berne: Walking Tree Publishers, 75-146.[10]

Harvey, Graham. 2006. *Animism*. New York: Columbia University Press.

Kane, Sean. 1998. *Wisdom of the Mythtellers*. Second edition. Peterborough: Broadview Press.

Latour, Bruno. 1993. *We Have Never Been Modern*. Translated by Catherine Porter. Hemel Hempstead: Harvester Wheatsheaf.

Shippey, Tom. 2000. *J.R.R. Tolkien: Author of the Century*. London: HarperCollins.

Toulmin, Stephen. 1990. *Cosmopolis: The Hidden Agenda of Modernity*. Chicago IL: University of Chicago Press.

---

9 Review in *The Fiddlehead* (Spring 2011) of *An Athabaskan Iliad: This Is What They Say: Stories by François Mandeville*, translated from Chipewyan by Ron Scollon (Toronto: Douglas & McIntyre, 2009).

10 Reprinted on pages 125-90 of the present volume.

The Critical Response to Tolkien's Fiction

Abstract

As it says on the tin, this essay concerns the critical response to Tolkien's fiction. The main part takes in "Tolkien criticism" – that is, work by critics with no specialised knowledge of Tolkien's work – but "Tolkien studies" by relative experts is also addressed. Responses are tracked in broadly chronological order from the 1950s through to the present before an attempt is made, under the rubric of "modernism", to understand and assess the largely hostile criticism, especially as compared with the overwhelmingly enthusiastic popular response.

For the purposes of this essay, I will use "Tolkien scholarship" as a generic term for all critical studies whose subject is Tolkien's work. That scholarship comprises two parts. One, the main subject of this essay, is "Tolkien criticism", in which the overwhelming majority of professional literary and cultural critics commenting on Tolkien's work have made no specialised study of it. The other is "Tolkien studies", undertaken by relative experts on his work, who themselves divide into professional critics on the one hand and informed "fans" on the other, with some qualifying as both. (Drout (2005) describes work by the latter group as "Middle-earth studies".)

The distinction between Tolkien criticism and Tolkien studies is not clear-cut, however, insofar as a few critical experts on Tolkien have had sufficient impact, both scholarly and popular, to affect mainstream critical opinion. The leading instance is Tom Shippey; others include Verlyn Flieger, Brian Rosebury, Michael D.C. Drout and John Garth. In discussing Tolkien criticism, I will therefore include their work, along with that of a few critics who, conversely, are not primarily Tolkien scholars but have nonetheless made a significant contribution to the field. Tolkien studies as such is not the subject here, however. Nor do I

First published in Stuart D. Lee (ed.). 2014. *A Companion to Tolkien*. Oxford: Wiley Blackwell, 369-88.

venture into non-Anglophone criticism, and within Tolkien criticism, we are only concerned with the response to his fiction.

Even within these strictures, the survey that follows, although it aims to be comprehensive, will necessarily be selective. But it is not enough simply to describe the critical reaction to Tolkien. Rather, it is our intellectual responsibility to reflect on and try to understand that reaction and the reasons for it, so space must be also be made for that. Furthermore, it is worth recognising that one of the factors that makes the critical reaction to Tolkien worth considering is his immense popular appeal. It is the combination of that and elite critical rejection that gives this subject much of its abiding interest. Tolkien's popular reception therefore cannot be ignored when considering his critics.

Any attempt to survey Tolkien criticism in a disinterested manner must conclude that the weight of critical opinion has been, and largely remains, negative. Indeed, the greater part seems not an attempt to understand Tolkien and his readers but rather to disqualify and humiliate them. In this context, Daniel Timmons's assessment (2000: 1-10) is admirably irenic but misleading. True, for every critical attack on Tolkien one can find a positive opinion; but that means little without taking into account the relative status, perceived authority, and scholarly as well as public impact of the critics concerned. I therefore make no apology for concentrating overall on the critical hostility to Tolkien's fiction.[1]

Finally, before we embark, it is vital to realise that we are all, plain public and professional critics alike, engaged in a common task, namely engaging with the meaning(s) of Tolkien's fiction. That is to say: the meanings resulting from how his books, as they are written, are taken up by readers. So there are two elements to any such process, analytically distinguishable but seamless in practice: production, or what went into his fiction, both the materials and his creative uses of them, and reception: what the results signify to its readers. There is no escaping what Drout and Wynne (2000: 107) call "the

---

1 Many of the critical attacks on *The Lord of the Rings*, up till 2000, are discussed in Shippey (1992, ch. 1, and 2000a, especially the Afterword; these should definitely be consulted). See also Hammond (1995); Pearce (1998: 1-10); Curry (2004, ch. 2, and 2005); and Lobdell (2007).

vital epistemological fact that all texts must be interpreted,"[2] and given both the set of skills and the related tendencies of many literary critics, questions of reception – what Tolkien (2006b: 128) called "the effect produced now by these old things in the stories as they are" – are arguably still the more challenging and therefore neglected of the two. (Shippey 2000a is a model in taking an integrated approach.)

What follows has four parts. First, I shall review what occurred in the chief phases of Tolkien criticism, before suggesting a way to understand their import. That will be followed by a look at Tolkien studies that overlap with Tolkien criticism, and I shall conclude with a brief discussion of some remaining work that deserves mention.

The principal phases of critical response are these. *The Hobbit* was published in 1937 to some acclaim, but Tolkien criticism started in earnest with publication of *The Lord of the Rings*, as a book for adults, in 1954-55. It stepped up with the book's spectacular success beginning in 1965, was given renewed impetus by the results of readers' polls in 1996-98, and again by Peter Jackson's films in 2001-3. Tolkien also received some critical notice with publication of *The Silmarillion* in 1977.

First wave: the 1950s and 60s

In several ways, the initial critical response to *The Lord of the Rings* set precedents which have continued, with remarkable continuity, into the present. One was the observation by W.H. Auden (1956: 5), one of Tolkien's staunchest defenders, that "I rarely remember a book about which I have had such violent arguments. Nobody seems to have a moderate opinion; either, like myself, people find it a masterpiece of its genre or they cannot abide it, and among the hostile there are some, I must confess, for whose judgement I have

---

2 It is therefore odd that later in the same paper, they refer to the "intrinsic quality" of Tolkien's fiction. "Intrinsic" here is an empty signifier which, to use Williams James's blunt metaphor, can never be cashed in as such. There are only ever interpretations, better and worse, and any qualities are a function of the work *plus* its readers, including critics, which interface is therefore where the real work of criticism must take place. It follows that any good critical practice must include reflexive awareness (which is why *ex cathedra* denunciations are always a bad sign).

great respect." Auden added, shrewdly, "I can only suppose that some people object to Heroic Quests and Imaginary Worlds on principle."

Praise was also forthcoming from Richard Hughes, Naomi Mitchison and, effusively but perhaps predictably, C.S. Lewis (1954, 1955), but others were less enthusiastic. Alfred Duggan (1954: 541), reviewing *The Lord of the Rings* anonymously in the *Times Literary Supplement*, opined that "This is not a work which many adults will read through more than once," thus marking the start of a long series of patrician critical judgements on Tolkien subsequently perceptible as clearly wide of the mark. Similarly, Philip Toynbee, writing in the *Observer* in 1961, recorded his spectacularly premature belief that "today these books have passed into a merciful oblivion."

In the second of three reviews in 1954-55, Edwin Muir, just appointed Norton Professor of English at Harvard University, declared that *The Lord of the Rings* disappointed because "all the characters are boys masquerading as adult heroes [...]" (1955) In other words, they are (1) immature, as signalled by what Muir curiously described as an uncomplicatedly happy ending; (2) one-dimensional, the good ones being thoroughly good and the bad utterly bad; and (3) problematically masculine and/or sexually immature. To anyone who knows the books, it is obvious that the first two points are wrong, and they have been refuted more than once (e.g. in Le Guin 1989: 57-58 and Shippey 2000a); the third is more complex (see Clark 1997, Green 1998, Curry 2005: 85-87[3]). What is more significant, however, is the durability of the charges.

Probably the most influential single review from this period was by one of the leading American literary critics of his day, a Marxist modernist, Edmund Wilson (1956). Its significance is not so much its questionable judgements (the books show "poverty of invention" and their hero "has no serious temptations") as its contemptuous mockery, extending from the title, "Oo, Those Awful Orcs!", to the dismissal of *The Lord of the Rings* as "juvenile trash". That tone remained a constant throughout the next half-century. (In a little-known rejoinder a few years later, Donald Davie (1969: 90) argued that Wilson's attack "quite fails to account for the seriousness of the undertaking, for the

---

3 Reprinted on pages 135-36 of the present volume.

pressure that drove the author through these thousand or more pages, as it has driven many readers (this reader among them) to follow through the same pages eagerly.")

Also in 1969, amid *The Lord of the Rings*'s popular success, Columbia University Press published a full-length academic critique. Catherine Stimpson excoriated Tolkien as "an incorrigible nationalist" celebrating a "bourgeois pastoral idyll" with one-dimensional characters who are "irritatingly, blandly, traditionally masculine." The (in)justice of these specific charges has been discussed in detail by Colebatch (2003: ch. 6) as well as Curry (2005: 83-85[4]), so they need not detain us. They will serve here to underline the predominantly Marxist, feminist and literary-modernist provenance of these attacks.

The Silmarillion: the 1970s

Christopher Tolkien's edited version of *The Silmarillion* was published in 1977. It was the first of Tolkien's works of fiction to meet with public bafflement and disappointment (in which connection it may be relevant that it was published posthumously, i.e. without his approval). It was a response which largely coincided, for once, with the critical reception. John Gardner reviewed it sympathetically and insightfully, however, in the *New York Times Book Review* (12.10.1977).

It is true, and by now almost a truism, that Tolkien studies must now include Tolkien's "legendarium" in understanding his work as a whole (see Flieger and Hostetter 2000 and Hammond 1995: 229-30). In terms of Tolkien criticism, however, that importance does not turn *The Silmarillion* into an accessible or even particularly readable text. It isn't, which has naturally served to sharply limit its impact on common apprehensions of Tolkien's fiction, and critics are under no obligation to pretend otherwise. (Tolkien himself (2006a: 333) noted one insuperable problem: *The Lord of the Rings* and *The Hobbit* depended for their sense of depth and antiquity on "glimpses of a large history in the background", which was not possible when presenting that background itself.)

---

4 Reprinted on pages 133-34 of the present volume.

Tolkien's Fiction in the 1980s

This decade began with two critiques of Tolkien in the mould of that of Stimpson but issuing from the new critical industries, recently ascendant within the academy, of structuralism and psychoanalysis respectively: Christine Brooke-Rose, *A Rhetoric of the Unreal* (1981) and Rosemary Jackson, *Fantasy: The Literature of Subversion* (1981). The former author, an eminent academic structuralist as well as author of "experimental" novels, turned the big guns of Theory on *The Lord of the Rings*, appropriating it as little more than grist to its preset mill (see Attebery 1992: 23-27 and Curry 2005: 110-11[5]). As with those of Wilson and Stimpson but even more so, Brooke-Rose's account of Tolkien was littered with both spelling and factual mistakes, suggesting that the difficulty these critics shared in reading Tolkien at all, let alone closely, and undermining confidence in her wider conclusions.

Jackson, a Marxist and psychoanalytic critic, argued that Tolkien's "sentimental" and "nostalgic" work functions as a conservative vehicle for repression supporting a ruling ideology. The remedy, in standard modernist (and crypto-Protestant) style, is demystification. Once again, as Attebery shows (1992: 20-23, 27, 31; see also Curry 2005: 106-8[6]), Jackson was more concerned to dispose of Tolkien's work than to comprehend it.

That same year, and again in 1983, Fred Inglis, a former student of F.R. Leavis, took Tolkien criticism to a new nadir, calling Tolkien a fascist (Inglis 1981: 197). I have discussed his critique elsewhere (2005: 104-6[7]); here it is only needful to point out the same phenomenon that Shippey (2000a: 306-8) has noted of Toynbee and Edmund Wilson, namely gross inconsistency between their self-professed critical ideals and their practice when they encounter Tolkien. In Inglis's case (1983: 3, 31-32), this takes the form of criticising the metropolitan "irony-stereotypewriter" while shamelessly patronising a "typical" Tolkien reader as the retired head of art in a market-town grammar-school, reading *The Lord of the Rings* to his young sons in a pine-panelled flat, etc.

---

5 Reprinted on pages 156-58 of the present volume.
6 Reprinted on pages 153-55 of the present volume.
7 Reprinted on pages 151-53 of the present volume.

Inglis was the respectful biographer of Raymond Williams, the leading Marxist literary critic of his time and a major influence on the new academic discipline of cultural studies. In the course of a critique of pastoralism, Williams (1985: 258) casually counted Tolkien as a practitioner of "country-based fantasy" that is "suburban" and "half-educated". Again, the most significant point is not that these criticisms, left unqualified, are mistaken, which can easily be shown; Tolkien was no more half-educated than he was a fascist. It is rather how very mistaken they are, and how consistently. That suggests that there is (as Marxists like to say) a structural or systematic bias at work.

Fortunately for Tolkien criticism, the early 1980s also saw publication of what is probably its most important single work, both in quality and (eventually) influence: Tom Shippey's *The Road to Middle-earth* (1982, with revised and expanded editions in 1992, 2003 and 2005). A year later, Verlyn Flieger's pioneering and insightful *Splintered Light: Logos and Language in Tolkien's World* (revised edition, 2002) appeared. Together, these books revealed the profound linguistic, cultural and metaphysical dimensions of Tolkien's work. It is doubtful that they significantly altered mainstream critical opinion upon publication, but less doubtful that they have done so over time. Since space is severely limited, however, and both these books are still widely available as well as unmissable in both Tolkien studies and (it is to be hoped) criticism, I won't discuss them directly here.[8]

The Polls: 1996-98

In 1996, *The Lord of the Rings* topped the poll by Waterstone's and BBC Channel 4 (26,000 readers) of the greatest books of the century. The same year, the Folio Society asked its members to decide upon their favourite books; in first place, with 10,000 votes, was *The Lord of the Rings*. The same finding emerged from follow-up polls in 1997 by the television programme *Bookworm* (c. 50,000 readers), readers of the *Daily Telegraph*, and in 1999 by MORI, although in the last *The Lord of the Rings* was finally pushed into second place – by the Bible. That same year, *The Lord of the Rings* topped a

---

8 Also in 1981, Isaacs and Zimbardo published another uneven collection of critical essays which failed to add very much to their earlier and innovative one of 1968.

poll conducted by Amazon.com as the book of the millennium. (In several of these polls, Orwell placed second, either directly or as the author of *Nineteen Eighty-Four*: an interesting fact to which we shall return.)

The critical response was explosively hostile. Auberon Waugh, editor of the *Literary Review*, Professor John Carey, and Mark Lawson on the BBC *Today* programme all concurred that Tolkien fans had orchestrated the outcome. (Tolkien, it seems, has "fans" rather than "readers".) This conspiracy theory was quietly dropped after the Folio Society poll. Susan Jeffreys, for the *Sunday Times* (26.01.1997), recorded the dismay at the Waterstones/Channel 4 result "up and down the country wherever one or two literati gathered together."[9] The *Times Literary Supplement* (24.01.1997) found it "horrifying", Howard Jacobson opined that "It's another black day for British culture" (see Pearce 1998: 2-3) and, not to be outdone, Germaine Greer (1997: 4) described the result as a "nightmare", adding that the books subsequently inspired by Tolkien "are more or less what you would expect; flight from reality is their dominating characteristic." The charge of escapism, reiterating those of immaturity, nostalgia and conservatism, is another hardy perennial to which we shall return. (At least it *is* a charge, as against inchoate exclamations of horror.)

The same pattern persisted into the next decade. In 2003, *The Lord of the Rings* won the BBC's *The Big Read* poll of readers' favourite book, with 174,000 votes (23% of the total of nearly ¾ million readers): by now, surely an unsurprising result except, it seems, to the three critics live on TV on the night, two of whom had apparently been unable to read it beforehand. All in all, such instances, together with Tolkien's critics' repeated inability to get the details or narrative meaning of what they are attacking right, point to an irrational revulsion. This is not irrelevant; it throws a very interesting light on the dominant literary mindset and, as such, it should form part of any truly critical consideration thereof.

Meanwhile, an authoritative work edited by John Clute and John Grant, *The Encyclopedia of Fantasy* (1997) offered an assessment of Tolkien's work as measured and reasoned, especially concerning both his literary influences and his own influence, as the public critics' had been the contrary.

---

9 Leading unavoidably to the thought, as Shippey (2000a: xxi) observes, that the literati sometimes talk to themselves.

The Good, the Bad and the Ugly: the 2000s

In Tolkien criticism, the new century and millennium opened with publication of Shippey's *J.R.R. Tolkien: Author of the Century*. Its quality combined with the backing of a major trade publisher, and Shippey's eminence in both Tolkien studies and criticism, makes it central in both, and I will only mention points made therein which directly concern our remit.

Shippey defends the bold claim of his title on three grounds: democratic, generic and qualitative (2000a: xvii-xx). These could be summarised by saying that for the last fifty years, Tolkien has found unignorable numbers of readers, many of whom have not only gone on to seek out similar works in the fantasy genre he unintentionally founded but "have been deeply and lastingly moved by Tolkien's works, and even if one doesn't share the feeling, one should be able to understand why" (Shippey 2000a: xix-xx).

Shippey also makes a convincing case that Tolkien should be considered a modern writer, in the company of Orwell, Golding, Vonnegut and others, with a thoroughly twentieth-century concern for and treatment of power and evil. (Two qualifications: Tolkien's understanding of them was often at variance with his contemporaries', and his work being modern in some respects does not preclude it from being non-modern in others.)

Finally, Shippey suggests (2000a: xxxiv) that "[v]ery probably the reason for the dislike has a good deal to do with the reasons for the success. Tolkien has challenged the very authority of the literati, and this will never be forgiven." In his "Afterword: The Followers and the Critics" (2000a: 305-28), Shippey usefully considers the phenomenon of "intense critical hostility to Tolkien, the refusal to allow him to be even a part of 'English literature' […]" (2000a: 305).

Despite the insights offered by Shippey, Flieger and others working in Tolkien studies, the various charges laid against *The Lord of the Rings* over several decades by his detractors in Tolkien criticism were prominently revived in 2001 in perhaps the leading organ of the British literary establishment, the *London Review of Books* (*LRB*), in an article by one of its editors, Jenny Turner. (For one of the few responses to Turner, see Galwey 2004.) Entitled, with heavy irony, "Reasons for liking Tolkien", Turner's essay seeks not so much to understand Tolkien or his readers as to place them beyond serious consideration. Nonetheless, it is illuminating because of what it reveals about the gut reactions and critical mindset of Wilson, Muir, Stimpson, Jackson and more recently Greer. It is thus invaluable as data.

Turner repeats some of her predecessors' elementary mistakes, e.g. describing the hobbits of the story as subordinate and powerless, and portraying the message of the book as one of reassuring safety resulting from a "cosy little universe". There is also the familiar snobbery according to which *The Lord of the Rings* isn't literature but "junk fiction", in the same relation to "literature and learning" as "astrology is to physics," written by someone who, if he hadn't been an Oxford scholar, might have been obsessed with "a model railway, or a record collection, or military history, or maps [...]."

Turner's principal subject, however, is her own reaction to *The Lord of the Rings*. She writes as an apostate who once read it with "an intensity I now find scary." She now finds it "silly and boring", yet "it still locks with my psyche in a most alarming way [...]. It's an infantile comfort that is also a black pit."[10] It seems *The Lord of the Rings* "has cubby-holes for all sorts of urges to hide in," and "[a]ll sorts of visceral needs and desires are involved" which make it "not just anti-intellectual but a sort of anti-book" and even "a little sinister." All Tolkien's fans are "vulnerable people" smitten by "soggy, yearny nostalgia," but "the swotty teenager" is particularly at risk.

Turner mentions Tolkien's "dreadful prose style" in passing (cf. Drout 2004), and takes it as read that "[o]bviously there are problems to do with women, and race and racism," not to mention "with the elves and so on" (recall in this connection Auden's point from 1956). But what she helpfully identifies as "the central problem" is that "[i]t's a whole world [...] You would expect elves to figure in Tolkien's story – if they had to figure at all – as creatures within a sub-creation,

---

10 I am vividly reminded of an incident in Vienna in 1910 when Sigmund Freud asked Carl Jung to promise that he would "never abandon the sexual theory." When Jung asked why, Freud hesitated before replying that they had to make it a "dogma", an "unshakeable bulwark" against the "black tide of mud, of occultism." Interestingly, Turner makes it clear that Freud is exemplary for her, and she too finds in his particular theory of sexual maturity a bulwark, one against the "black pit" of Tolkien's fiction.

characters in a story, fictions inside a frame. But actually, they are given much more credence, more constitutive importance, more ontological weight." In consequence, "[y]ou find yourself thirsting for some nice sensible wipe-down concepts like 'metaphor' or 'fiction'."

Why is this a serious problem for Turner and like-minded critics? Certainly the metaphysical realism and rationalism that dominates so much of mainstream Western culture are obvious in her response; although to apply a little of her hero Freud, why do we need constant reminders that elves, say, are not real? In any case, there is clearly a programme involved – in this case, rationalist, naturalist and secularist – along the lines of what Barbara Herrnstein Smith (1988: 179) has anatomised as the enduring effort "to identify the presumptively universally compelling Truth and Way and to compel it universally." When the Truth is at stake in this way, living and letting live is not a critical option, and any one claiming to sincerely love, say, the work of Tolkien, Proust *and* George Eliot, must be either deluded or dissembling.

In more strictly literary terms, it seems that Turner – and given that she is on its editorial board, one wonders about the *LRB* – fails to understand two of the most important things about art, literary or otherwise: that reality is (also) ineluctably fictional, and that fiction and its referents are (also) unavoidably real. Turner and her allies evidently want to keep reality and fiction on hermetically separate levels except for what they, the gatekeepers, will allow through.[11] As for metaphor, Paul Ricoeur showed more than three decades ago that "[t]here is no non-metaphorical standpoint [...]. [M]etaphoricity is absolutely uncontrollable" (2003: 339). In other words, any critique of fiction has fiction at its heart, and any critique of metaphoricity can only draw upon metaphor. So much for "a sensible wipe-down".

---

11 Behind nearly all such efforts stands the ghost of Plato, that great advocate of a single and universal truth, and enemy of popular unlicensed fictions; and, at no great distance, St Paul. In terms of their *mode*, this applies to most modern Western secularists as much as it does to theists.

Modernism

This review of the dominant critical reception of Tolkien's fiction consistently shows two characteristics which seem especially significant: a visceral hostility and emotional animus, and a plethora of mistakes showing that the books had not been read closely (or in a few cases, at all). Taking these together suggest that the inability to really engage resulted from the loathing, although without inhibiting the same critics from pronouncing anathema. As the critic J.P. Stern once observed: "Contempt is a poor guide." We must go beyond that conclusion, however, in search of an explanation. Why such contempt, and for these particular books?

Shippey (2000a: 316) argues that "at the heart of the critical rage, and fear, which Tolkien immediately and ever after provoked" is the fact that he "threatened the authority of the arbiters of taste, the critics, the educationalists, the literati. He was as educated as they were" – (Oxford professors usually are) – "but in a different school." Furthermore, *The Lord of the Rings* "showed an improper ambition, as if it had ideas above the proper station of popular trash." (The critics' assumption is often actually that simple: it's popular, so it must be trash.) Shippey adds: "It was the combination that could not be forgiven."

This explanation undoubtedly goes far towards explaining the unusual critical response, but as it stands, it is an excellent summary that awaits more elaboration. I shall attempt just that under the umbrella term (to be explained) of "modernism". First, however, we need briefly to review other relevant factors which are not captured by even a broad definition of modernism, although they may well overlap with it.

One is that *The Lord of the Rings* will never have universal appeal (properly so-called). That hardly marks it out from any other book, but in terms of content, you wouldn't go to it, for example, for subtle insights into relationships between the sexes. Furthermore, there remain stubborn issues, potentially problematic, with the way *The Lord of the Rings* treats race and politics as well as sex/gender.[12] Respecting style, Tolkien's tone (not unlike that of Dickens) is sometimes

---

12 On the last, see the references already supplied when discussing Muir's charges. On race and racism, see Luling (1995), Fimi (2010) and in general, Eaglestone (2005).

sentimental, and its occasional archaic and "high" style will never be to some readers' tastes. It is perfectly understandable that some would prefer other work (which differs from deploring anyone at all reading it).[13]

To some extent, a negative response to Tolkien's fiction may be simply a function of personal disaffinity. Temperaments, even to the extent they are a matter of nurture as well as nature, vary widely, and with them, tastes: *de gustibus non est disputandum*. But taste alone won't carry all the weight of the emotive reactions; alternatively, there must be more to "mere taste" than meets the eye. In either case, there is more to be said.

In this connection, another potential stumbling-block has been thoroughly explored by Shippey (1992, 2000; see also Honegger 2005): the problems posed, perhaps particularly for intellectuals, by a literary artefact suffused with a philological concern for words and a particular understanding of language (strongly influenced by Owen Barfield: see Flieger 2002) as rooted in and indicative of corresponding worlds/mentalities, past and present. That understanding has almost vanished from the contemporary intellectual world. As a result, as Shippey (1992: 291) says, "there is an enormous 'culture-gap' between him and his critics" – admirers, often, as much as detractors. Among critics, I believe Harold Bloom (2000) falls in this category; he evinces more bafflement than hatred.[14] As a sign of this problem for literary critics, see the ongoing struggle to place *The Lord of the Rings* in a category: it is clearly not a novel, so is it a romance, an epic, mythopoeic fiction or simply junk fiction? It has often proved easier to simply opine that whatever it is, to quote Humphrey Carpenter, it "doesn't really belong to literature" (BBC *Bookshelf*, 22.11.1991; see Simonson 2008).

Another consideration is simple snobbery, itself fed by fear (see Carey 1992). The power of this attitude, contributing to and fed by membership in a critical elite, particularly when institutionalised in an academic or media forum, should not be underestimated – particularly where popular success is also part

---

13 Respecting any defence of Tolkien here, however, Drout and Wynne (2000: 123) identify as "[t] he biggest failing in Tolkien criticism […] its lack of discussion of Tolkien's style, his sentence-level writing, his word choice and syntax."

14 It is amusing to imagine Bloom trying to find any "anxiety of influence" in Tolkien. But did it never occur to him that Joyce's *Ulysses* is a much better candidate than *The Lord of the Rings* for a work "fated to become only an intricate Period Piece" (Bloom 2000: 2)?

of the mix. I think Auberon Waugh's contempt for Tolkien was primarily a function of snobbery, and no doubt it also figured strongly in that of Wilson, Greer, Turner, Carpenter and others.

Nonetheless, more still seems needed to account for the sheer animus. For that, I think we need to invoke something like a worldview, ideology or set of values, relatively coherent and strongly-held (if not necessarily consciously so). Such values are ultimate in two senses: they cannot be further grounded or justified, yet they are also what their bearer feels (more than thinks) are what he or she is "all about". They are therefore often defended with quasi-religious or, in the case of values which entail denying religion, crypto-religious fervour. (They can change, of course, but any major shift amounts to a conversion experience.) It is at this level, respecting the critical response to Tolkien's fiction, that modernism enters the picture.

What do I mean by "modernism"? In answering that question, we first need a working definition of "modernity" and "modern". These embrace a sensibility and set of values which include, prominently:

- A belief in the "right" and ability, in principle, at least, of humanity to determine its own fate (rather than, say, God or nature), usually through science and technology.
- Secularism and materialism, as opposed to the sacrality of theism (whether mono- or poly-), animism or sacred nontheism (e.g. Buddhism).
- Considerable confidence, if not indeed faith, in reason, and relatedly in modern science, both instrumentally and substantively conceived, as the "highest" version of reason, along with efficient administration as its practical expression.
- All of which coalesces into a narrative ideology of Progress and its enemies (chief among them, "superstition", a.k.a. "tradition") that bears a significant but unacknowledged debt to Christian eschatology.

Secondarily, modernity is also an historical period, albeit necessarily broadly construed, in which that sensibility and set of values finds dominant or pre-eminent expression and influence. (The best single guide here is Toulmin 1990, but see also Latour 1993 and Horkheimer and Adorno 2002.)

"Modern*ism*" and "modern*ist*", then, refer to the valorisation and advocacy of modern values – that is, the chief values of modernity – whether in politics, culture, literature, architecture, music, etc. They do not necessarily describe a particular school or movement within art, architecture, literature, etc. (Thus, literary modernists need no longer hold up Joyce, Eliot and Woolf as exemplars, although they may do so.)

Now as Veldman (1994: 107) perceptively notes: "Not all the reviewers who stood outside Narnia and Middle-earth did so because they misunderstood what Lewis and Tolkien were about. Many did so precisely because they perceived the protest at the heart of these works."[15] It is my contention that the dominant ideology of the literati, as self-appointed guardians of literature, is modernism; that those most aggrieved by Tolkien are or were, personally as well as professionally, modernists; and that given Tolkien's uncompromising, erudite and popularly-received rejection of modernism, this makes sense not only of the most consistent charges – infantilism, nostalgia, escapism, etc. – but also of the casual vehemence with which they have been made.[16] As Tolkien himself realised, his chief crime was not even "the Escape of the Prisoner"; it was for encouraging "the Flight of the Deserter" (2006b: 148). (In this connection, it makes perfect sense that the most frequent runners-up in the polls of readers were Orwell and *Nineteen Eighty-Four*: an author and a book equally agonised over pathological modernity, although from a socialist rather than conservative perspective.)

As evidence and elucidation of this contention, let us examine the issues, as they appear in the critical texts, of modernism itself and of irony. Starting with modernism, I have already seconded Shippey's firm placing of *The Lord of the Rings* as a work with characteristically modern concerns, particularly respecting power. (See Shippey 2000a: 312-18 for an analysis of "Tolkien and modernity", and Honegger and Weinreich 2006.) At the same time, I also agree with Turner (2001) that "[i]n form, in content, in everything about it, *The Lord of the Rings* is the most anti-Modernist [*sic*] of novels." Andrew O'Hehire (2001) makes the

---

15 Lumping Tolkien and Lewis together should be done with care, as it can be quite misleading.
16 Although he doesn't discuss Tolkien specifically, Frederic Jameson, who dismisses all contemporary "magical narratives" as "archaic nostalgia" (1975: 61), will serve as a paradigmatic example of a dogmatic modernist literary and cultural critic.

same point; "the crux of the matter", he writes, "lies in Tolkien's wholehearted rejection of modernity and modernism. This is what so powerfully attracts some readers, and just as powerfully repels others […]." Anthony Lane (2001) sees the same dynamic in Tolkien's "high" style: "Hardly anyone had used it unironically since Tennyson's 'Idylls of the King,' and to revert to it with a straight face in the nineteen-fifties was to mount a head-on challenge to modernity […]." Finally, I have argued elsewhere (2004) that it is *The Lord of the Rings*'s *non*-modernism, presenting "a Europe that has not been 'Europeanised'" (Luling 1995: 53), that has powerfully attracted many readers.

There are no necessary contradictions here, if we recall the distinction between modernism and modernity. First, Tolkien himself was definitely anti-modernist; his deep reservations about advanced technology and industrialism, representative democracy and bureaucracy are well-documented. It would be simple-minded, however, to assume that his *books* are therefore straightforwardly anti-modernist. Second, Tolkien's fiction is certainly modern, but it is far from purely so. Both Shippey (1982/1992, 2000) and Flieger (especially 1997) have enabled us to analytically disentangle the modern and non-modern ingredients in the cauldron of Tolkien's story. Third (notwithstanding Mortimer's (2005) useful essay), that story is not modern*ist*; no advocacy of modernity is present. In short, *The Lord of the Rings* is a modern book, much of the import of which is also non-modern, written by an anti-modernist.

Rosebury also concludes that *The Lord of the Rings* "could not plausibly be called a modernist work, because it lacks a crucial quality universal within modernism: irony" (2003: 154). That brings us to our second key consideration. Pre-eminently, modernist irony functions as a signal that the writer subscribes to what Latour (1993: 22) calls the Modern Constitution: "1st […] even though we construct Nature, Nature is as if we did not construct it. 2nd: even though we do not construct Society, Society is as if we did construct it. 3rd: Nature and Society must remain absolutely distinct." Being ironic, especially about what one is writing oneself, says: being intelligent and highly-educated, I know that what I am doing (writing, i.e. cultural construction) isn't real (i.e. natural) – even, indeed especially, if I am writing about nature – and that the two are completely different. And anyone whose art is unselfconscious, thus ignoring (or should I say, disrespecting?) this convention, becomes fair game for mockery and contempt.

Like Rosebury, Drout too (2005: 653) notes Tolkien's failure, or refusal, to meet "the modernist expectation of pervasive irony." Attebery (1992: 39) concurs that "[t]he course of twentieth-century literature can be viewed as the gradual spread of irony into every phase of storytelling." Moorcock, one of Tolkien's bitterest critics ("Epic Pooh"), inadvertently confirms the point: "I think my own dislike of J.R.R. Tolkien lies primarily in the fact that in all those hundreds of pages, full of high ideals, sinister evil and noble deeds, there is scarcely a hint of irony anywhere" (1987: 107). (For a recent unconvincing attempt to enlist Tolkien as a "theorist of the ironic imagination", see Saler 2012.)

Ironies abound *within The Lord of the Rings*, of course, not least that it turns out to be not Frodo or Sam who finally destroy the Ring, nor any of the great and good, but Gollum. But Tolkien is not ironic *about The Lord of the Rings*; nor does he offer the slightest opening or invitation to readers to be so. He and his readers are, so to say, post-ironic. That is not something that will endear them to critics who pride themselves on being the critical avant-garde and can't stop using irony to signal it, or checking what they are reading for such signals. Infuriatingly for some, post-ironists – which, in Tolkien's case, is evidently the majority of readers – simply don't care.

Taking Turner again as an unusually articulate but otherwise representative critic of Tolkien, recall, in this connection, what she identifies as "the central problem": the "ontological weight" given by Tolkien to fictional creatures like elves. (As Shippey (1992: 251) points out, "Most novels are about 'people who never existed'," but let that pass.) Turner's cosmopolitan sophistication vanishes when realism, rationalism and secularism are at stake. The only alternative, it seems, is "the vague warm surges of feeling associated with religion and religion substitutes." Indeed, in a kind of modernist evocation of cold showers and mittens at night, she warns that "[t]hese responses can be touched off with a dangerous ease – every self-aware person finds that he has to train himself from adolescence in withstanding them." As Galwey

(2004: 10) comments: "Perhaps if one had staked one's all on modernity, one would feel like that."

Turner writes: "When I was young [...] I really did believe that the world inside the book had taken over the world outside," and such literature "plays on the reader's desire to believe that the world Tolkien is writing about is in some way real." When you grow up, however, "[y]ou know too much about how the world works to be so easily taken in." Notice how she resorts to classical epistemology in order to disqualify and domesticate others' as well as her own ontological experience of, and as, reality: they ("fans"; it used to be "natives") *believe*, but we literati *know*. From there it is a short step to associate such "realism" with maturity, growing up, and Muir's and Wilson's anxious concern to be the Adult in the room. But that is pure rhetoric, not logic or universal experience; and swollen into an ideology of Progress, on both an individual and collective level, it encourages an all-too-familiar obligation to chastise heretics, apostates, backsliders and "escapists".

It is hardly surprising, then, that "Tolkien's perfectly sincere, perfectly impossible narrative" (Atteberry 1992: 46) so provokes. As the Irish writer Nuala O'Faolain once remarked: "The language of highbrow criticism can only cope with a certain kind of fiction. It has no vocabulary with which to discuss a world where neither the individual nor the society is self-conscious, and the author pretends not to be either [...]. The ordinary reader is far ahead of the critics in ease with such a world."[17] In another genuine irony, it was one of the heroes of modernism, Walter Benjamin (1969: 83, 102), who remarked on modern "embarrassment all around when the wish to hear a story is expressed", and added approvingly that "[t]he first true storyteller is, and will continue to be, the teller of fairy tales." As Tolkien wrote in 1955, "the 'fairy-story' is really an adult genre" – that is, a genre for the ordinary reader – "and one for which a starving audience exists" (2006a: 209).

The Lord of the Rings is thus fundamentally not one but several things: a story told by a master story-teller; a story inspired by philology; a story suffused with Catholic values; and a mythic (or mythopoeic) story with a North European

---

17 *The Irish Times* (07.11.1992).

pagan inflection. It is also a story that enables the contemporary reader to imaginatively inhabit a non-modern world, one that throws into question some central modern values and assumptions.

There remains one important point to discuss in this connnection. Le Guin has pointed to "a deep puritanical distrust of fantasy." To such critics, fantasy "is escapism [...]. They confuse fantasy, which in the psychological sense is a universal and essential faculty of the human mind, with infantilism and pathological regression" (and not always by sincere error, I would add) – "as if evil were a problem, something that can be solved, that has an answer [...]" "*That*" she adds, "is escapism [...]" (1989: 58-59; emphasis in original).

Laura Miller (2008: 101) recounts a conversation in which Tolkien asked Lewis rhetorically, "What class of men would you expect to be most preoccupied with, and most hostile to, the idea of escape?" The answer, of course, is jailers. (Cf. Tolkien 2006b: 148.) Now Miéville (2002) has cited Moorcock to the effect that "this is precisely untrue. Jailers love escapism. What they hate is escape." But that rejoinder turns on whether you think imaginatively inhabiting an essentially non-modern world is already a form of escape, rather than mere escapism. Of course, any literature, or indeed art, *could* constitute escapism. Given the phenomenon of radical nostalgia, however (Curry 2004: 15-16) – which I take to be empirically confirmed in Tolkien's case by *The Lord of the Rings*'s influence in various movements of political and environmental resistance – his fiction is certainly not necessarily escapist or even quietist, sometimes proving rather to be activist.

From Tolkien Studies

This section is intended to bring attention to contributions to Tolkien scholarship from Tolkien studies, in addition to those already mentioned by Shippey, which have also figured in, and affected, Tolkien criticism. I shall assume without discussion the importance of Douglas A. Anderson's annotated edition of *The Hobbit* (1988), the biography by Humphrey Carpenter (1977), Tolkien's *Letters* (2006a) and essays (2006b), the posthumous *Unfinished Tales of Númenor and Middle-earth* (1980), and the twelve volumes of the *History of Middle-earth* series

(1983-96). To these should be added two collections from major conferences, edited by Reynolds and GoodKnight (1995) and Wells (2008), and at least two edited collections: Salu and Farrell (1979) and Clark and Timmons (2000).

First mention must be of the work of Verlyn Flieger (1997, 2002), and its sensitive analysis of the metaphysical and theological dimensions (which are vast and intricate) of Tolkien's work, both fiction and nonfiction. In addition, Flieger has provided definitive editions of Tolkien's *Smith of Wootton Major* (2005) and his landmark essay "On Fairy-stories" (2008, with Douglas A. Anderson), and a collection of essays on the *Silmarillion* (2000, with Carl F. Hostetter). She is also the best guide to the vital place of *Faërie* or enchantment in Tolkien's work.

Brian Rosebury (1992) pioneered the first good study of Tolkien's work as a cultural phenomenon, and the later edition (2003) is still more useful and insightful. For other recent work of good quality on Tolkien's fiction in the light of contemporary literature and especially cultural studies, see Hughes (2004), Eaglestone (2005) and Fimi (2010).[18]

Also in 1992, Brian Attebery's *Strategies of Fantasy* set the bar high for such studies. Starting from the premiss that "the task of literary theory is to provide a framework capable of accounting for the story's success on its own terms, rather than denying that its aims are achievable or worth the attempt" (17), his discussion of Tolkien draws upon the unjustly neglected approach of Meeker (1974) and subsequently Elgin (1985) to show convincingly that Tolkien's epic is life-affirmingly "comic" and ecological, as opposed to despairingly "tragic" and Promethean. As such, it is "neither nostalgic nor transcendental. Tolkien draws on the ancient magical worldview and the comic narrative structure because they offer something to the present […] an affirmative, integrative worldview, which is not necessarily naïve, escapist, or reactionary" (Attebery 1992: 34). (I would say the failure to follow through this insight is the biggest single lapse to date in Tolkien studies and criticism alike.)

---

18 For an interesting collection on *The Lord of the Rings* by philosophers, see Bassham and Bronson (2003). It is marred, however, by an annoyingly arch tone which seems to indicate a need to show that they are not taking Tolkien *too* seriously. Much more serious and driven by truly scholarly passion is the most recent volume edited by Roberto Arduini and Claudio Testi, *Tolkien and Philosophy* (2014).

Michael Drout is a critic and scholar in Tolkien studies whose comprehensive and acute metacritical essays (2005 and, with Wynne, 2000) should also be read by anyone engaged in Tolkien criticism. He has also edited a Tolkien encyclopedia (2007). His and Wynne's bibliography (2000) is another major resource, along with those of Johnson (1986), Hammond (1993, with Douglas A. Anderson) and West (1981, 2004). (See also Wynne 2007 and Lobdell 2007.)

John Garth's exemplary biography of the first part of Tolkien's life (2003) overlaps both Tolkien studies and criticism, and it has been deservedly praised. One can only hope Garth will one day be able to give similar treatment to Tolkien's entire life, superseding Humphrey Carpenter's earlier and useful but flawed biography of 1977.[19]

Finally, mention must be made of the excellent series of books produced by Walking Tree Publishers, founded in 1997, under the direction of Thomas Honegger, and of the annual refereed journal *Tolkien Studies* established in 2004.

Others

This concluding section will mention contributions by writers not Tolkien scholars as such, nor even all literary critics, but which have nonetheless enriched Tolkien criticism. Pride of place here, on account of her unimpeachable status as both writer and critic and her close relationship, equally personal and professional, with Tolkien's fiction, goes to Ursula Le Guin. Her reflections in the collection of her essays from 1989 on the vexed questions of fantasy and escapism, the complexity of the characters in *The Lord of the Rings*, and its treatment of the nature of evil, remain evergreen.

The historian Ronald Hutton (2003, 2011) treats the pagan dimension of Tolkien's work, an important but neglected topic, with originality and insight. The result throws an interesting light in turn on its Christian dimension, which has received considerably more (and sometimes uncritical) attention.

---

19 For interesting reflections on the relatively neglected topic of Tolkien and the Second World War, see also Manni and Bonechi 2008.

Another social and cultural historian, Meredith Veldman, wrote an early consideration of Tolkien's social and environmental commitments and influence that stands up very well and should be better known. She was the first to note that "[d]ecades before the Greens, he denounced the exaltation of mechanization and the narrow definition of economic progress that resulted in the degradation of the natural environment, and he did so in romantic terms: in Tolkien's Middle-earth, nature expressed a reality beyond human comprehension and worthy of human respect" (1994: 90). In this context, *The Lord of the Rings* "could serve as a text of not only withdrawal but also engagement" (1994: 108), and the elective affinity between it and the countercultural movements of the 1960s, 70s and 90s was far from an anomaly.

Turning to other literature and literary criticism, we should be grateful to a critic for *The Guardian* (03.04.10), Nicholas Lezard, for finally admitting in print that "of all the means for professional suicide that are available to the writer, expressing affection for Tolkien is one of the most effective." It is depressing (if you think Tolkien deserves better) that this should still be the case in 2010. On the other hand, there are signs that the wind is changing. Among the newer generations of contemporary writers, a few are evidently unafraid to include casual and favourable references to Tolkien in their own work. These include Junot Díaz, Michael Chabon and, among literary critics, Anthony Lane (2001) in *The New Yorker*, Andrew O'Hehire (2001) in the online *Salon*, and another writer for *Salon*, Laura Miller (2008).

China Miéville is an accomplished fantasy/science fiction writer himself. In 2002, he published a sharp critique of Tolkien in the *Socialist Review*, an internet journal, but followed this up with a lighter and more tolerant treatment in 2009, giving "Five Reasons Tolkien Rocks", which I recommend. Among the acute and amusing points he makes is one that breaks through just the modernist barrier erected by Turner and others, which she sees as Tolkien's "central problem": "Tolkien refused the notion that a work of fiction is, in some reductive way, primarily, solely, or really 'about' something else, narrowly and precisely [...] his 'cordial dislike' [of allegory] is utterly key for the project of creating a fantastic fiction that both means and is vividly and irreducibly itself, and is thereby fiction worthy of the name."

Miéville, Lane, O'Hehire and Miller show that it is perfectly possible to subject Tolkien's work to serious criticism and/or even poke fun at it while still recognizing its virtues, respecting its strengths and retaining affection for the old monster, as it were. In support of the best of the Tolkien criticism and studies discussed above, they offer hope for Tolkien scholarship continuing to put flesh on the bones of perhaps the most pithy and accurate critical judgement ever delivered on *The Lord of the Rings*, by its first publisher Rayner Unwin (quoted in Carpenter 1977: 210): "a very great book in its own curious way."

Bibliography

ARDUINI, Roberto and Claudio A. TESTI (eds.). 2014. *Tolkien and Philosophy*. Zurich and Jena: Walking Tree Publishers.

ATTEBERY, Brian. 1992. *Strategies of Fantasy*. Bloomington IN: Indiana University Press.

AUDEN, W.H. 1954. "The Hero is a Hobbit." *New York Times Book Review* (31.10.1954) 37.

1956. "At the End of the Quest, Victory." *New York Times Book Review* (22.1.1956) 5.

1962. "The Quest Hero." *The Texas Quarterly* IV: 81-93; reprinted in ISAACS and ZIMBARDO 1968, 40-61.

BASSHAM, Gregory and Eric BRONSON (eds.). 2003. *The Lord of the Rings and Philosophy*. La Salle IL: Open Court.

BENJAMIN, Walter. 1969. "The Storyteller." In *Illuminations*. Edited by Hannah ARENDT. New York: Schocken Books, 83-109.

BLOOM, Harold. 2000. "Introduction." In Harold BLOOM (ed.). 2000. *J.R.R. Tolkien: Modern Critical Views*. Philadelphia PA: Chelsea House, 1-2.

BROOKE-ROSE, Christine. 1981. *A Rhetoric of the Unreal*. Cambridge: Cambridge University Press.

CALDECOTT, Stratford and Thomas HONEGGER (eds.). 2008. *Tolkien's The Lord of the Rings. Sources of Inspiration*. Zurich and Jena: Walking Tree Publishers.

CAREY, John. 1992. *The Intellectuals and the Masses*. London: Faber and Faber.

CLARK, Craig. 1997. "Problems of Good and Evil in Tolkien's *The Lord of the Rings.*" *Mallorn* 35: 15–19.

CLARK, George and Dan TIMMONS (eds). 2000. *J.R.R. Tolkien and his Literary Resonances: Views of Middle-earth.* Westport CT: Greenwood Press.

CLUTE, John and John GRANT. 1997. *The Encyclopedia of Fantasy.* London: Orbis.

COLEBATCH, Hal G.P. 2003. *Return of the Heroes: The Lord of the Rings, Star Wars, Harry Potter, and Social Conflict.* Second edition. First edition 1999. Christchurch: Cybereditions.

CURRY, Patrick. 2004. *Defending Middle-earth: Tolkien, Myth and Modernity.* Second edition. First edition 1997. Boston PA: Houghton Mifflin.

2005. "Tolkien and his Critics: A Critique." In Thomas HONEGGER (ed.). 2005. *Root and Branch: Approaches Towards Understanding Tolkien.* Second edition. First edition 1999. Zurich and Berne: Walking Tree Publishers, 75-146.[20]

DAVIE, Donald. 1969. "On Hobbits and Intellectuals". *Encounter* (October 1969): 90-92.

DROUT, Michael D.C. and Hilary WYNNE. 2000. "Tom Shippey's *J.R.R. Tolkien: Author of the Century* and a Look Back at Tolkien Criticism since 1982." *Envoi* 9.2: 101-134.

Hilary WYNNE and Melissa HIGGINS. 2000. "Scholarly Studies of J.R.R. Tolkien and His Works (in English): 1984-2000." *Envoi* 9.2: 135-167.

2004. "Tolkien's Prose Style and its Literary and Rhetorical Effects." *Tolkien Studies* 1: 137-163.

2005. "Towards a Better Tolkien Criticism." In Robert EAGLESTONE (ed.). 2005. *Reading The Lord of the Rings: New Writings on Tolkien's Classic.* London: Continuum, 15-28.

(ed.). 2007. *J.R.R. Tolkien Encyclopedia. Scholarship and Critical Assessment.* London: Routledge.

DUGGAN, Alfred. 1954. "Heroic Endeavour." *Times Literary Supplement* (27.8.1954): 541.

EAGLESTONE, Robert (ed.). 2005. *Reading The Lord of the Rings: New Writings on Tolkien's Classic.* London: Continuum.

ELGIN, Don D. 1985. *The Comedy of the Fantastic: Ecological Perspectives on the Fantasy Novel.* Westport CT: Greenwood Press.

---

20 Reprinted on pages 125-90 of the present volume.

FIMI, Dimitra. 2010. *Tolkien, Race and Cultural History*. Basingstoke: Palgrave Macmillan.

FLIEGER, Verlyn. 1997. *A Question of Time: J.R.R. Tolkien's Road to Faërie*. Kent OH: Kent State University Press.

2002. *Splintered Light: Logos and Language in Tolkien's World*. Second edition. First edition 1983. Kent OH: Kent State University Press.

and Carl F. HOSTETTER (eds). 2000. *Tolkien's Legendarium: Essays on The History of Middle-earth*. Westport CT: Greenwood Press.

and Douglas A. ANDERSON (eds). 2008. *Tolkien on Fairy-Stories*. London: HarperCollins.

GALWEY, Caroline. 2004. "Reasons for not Liking Tolkien". *Mallorn* 42: 5-10.

GARTH, John. 2003. *Tolkien and the Great War: The Threshold of Middle-earth*. London: HarperCollins.

GREEN, William. 1998. "'Where's Mama?' The Construction of the Feminine in *The Hobbit*." *The Lion and the Unicorn* 22: 188-195.

GREER, Germaine. 1997. "The Book of the Century?" *W: The Waterstone's Magazine* 8: 2-9.

HAMMOND, Wayne G. with Douglas A. ANDERSON. 1993. *J.R.R. Tolkien: A Descriptive Bibliography*. Winchester: St Pauls' Bibliographies.

1995. "The Critical Response to Tolkien's Fiction." In Patricia REYNOLDS and Glen H. GOODKNIGHT (eds.). 1995. *Proceedings of the J.R.R. Tolkien Centenary Conference*. Milton Keynes: The Tolkien Society/Altadena CA: The Mythopoeic Press, 226-232.

HONEGGER, Thomas. 2005. "Tolkien Through the Eyes of a Mediaevalist." In Thomas HONEGGER (ed.). 2005. *Reconsidering Tolkien*. Zurich and Jena: Walking Tree Publishers, 45-66.

and Frank WEINREICH (eds.). 2006. *Tolkien and Modernity*. 2 volumes. Zurich and Jena: Walking Tree Publishers.

HORKHEIMER, Max and Theodor ADORNO. 2002. *Dialectic of Enlightenment*. Translated by Edmund JEPHCOTT. Stanford CA: Stanford University Press.

HUGHES, Shaun F.D. 2004. "Introduction: Postmodern Tolkien." *Modern Fiction Studies* 50.4: 807-813.

HUTTON, Ronald. 2003. "The Inklings and the Gods". In Ronald HUTTON. 2003. *Witches, Druids and King Arthur*. London: Hambledon and London, 215-238.

2011. "The Pagan Tolkien" and "Can We Still Have A Pagan Tolkien?" In Paul E. KERRY (ed.). 2011. *The Ring and the Cross: Christianity and The Lord of the Rings*. Madison WI: Fairleigh Dickinson University Press, 57-70 and 90-105.

INGLIS, Fred. 1981. *The Promise of Happiness: Value and Meaning in Children's Fiction*. Cambridge: Cambridge University Press.

1983. "Gentility and Powerlessness: Tolkien and the New Class." In Robert GIDDINGS (ed.). 1983. *J.R.R. Tolkien: This Far Land*. London: Vision Press, 25-41.

ISAACS, Neil D. and Rose A. ZIMBARDO (eds). 1968. *Tolkien and the Critics: Essays on J.R.R. Tolkien's The Lord of the Rings*. Notre Dame IN: University of Notre Dame Press.

and Rose A. ZIMBARDO (eds). 1981. *Tolkien: New Critical Perspectives*. Lexington KT: University Press of Kentucky.

JACKSON, Rosemary. 1981. *Fantasy: The Literature of Subversion*. London: Methuen.

JAMESON, Frederic. 1975. "Magical Narratives: Romance as Genre." *New Literary History* 7.1: 135-163.

JOHNSON, Judith A. 1986. *J.R.R. Tolkien: Six Decades of Criticism*. Westport CT: Greenwood Press.

LANE, Anthony. 2001. "The Hobbit Habit: Reading *The Lord of the Rings*." *The New Yorker* (10.12.2001), online at http://www.newyorker.com/archive/2001/12/10/011210crat_atlarge (accessed 24.6.11).

LATOUR, Bruno. 1993. *We Have Never Been Modern*. Translated by Catherine PORTER. Hemel Hempstead: Harvester Wheatsheaf.

LE GUIN, Ursula K. 1989. *The Language of the Night: Essays on Fantasy and Science Fiction*. Revised edition. London: The Women's Press.

LEWIS, C.S. 1954. "The Gods Return to Earth." *Time and Tide* (14.8.1954).

1955. "The Dethronement of Power." *Time and Tide* (22.10.1955).

LOBDELL, Jared. 2003. "Postscript." In Jared LOBDELL (ed.). 2003. *A Tolkien Compass*. Revised edition. First edition 1975. Chicago and La Salle: Open Court, 151-158.

2007. "Criticism of Tolkien, Twentieth Century." In Michael D.C. DROUT (ed.). 2007. *J.R.R. Tolkien Encyclopedia. Scholarship and Critical Assessment*. London: Routledge, 109-110.

LULING, Virginia. 1995. "An Anthropologist in Middle-earth." In Patricia REYNOLDS and Glen H. GOODKNIGHT (eds.). 1995. *Proceedings of the J.R.R.*

Tolkien Centenary Conference. Milton Keynes: The Tolkien Society/Altadena CA: The Mythopoeic Press, 53-57.

MANNI, Franco and Simone BONECHI. 2008. "The Complexity of Tolkien's Attitude Towards the Second World War." In Sarah WELLS (ed.). 2008. *The Ring Goes Ever On. Proceedings of the Tolkien 2005 Conference: 50 Years of The Lord of the Rings*. 2 vols. Coventry: The Tolkien Society, vol. 1: 33-51.

MEEKER, Joseph. 1974. *The Comedy of Survival: Studies in Literary Ecology*. New York: Scribner's.

MIÉVILLE, China. 2002. "Tolkien – Middle Earth Meets Middle England." *The Socialist Review* (January 2002). Online at http://www.socialistreview.org.uk/article.php?articlenumber=7813 (accessed 24.6.11).

2009. "There and Back Again: Five Reasons Tolkien Rocks." (15.6.2009). Online at http://www.omnivoracious.com/2009/06/there-and-back-again-five-reasons-tolkien-rocks.html (accessed 22.6.2011).

MILLER, Laura. 2008. *The Magician's Book: A Skeptic's Adventures in Narnia*. New York: Little, Brown.

MOORCOCK, Michael. 1987. *Wizardry and Wild Romance: A Study of Epic Fantasy*. London: Gollancz.

MORTIMER, Patchen. 2005. "Tolkien and Modernism." *Tolkien Studies* 2: 113-129.

MUIR, Edwin. 1955. "A Boy's World." *The Observer* (27.11.1955), 11.

O'HEHIRE, Andrew. 2001. "The Book of the Century." *Salon* (4.6.2001), Part 1: online at http://www.salon.com/books/feature/2001/06/04/tolkien and Part 2: online at http://www.salon.com/books/feature/2001/06/05/tolkien2 (accessed 30.6.11).

PEARCE, Joseph. 1998. *Tolkien: Man and Myth. A literary life*. London: HarperCollins.

REYNOLDS, Patricia and Glen H. GOODKNIGHT (eds). 1995. *Proceedings of the J.R.R. Tolkien Centenary Conference*. Milton Keynes: The Tolkien Society/Altadena CA: The Mythopoeic Press.

RICOEUR, Paul. 2003. *The Rule of Metaphor*. Translated by Robert CZERNY. First published 1975. London: Routledge.

ROSEBURY, Brian. 2003. *Tolkien: A Cultural Phenomenon*. Basingstoke: Palgrave Macmillan. First edition 1992 as *Tolkien: A Critical Assessment*. Basingstoke: Macmillan.

SALER, Michael. 2012. *As If: Modern Enchantment and the Literary Prehistory of Virtual Reality*. Oxford: Oxford University Press.

SALU, Mary and Robert T. FARRELL (eds). 1979. *J.R.R. Tolkien: Scholar and Story-teller*. Ithaca NY: Cornell University Press.

SHIPPEY, Tom. 1992. *The Road to Middle-earth*. London: HarperCollins. First edition 1982; further revised editions in 2003 and 2005.

2000a. *J.R.R. Tolkien: Author of the Century*. London: HarperCollins.

2000b. "Orcs, Wraiths, Wights: Tolkien's Images of Evil." In George CLARK and Dan TIMMONS (eds). 2000. *J.R.R. Tolkien and his Literary Resonances: Views of Middle-earth*. Westport CT: Greenwood Press, 183-198.

2003. "Foreword." in Jared LOBDELL (ed.). 2003. *A Tolkien Compass*. Revised edition. Chicago and La Salle IL: Open Court, vii-xi.

2007. "Literature, Twentieth Century: Influence of Tolkien." In Michael D.C. DROUT (ed.). 2007. *J.R.R. Tolkien Encyclopedia. Scholarship and Critical Assessment*. London: Routledge, 378-382.

SIMONSON, Martin. 2008. *The Lord of the Rings and the Western Narrative Tradition*. Zurich and Jena: Walking Tree Publishers.

SMITH, Barbara Herrnstein. 1988. *Contingencies of Value. Alternative Perspectives for Critical Theory*. Cambridge MA: Harvard University Press.

STIMPSON, Catherine R. 1969. *J.R.R. Tolkien*. New York: Columbia University Press.

TIMMONS, Dan. 2000. "Introduction." In George CLARK and Dan TIMMONS (eds). 2000. *J.R.R. Tolkien and his Literary Resonances: Views of Middle-earth*. Westport CT: Greenwood Press, 1-10.

TOLKIEN, J.R.R. 1988. *The Annotated Hobbit*. Edited by Douglas A. ANDERSON. London: Unwin Hyman; Boston: Houghton Mifflin.

2005. *Smith of Wooton Major*. Extended edition, edited by Verlyn Flieger. London: HarperCollins.

2006a. *The Letters of J.R.R. Tolkien*. Edited by Humphrey CARPENTER, with the assistance of Christopher TOLKIEN. London: HarperCollins.

2006b. *The Monsters and the Critics and Other Essays*. Edited by Christopher TOLKIEN. London: HarperCollins.

TOULMIN, Stephen. 1990. *Cosmopolis: The Hidden Agenda of Modernity*. Chicago: University of Chicago Press.

TOYNBEE, Philip. 1961. "Review." *The Observer* (6.8.1961).

TURNER, Jenny. 2001. "Reasons for Liking Tolkien." *London Review of Books* 23.22 (15.11.2001). Online at http://www.lrb.co.uk/v23/n22/jenny-turner/reasons-for-liking-tolkien (accessed 21.6.11).

VELDMAN, Meredith. 1994. *Fantasy, the Bomb, and the Greening of Britain: Romantic Protest, 1945-1980*. Cambridge: Cambridge University Press.

WELLS, Sarah (ed.). 2008. *The Ring Goes Ever On. Proceedings of the Tolkien 2005 Conference: 50 Years of The Lord of the Rings*. 2 volumes. Coventry: The Tolkien Society.

WEST, Richard C. 1981. *Tolkien: An Annotated Checklist*. Second edition. Kent OH: Kent State University Press.

2004. "A Tolkien Checklist: Selected Criticism 1981-2004." *Modern Fiction Studies* 50.4: 1015-1028.

WILLIAMS, Raymond. 1985. *The Country and the City*. London: Hogarth Press.

WILSON, Edmund. 1956. "Oo, Those Awful Orcs!" *The Nation* 182.15 (14.04.1956): 312-314; reprinted in his *The Bit between My Teeth*. New York: W.H. Allen, 326-332.

WYNNE, Hilary. 2007. "Tolkien Scholarship: Since 1980." In Michael D.C. DROUT (ed.). 2007. *J.R.R. Tolkien Encyclopedia. Scholarship and Critical Assessment*. London: Routledge, 659-662.

Review of *Reading 'The Lord of the Rings': New Writings on Tolkien's Classic*, edited by Robert Eaglestone. London: Continuum, 2005

My first impression of this book evoked uncomfortable memories of an earlier effort: *J.R.R. Tolkien: This Far Land*, edited by Robert Giddings (1984). This deeply eccentric if pioneering collection included papers which verged on parody, evoking images of earnest young academics, mostly in polytechnics, for whom Tolkien functioned mostly as grist for new critical mills. It is clear from the present volume, however, that things have moved on. Compared with two decades ago, there have been two signal improvements: Eaglestone and his contributors evince much greater theoretical sophistication, and they take Tolkien's work more seriously. In short, *Reading 'The Lord of the Rings'* realizes its goal – "to reintegrate *The Lord of the Rings* into the broad sweep of current literary critical and theoretical interests" (2) – with impressive success.

Eaglestone's introduction offers a useful supplement to Shippey's analysis of *The Lord of the Rings* as a quintessentially twentieth-century work, including new insights into Tolkien's rhetoric. His own chapter, "Invisibility", draws on Emmanuel Levinas and Alasdair MacIntyre to reveal the integral connection between evil and invisibility. This point is ably contextualized in terms of the modernist and especially Cartesian valorization and project of instituting a freedom which is radically non-participative – and, as such, ontologically inauthentic if not impossible.

Michael Drout's offering, "Towards a Better Tolkien Criticism", offers some valuable pointers in that regard although, being confined to chapter-length, it is unavoidably more programmatic than substantive. Even so, it is highly refreshing to encounter Roland Barthes, Michel Foucault and Stanley Fish, all skilfully handled, in the context of Tolkien studies. And one can only agree that "Tolkien Studies" (by scholars) and "Middle-earth Studies" (by fans), instead of indulging in mutual hostility, should be mutually enriching.

First published in *Tolkien Studies* 4 (2007) pp. 297-302.

Drout also criticizes some scholars as "over-invested in the truth of [Tolkien's] *Letters*" as "a transparent, unambiguous guide to the 'real meaning' of Tolkien's literature" (20). That would indeed be a mistake; however, is such a use of the *Letters* really that common? And surely it is defensible to use them as a guide to Tolkien's own conscious intentions, beliefs and values, and how those affected what he wrote. That, at any rate, is my practice (which, in addition, does not extend to equally naïve assertions of *The Lord of the Rings*'s "real meaning").

Certainly Barry Longford, in the following chapter on "Time", has no hesitation in drawing on the *Letters* in order to break down the "narrative extension" of *The Lord of the Rings* into its linguistic, geographical and temporal components. He then uses this analysis to identify Jackson's films as "relentlessly present-tense and ruthlessly goal-oriented," the effect of which is to close down the possibility "for critical reflection or ethical engagement" that is such a distinctive mark of the book (43, 46). Again, it is hard to disagree. One bad academic habit is in evidence here, however, if not egregiously so: if specialist jargon such as "lisible" and "scriptable" is going to be used – neither of which appear in the *Shorter OED* – then it should also be explained. (True, one could infer their meaning; but with technical terms that is not always reliable.)

Sue Zlosnik's "Gothic Echoes" is one of the weaker papers in this collection. In distinctively modernist manner, she refers to "those who find solace in Tolkien's fake mythology" (58; a phrase repeated from page 50). Not only is this the sort of dismissively patronizing attitude we know too well from Greer and Waugh et al., it also betrays a curiously positivist attitude. What is "real" mythology, from which the contrast must draw its force? Even Homer and Herodotus were interpreters of myth. But in that case, what is "fake"? And her remark that *The Lord of the Rings* encourages "a willing suspension of disbelief in its readers" (50) might carry more conviction if it showed some awareness at least of Tolkien's contrary point, in "On Fairy-Stories" (37), that if disbelief must be suspended by an act of will then the fantasy has already failed.

Zlosnik concludes by quoting, with implicit approval, Ken Gelder, who has attacked contemporary fantasy as a "'literary form of fundamentalism that troubles secular ideals'" and is "'terroristic' in its attack on the modern world"

(58). This sort of unselfcritical literary modernism, with its crypto-religious secularism, was the reason why I once published an essay entitled "Tolkien and his Critics: a Critique" (Curry 2005[1]). To judge by its reception, it filled a much-needed gap and now appears somewhat dated, not least in its over-enthusiastic embrace of postmodernism. But Gelder, and Zlosnik's endorsement of him, makes me think there might be a place for it still.

Adam Roberts, in "The One Ring", reveals a new dimension to Tolkien's choice and use of a ring as the central symbol of his narrative. The result is a fascinating study of the way Tolkien's Catholicism – specifically, the sacramental dimension of the One Ring – found literary expression which deepened that meaning for readers mostly quite unaware of its source.

In "Home", Simon Malpas makes a plausible and tantalizing connection between Martin Heidegger's and Tolkien's responses to what they both perceived (arguably with perspicacity) as the threat of runaway modernity and especially techno-science. This is potentially a rich vein but Malpas's exploration contains an uneasy lacuna. He relies in particular upon Martin Heidegger's lectures on Hölderlin. Does the fact that these were delivered in Germany in the summer of 1942 by a member of the Nazi Party signify nothing? Particularly when, to quote Roz Kaveney later in this collection, there are "attitudes in *The Lord of the Rings* that are sufficiently cognate with racism to have appealed to neo-Nazis" (174)? I myself have defended *The Lord of the Rings* against the charge of racism, but it is worryingly selective to pretend there is no issue here to be discussed.

Malpas also urges upon us the unavoidability of accommodating technological change, arguing that "Tolkien is quite explicit [...] that nothing can simply resist or ignore change" (88). But Tolkien's reluctant embrace of change was principally metaphysical; and metaphysics – as we ought to know from the case of Heidegger – is an unreliable guide to political and social actions. In any case, Malpas may be right, but he is rather too quick to dismiss resistance, if only as a vital part of any eventual positive compromise. Elrond, for one, held a contrary view: "There is nothing you can do, other than to resist, with hope or without it."

---

1 This essay is reprinted on pages 125-90 of the present volume.

Jennifer Neville, on "Women", shows convincingly that the relative marginality of women in Tolkien's fiction is, to a very significant extent, a function not of the literary texts he drew upon but of nineteenth- and twentieth-century literary scholarship. This argument includes both considerable specific detail in *The Lord of the Rings* and a nuanced conclusion regarding the implications for the dimension of gender in Tolkien studies.

In "Masculinity", Holly A. Crocker nearly succumbs to bad academic prose (the pernicious effects of one of her sources, Homi Bhabha on postcolonialism, seem evident), e.g.: "Functioning as an unlocated mode of becoming that subsumes all those who subscribe to its principles, this masculinity compels others to see it as invisible" (113). But this passage, like the paper itself, is far from meaningless; it is simply unnecessarily difficult to follow. And as a matter of fact, what Crocker reveals about masculinity as an organizing principle of, and in, *The Lord of the Rings* is acute and fruitful. My only caveats are that it surely also requires something to be said about the contrary pole, unexamined here, of femininity; and that the whole exercise would be greatly enriched by *adding* the political dimension – unremarked but unmistakably present – of hegemony. (That is, hegemonic gendering, and gendered hegemony.) The best guides here are undoubtedly the post-Marxists Ernesto Laclau and Chantal Mouffe in their now-classic *Hegemony and Socialist Strategy* and subsequent work.

Esther Saxey, in "Homoeroticism", asks whether Frodo and Sam can and should be considered a sexual/romantic couple. There is, of course, no good reason why this should not be a matter for discussion. Unfortunately, however, Saxey falls back on some questionable tactics in order to answer in the affirmative. One is to maintain that the resistance among Tolkien fans to the idea of Frodo and Sam as sexually involved "is a good reason [...] for me to insist on the sexual nature of their relationship" (131). But is that alone *sufficient* reason? Even the most hardened critical theorist would think twice before asserting so. Another problem is castigating objections as "attempts to avoid homosexuality" – a notorious rhetorical ploy to problematize any disagreement. Thus, "the use of Elven language as a token of love between Aragorn and Arwen adds a suggestive note to his exchanges with Legolas, at Helm's Deep and elsewhere" (136). But if I reply, "Not necessarily; after all, Arwen and Legolas are both elves," then I open myself to the charge of engaging in a "heterosexualizing" strategy (with the added possibility of doing so for dubious psychosexual motives of my own). This is no way to enable or conduct intellectual dialogue. It is also curious that Saxey makes no historical allowances for the difficulty, since the early twentieth century, of understanding the hitherto more common reality of socially hierarchical and emotionally intense but non-sexual relationships between men, often Englishmen, without stretching the meaning of "sexual" beyond what makes it useful and meaningful.

Scott Kleinman's "Service" is a useful and original analysis of the confusing and confused intertwining of service (preferable to the more loaded and patronizing "servility") and eroticism in the relationships between Éowyn and Aragorn and Sam and Frodo.

The subject of Barry Atkins's chapter is "Games": that is, "the games of the films of the books" (155). He concludes by suggesting the possibility that computer games might "finally satisfy that desire to enter a fictional world that Tolkien's text has always provoked" (161). Against this, it is worth at least noting Tolkien's own opinion that the desire for fantasy "is only cheated by counterfeits, whether the innocent but clumsy devices of the human dramatist, or the malevolent frauds of the magicians. In this world it is for men unsatisfiable, and so imperishable" ("On Fairy-Stories", 50). When it is ever-increasingly difficult to distinguish between those two elements in the games, and the entire industry is predicated on enormous amounts of money changing hands – a sure sign, to use Tolkien's terminology, of Magic rather than Enchantment – then I know which outcome I would back.

Roz Kaveney concludes the collection with "In the Tradition…". Kaveney once opined (in 1991) that Tolkien's work deserves "intelligent reading but not passionate attention." (I am indebted to her for this, since it was a major spur for my own writings, albeit in an attempt to prove her wrong.) Perhaps for that reason, she demonstrates a lack of the sure touch that one associates with Tolkien's best critics. Is there, for example, really a "sense that all will, in the end, be well that pervades *The Lord of the Rings*" (164)? Or is not *The Lord of the Rings* pervaded by just the opposite: an unassuagable sense of loss, even in apparent victory? Perhaps both; but then a balanced assessment would address both. She also remarks that Tolkien's success inaugurated fantasy as "a literature of comfort" (169). But is it not possible, borrowing from Geoffrey Grigson, to be comforted without being content? I persist in believing that the idea of "radical nostalgia", which I discussed in *Defending Middle-earth*, remains a more promising and under-valued one for understanding much of Tolkien's appeal.

Regrettably, then, there is, in Kaveney's contribution and elsewhere here, a lingering sense of elitist modernism about which Tolkien's pointed remark about critics "confusing, not always by sincere error, the Escape of the Prisoner with the Flight of the Deserter" ("On Fairy-Stories", 56) remains the aptest comment. Yet I would myself be guilty of ideological one-sidedness if I did not recognize the quality of Kaveney's discussion of post-Tolkienian fantasy, especially the work of Terry Brooks, Stephen Donaldson, Robert Jordan, Terry Goodkind and Tad Williams. She is particularly acute on Ursula Le Guin's complex relationship with and debts, both positive and reactive, to Tolkien. And the same general point applies to the collection as a whole. In short, then, it is indisputably a good thing, and a sign of the rude new health of Tolkien studies.

Works Cited

CURRY, Patrick. 2004. *Defending Middle-earth: Tolkien, Myth and Modernity.* Second edition. First edition 1997. Boston MA: Houghton Mifflin.

2005. "Tolkien and his Critics: a Critique." In Thomas HONEGGER (ed.). 2005. *Root and Branch: Approaches Towards Understanding Tolkien.* Second edition. First edition 1999. Zurich and Berne: Walking Tree Publishers, 75-146.[2]

KAVENEY, Roz. 1991. "The Ring Recycled." *New Statesman and Society* (20 & 27.12.1991).

LACLAU, Ernesto and Chantal MOUFFE. 1985. *Hegemony and Socialist Strategy: Towards a Radical and Plural Democracy.* London: Verso.

TOLKIEN, J.R.R. 1988. "On Fairy-Stories." In J.R.R. TOLKIEN. 1988. *Tree and Leaf.* London: Unwin Hyman, 9-73.

---

2 Reprinted on pages 125-90 of the present volume.

PART IV

VARIA

Approaches to Myth in Middle-earth

Abstract

In this paper, I discuss the intellectual resources and their approaches – including both their theories and values – that I have found most useful in understanding myth in Tolkien's work, especially *The Lord of the Rings*. I am primarily concerned not with his sources, nor even his uses, but rather the mythic resonances that readers find in his literary myth. Those resources are principally the work of Roberto Calasso, Milton Scarborough, Max Horkheimer and Theodor Adorno, and Sean Kane. These are contrasted (favourably) with that of Frederic Jameson. I also distinguish between the myths of Paleolithic/Mesolithic hunter-gatherers and those of Neolithic/Bronze Age agricultural and increasingly urban origin; both are present in *The Lord of the Rings*, but the former occupy a particularly important place in the context (or so I argue) of the increasingly pathological effects of "late modernity", of which that book constitutes an implicit critique.

I am not going to try to present a fully worked-out position here on mythology in the work of Tolkien (and by "work" I mean primarily that which has most taken the public imagination: in other words, principally, *The Lord of the Rings*). To some extent I have already tried to do so in my *Defending Middle-earth: Tolkien, Myth and Modernity*, albeit one written in more popular than academic mode.[1] My concern, both there and here, is not with the sources of Tolkien's literary mythology, nor even what he rightly claimed as more interesting, his use of them, but with the "applicability" (as he termed it, to distinguish it from deliberate allegory) that many readers find in his books; and although nothing I say should be taken to deny the importance of other dimensions or meanings, I do want to suggest that in this applicability, myth plays a crucial role. So I would like to tell you about the sources, including their approaches – which in turn, it is important to acknowledge,

First published in Maria Kuteeva (ed.). 2000. *The Ways of Creative Mythologies. Imagined Worlds and Their Makers*. Two volumes. Telford: The Tolkien Society, volume 1: 45-52.

1 See also my paper "Tolkien and his Critics: a Critique" (pages 125-90 of this volume).

includes not just their theories but their values – which I found most helpful in doing justice to this subject.

That simply cannot be done without first also admitting a crucial fact: in Tolkien's work, myth is still alive. Or as he put it, "myth is alive at once and in all its parts, and dies before it can be dissected" (Tolkien 1997: 15). (Which is not to say, of course, that it cannot be dissected; only that the results will do nothing to explain what it was and does when it is alive.) This is still a radical position in the academy. Among probably thousands of other professional intellectuals, for example, Habermas has spoken of "the conditions of a disenchanted and demythologized world." Unlike many, he has warned that we must therefore guard against "losing the illumination of the semantic potential which was once preserved in myth" (Dews 1995: 11). I am sympathetic, but who is "we", and where is this world?[2] I suppose it could be argued that myth is no longer a central cultural organizing force to the extent it was a couple of thousand years ago, although that would actually be a very difficult proposition to establish. But in any case, to pick the example closest to hand, many of Tolkien's millions of readers have no difficulty in experiencing his enchanted and mythologized fictional world as alive: and they don't have to leave this world or their present lives to do so. Nor is there is any good reason why this should not be the case, rather than amounting to some kind of aberration or illusion.

The kind of attitude thus required was wonderfully put by the Indologist Heinrich Zimmer (1948: 1-3):

> The dilettante – Italian "dilettante" (present participle of the verb "dilet-tare", "to take delight in") – is one who takes delight in something [...]. The moment we abandon this dilettante attitude toward the images of folklore and myth and begin to feel certain about their proper interpretation (as professional comprehenders, handling the tool of an infallible method), we deprive ourselves of the quickening contact, the demonic and inspiring as-sault that is the effect of their intrinsic virtue. We forfeit our proper humility and openmindedness before the unknown, and refuse to be instructed. [...] What they demand of us is not the monologue of the coroner's report, but the dialogue of a living conversation.

---

2 Cf. Bruno Latour, *We Have Never Been Modern*.

Now a powerful more recent work on myth which takes this attitude as a starting-point, and which, for that reason, casts some useful light on Tolkien, is Roberto Calasso's *The Marriage of Cadmus and Harmony* (1988). He writes:

> We shouldn't be too concerned about having lost many of the secrets of the myths, although we must learn to sense their absence, the vastness of what remains undeciphered. To be nostalgic would be like wanting to see, on raising our eyes to the sky, seven Sirens, each intoning a different note around each of the seven heavens. Not only do we not see the Sirens but we can't even make out the heavens any more. And yet we can still draw that tattered cloth around us, still immerse ourselves in the mutilated stories of the gods. And in the world, as in our minds, the same cloth is still being woven. (Calasso 1988: 280)

The remarkable thing, as you will discover if you read Calasso, is that he is not merely being polite here; he means it. Perhaps that is why he unintentionally provides a wonderfully apt description of Tolkien's despairing efforts to put his own attempt at "primary myth" – *The Silmarillion* – in order:

> The mythographer lives in a permanent state of chronological vertigo, which he pretends to want to resolve. But while on one table he puts generations and dynasties in order [...] you can be sure that on another table the muddle is getting worse and the threads ever more entangled. No mythographer has ever managed to put his material together in a consistent sequence, yet all set out to impose order. In this they have been faithful to the myth. The mythical gesture is a wave which, as it breaks, assumes a shape, the way dice form a number when we toss them. But, as the wave withdraws, the unvanquished complications swell in the undertow, and likewise the muddle and the disorder from which the next mythical gesture will be formed. So myth allows of no system. Indeed, when it first came into being, system itself was no more than a flap on a god's cloak, a minor bequest of Apollo. (Calasso 1988: 281)

(There was another and more particular reason for Tolkien's failure too, which we shall come to later.) Calasso sees that "myth is the precedent behind every action, its invisible, ever-present lining" (Calasso 1988: 383) – a statement one can well imagine Tolkien approving. In this sense, myth is practically (I mean, in practice) indistinguishable from metaphysics. As Peter Dews' book on that subject concurs, "the end of myth can itself only be recounted as myth" (Dews 1995: 13). This leads me to another work which I found indispensable: Milton Scarborough's *Myth and Modernity: Postcritical Reflections* (1994). "Postcritical" refers here to the work of Michael Polanyi, who showed that the grounds of our knowledge-claims can never be exhaustively or ultimately specified (but not, *pace* some versions of poststructuralism, that knowledge-claims cannot be made at all). As Scarborough points out, since theories and criteria of truth are already myth-dependent, the

> ultimate assessment of myth must be of a kind suited to the nature of myth as giving expression to apprehensions of the life-world and as functioning to provide an orientation for living in that world. Within those strictures myth is neither true nor false *in a theoretical sense* but viable or not viable for the tasks (both theoretical and otherwise) which confront us. This viability is not determined in intellectual terms but in the very process of living, by whether or not one is energized, whether or not problems are being solved, whether or not it is endowed with a significance that pulls one toward the future in hope. (Scarborough 1994: 110)

I need hardly stress the resonances of this suggestion with the experience of Tolkien's readers that that is precisely what his books do. And as Scarborough adds, "Viability is not determined in advance of inhabiting a myth" (1994: 110) – which is precisely what the great majority of Tolkien's hostile professional literary critics try to do: and why they so consistently miss the mark. Incidentally, Scarborough has other fascinating and tantalizing suggestions to make, notably that myth is not metaphorical (cf. Scarborough 1994: 90-93). I cannot follow this up here, partly because of lack of space and partly because I don't altogether understand it myself.

The theoretical assumption of a single, completely and unproblematically disenchanted world, as revealed in Habermas's remark, is not only typical in its arrogance of this professional caste; even when "defending" myth, as he seems to be trying to do, it starts by already conceding just that central, deeply self-interested and erroneous claim to those trying the hardest to destroy mythic enchantment: trying, that is, under cover of strenuously asserting that it *is* true, to *make* it true. This is an enormous and complicated issue, and for that reason I am going to be irritating and refer you to elsewhere for an explication,[3] but my umbrella term for this anti-mythic programme is "modernism": *not* as a particular cultural, architectural, literary or whatever movement but as, so to speak, the self-consciousness of modernity. (Another strong candidate is "humanism", provided that it is understood in contemporary and not, for example, classical terms.) Modernism in this sense can be seen to comprise three

---

3 Namely *Defending Middle-Earth*, where it is a principal argument, and "Tolkien and his Critics".

interlocking empires: international financial capital, state-power, and modern science and technology. Insofar as the last represents the "intellectual" wing of modernity (and as such, is further analyzable in terms of philosophical realism and rationalism), it is the mode most directly and violently involved in what Barbara Herrnstein Smith memorably summarized as "the effort to identify the presumptively universally compelling Truth and Way and to compel it universally" (Smith 1991: 179). For brevity, let's call this programme "scientism", the cult of science.

Here is where another remarkable book comes into its own: Max Horkheimer and Theodor W. Adorno's *The Dialectic of Enlightenment* (first published in 1944). I am not going to try to sum up this extraordinarily bleak blast against the modern myth of enlightened scientific, technological and managerial progress. It managed to embarrass almost everyone, from Horkheimer and Adorno's own Marxist colleagues to the massed ranks of post-war enlightened administrators and their adjutants themselves; even, it seems, its own older and more sensible authors. But there is still a great deal to learn from Horkheimer and Adorno's chilling account. They argue that the "program of the Enlightenment was the disenchantment of the world; the dissolution of myths and the substitution of knowledge for fancy" (Horkheimer and Adorno 1994: 20). So far so good, perhaps, except that this brave new knowledge, which they identify as "instrumental reason", successfully disguises its own mythicity. This bad faith "turns it into an instrument of rational administration by the wholly enlightened as they steer society toward barbarism" (Horkheimer and Adorno 1994: 18). And note that to agree that Enlightenment reason, in its various forms from political to economic to scientific, is really disenchanted – that is, disinterested, objective, universal and so on – to do so is to open wide the door to such barbarism. So it must be seen in its true colours: a counter-spell, not just a modern form of willed magic but the most powerful, as Tolkien recognized, in Middle-earth.

As Horkheimer and Adorno point out, drawing directly on Weber, such a campaign, in its aspirations to universality, requires both reason and religion to "condemn the principle of magic enchantment" (1994: 5). A fundamental prerequisite of the disenchantment of the world is "the extirpation of animism […] [and the] destruction of gods and qualities alike" (Horkheimer and Adorno 1944: 7). Why? Because, to put it simply, a single universal truth, whether spiritual or material, cannot permit any exceptions let alone rivals. And the point about animistic spirits, gods and qualities is that they are plural and unique.

The battleground for this campaign is typically nature. Is nature single, entirely material and inanimate (that is, even living beings operate essentially mechanically and are not meaningfully sentient); or is it ultimately mysterious and alive – in the words of Louis MacNeice, "incorrigibly plural"? As Alkis Kontos (1994: 224-25) has pointed out, a still enchanted (or re-enchanted) nature is inexhaustible, mysterious, imbued with spirits: "It was the spiritual dimension of the world, its enchanted, magical quality that rendered it infinite, not amenable to complete calculability [...] it permitted and invited mythologization."

One such world is, of course, precisely Middle-earth. I have argued elsewhere that nature is absolutely central to Tolkien's literary *mythos* in such a way as to include both spirit, just as Kontos specifies, and community (paradigmatically, the Hobbits). There is only one regime attempting to impose a single, rigid order upon all of Middle-earth, which requires the obliteration of all differences, localisms and meaningful particularities; that is Mordor.

This point brings me to my last book, Sean Kane's *Wisdom of the Mythtellers* (1994). This is itself a wise book. It recognizes with Calasso that myth is alive today, with Scarborough that myths must be inhabited in order to be judged, and with Horkheimer and Adorno that the onslaught of modernist/humanist reason "is the account of an increasing privatization of the narratives of the earth" (Kane 1994: 248). But as the last quotation implies, Kane gives the subject of myth a twist which is particularly illuminating for Tolkien (and much else besides).

In relation to mythology, we usually think of those of the agricultural Neolithic peoples and their increasingly urbanized and sophisticated Bronze Age heirs, with their humanoid gods and goddesses familiar to us from the Greek, Celtic and Norse pantheons. But Kane points out that underlying, coexisting with and in some places surviving these myths is the much older mythology of Paleolithic and Mesolithic hunter-gatherers, for whom all life on earth was "intelligent kin"

(Kane 1994: 19), and the countless living power-sites and sanctuaries had not yet been increasingly replaced by a single, increasingly rigid boundary between human and nonhuman world. In this way, moving backwards in time, we pass from a working definition of myth as "stories about the gods" (Kane 1994: 240), through stories about (in Kane's words) "'something mysterious', invisible and whole" (Kane 1994: 45; which I think Calasso would also accept), to "stories about nature" (Kane 1994: 33), whereby "The proper subject of myth is the ideas and emotions of the earth" (Kane 1994: 34).

But there is also a strong if ultimately inexplicable sense of moving forward to arrive at the same kind of understanding. For as global ecological crisis deepens, as the human race as a whole becomes increasingly mired in a way of life – call it international consumer capitalism, for short – that is the acme of destructive unsustainability, a few of its members are groping towards an ethos (both a perception and an ethic) by which we may truly live and let live. And this movement is a re-discovery of something, simultaneously mythic and intensely practical, that people once knew. As Kane (1994: 50) puts it:

> Wisdom about nature, that wisdom heard and told in animated pattern, that pattern rendered in such a way as to preserve a place whole and sacred, safe from human meddling: these are the concepts with which to begin an exploration of myth. Of these, the notion of the sanctity of place is vital. It anchors the other concepts [...] Once the power of the place is lost to memory, myth is uprooted; knowledge of the earth's processes becomes a different kind of knowledge, manipulated and applied by man.

I suggest that such wisdom, in what Tolkien called "the mythical mode of imagination" (Tolkien 1997: 15), is at the heart of Tolkien's work; and that it turns most vitally, for his readers, on restoring a sense of the sanctity of place. As Kane (1994: 256) remarks, "the wisdom of the Earth has ways of re-seeding itself." I think *The Lord of the Rings* is just such a re-seeding.

Despite its local origins, then – Sarehole, the West Midlands, and the North-West of the Old World – Tolkien's literary mythology has acquired relative universality in two ways. One is through the contingent fact that the economic, political and cultural process of modernization is now truly global. To the extent that Tolkien's fiction is, in the experience of his readers and among other things, a mythic critique of that process – and what more effective way to counter a scientistic and utilitarian world-view than in a mythically imaginative way? – it too acquires global meaning. Relevant here is Virginia Luling's shrewd suggestion that Middle-earth is a Europe that has never been Europeanized or (what amounts to the same thing) modernized: a Fourth World Europe of indigenous peoples where imperialism, the Industrial Revolution and nation-state power has never seen the light of day – except, of course, through Mordor (cf. Luling 1995).

Tolkien's other route to universality, probably equally unintentionally, is through the fact that there is nowhere in the world without some indigenous tradition of a mythical way of relating to the world in which it is alive and saturated with spiritual meaning: enchanted, in a word. Those traditions may be deeply buried; they may only exist in most readers' minds now as a dim ancestral memory of a "small" and ostensibly primitive rural or wild folk who knew how to live on nature's terms. Nonetheless, as Kane (1994: 238) notes, the "gods have not been silenced; in fact, they have been driven underground." They can still be revived by recognition. And as the first, negatively driven kind of universality grinds on, the second positive kind of rediscovery becomes ever more urgently relevant – which is at least one reason why Tolkien's books, so extremely unlikely on the face of it, have had about 100 million readers with no sign of let-up. (Credit where it's due, even if the irony is awful: Rupert Murdoch perceived this as a good bet where countless literary critics have failed.)

This is not to suggest that the mythicity of *The Lord of the Rings* isn't complex, or – although it is not my real interest – that Tolkien himself felt unambivalent about it. It seems to me that Tolkien's *mythos* is balanced between, and includes, both the powerful anthropocentric sky-gods of Neolithic myth and the more ancient Paleolithic earth-mysteries and vegetable gods and goddesses. The Valar, for example, are plainly enough the former; whereas the Ents are not people in tree-form, but trees that happen to speak and walk – that is their very point, and wonder – while the Drúedain, whom Théoden and Merry encounter on the way to Minas Tirith, are the indigenous hunter-gatherers themselves. Tolkien's Elves are balanced on the very fulcrum of this shift: humanoid but chthonic, and even if killed, potentially returning to the Earth through reincarnation.

Tolkien personally found this positioning deeply uncomfortable. In the original cosmogonic myth of *The Silmarillion*, the Two Trees of Valinor, Telperion and Laurelin, bore as fruit and blossom the Moon and the Sun before they succumbed to Morgoth's poison. Beginning in the late 1950s, however, he was assailed by self-doubts as to "the astronomically absurd business of the making of the Sun and Moon" and tried to purify this *legendarium*. But the vegetable birth of the luminaries was integrally related to other elements which he needed to retain, and Tolkien died without ever having succeeded in resolving the resulting inconsistencies. As his son Christopher (Tolkien 1993: 371-72) remarked:

> I think it possible that it was the actual nature of this myth that led him finally to abandon it. It is in conception beautiful, and not absurd; but it is exceedingly "primitive" [...] [Tolkien's] grave and tranquil words cannot entirely suppress a sense that there emerges here an outcropping, as it were, uneroded, from an older level, more fantastic, more bizarre.

I would be remiss if, before concluding, I didn't give you some idea of the kind of approach to myth that I didn't find helpful. Since this is less interesting and important, however, I shall content myself with mentioning only one: Frederic Jameson's "Magical Narratives: Romance as Genre" (1975). The perfect example of a coroner's report, *de haut en bas*, over the corpse of myth, Jameson's dissection commends Vladimir Propp's structuralist analysis of folktales as "a process of abstraction, whereby surface events or elements are assimilated to emptier and ever more general categories." But he then criticizes it as "still too meaningful". He wants "a type of analysis which aims at seeing the entire narrative in terms of a single [...] mechanism" (Jameson 1975: 146-48). But myth allows of no system ... while still alive. And what better statement of the modernist dream, with its monistic and universalist fanaticism, could be imagined? As Horkheimer and Adorno (1994: 7) pointed out, "its ideal is the system from which all and everything follows." Wouldn't that just make everything simpler for "the high and ultimate purpose: Knowledge, Rule, Order"?[4] Gandalf recognized in the grand words of this overture the voice of Mordor; and if we are wise, so will we.

---

4 Saruman to Gandalf (FR.II.ii).

Bibliography

CALASSO, Roberto. 1988. *The Marriage of Cadmus and Harmony*. Originally published 1983. London: Jonathan Cape.

DEWS, Peter. 1995. *The Limits of Disenchantment*. London: Verso.

JAMESON, Frederic. 1975. "Magical Narratives: Romance as Genre." *New Literary
History* 7.1: 135-163.

KANE, Sean. 1994. *Wisdom of the Mythtellers*. Peterborough: Broadview Press.

KONTOS, Alkis. 1994. "The World Disenchanted, and the Return of Gods and
Demons." In Asher HOROWITZ and Terry MALEY (eds.). 1994. *The Barbarism
of Reason: Max Weber and the Twilight of Enlightenment*. Toronto: University of
Toronto Press, 223-247.

LATOUR, Bruno. 1993. *We Have Never Been Modern*. Hemel Hempstead: Harvester
Wheatsheaf.

LULING, Virginia. 1995. "An Anthropologist in Middle-earth." In Patricia
REYNOLDS and Glen H. GOODKNIGHT (eds.). 1995. *Proceedings of the J.R.R.
Tolkien Centenary Conference*. Milton Keynes: The Tolkien Society/Altadena
CA: The Mythopoeic Press, 53-57.

SCARBOROUGH, Milton. *Myth and Modernity: Postcritical Reflections*. Albany NY:
SUNY.

SMITH, Barbara Herrnstein. 1991. *Contingencies of Value: Alternative Perspectives for
Critical Theory*. Cambridge MA: Harvard University Press.

TOLKIEN, Christopher (ed.). 1993. *Morgoth's Ring*. London: HarperCollins.

TOLKIEN, J.R.R. 1997. "Beowulf: The Monsters and the Critics." In Christopher
TOLKIEN (ed.). 1997. *The Monsters and the Critics and Other Essays*. London:
HarperCollins, 5-48.

ZIMMER, Heinrich. 1948. *The King and the Corpse: Tales of the Soul's Conquest of
Evil*. Princeton NJ: Princeton University Press.

On Hobbits & Elves: or, Took and Baggins Again

Good evening. It may not be very original to say so, but it's true – I am honoured to be here. And I would like to start by talking a little about originality. In the first place, it is overrated. The desperate search to say (write, paint, record) something that no-one else ever has, has produced a lot of boring and/or trivial art. It has also encouraged people to ignore the well-springs of immense value – cultural, but also personal – which are common, which we all potentially share, and from which people have returned refreshed throughout history. I hardly need to add that Tolkien, as a conservative in the best sense of the word, was well aware of this fact.

Second, originality, when properly understood, is unavoidable anyway. Let me take the handiest example: myself. I have lived with Tolkien's work nearly all my life. But so too, probably, have all of you. I also know a thing or two about it – although, probably, less than all of you. But given that my life is not precisely the same as anyone else's, my perspective on it, "properly understood" – that is, if I am really paying attention – cannot but be original.

Finally, on this particular theme, I thought I would take this opportunity to present my revolutionary and completely new theory that J.R.R. Tolkien was *actually* … a Buddhist. That's right. And what is extraordinary is that no-one ever noticed this before, because once you begin to look, it's obvious. Admittedly, there is little supporting evidence – to date – that Tolkien actually practised Buddhism. But let's just take its canonical starting-point, the first Noble Truth. It states, "Life entails suffering". Now I ask you: did not Tolkien subscribe to this tenet? And where the second Noble Truth holds that suffering has a cause, which is attachment; and the third that attachment can be eliminated; the fourth concerns how to do so – which is by each of us

Given as an After Dinner speech for the Tolkien Society (15.04.2000); first published in Helen Armstrong (ed.). 2001. *Digging Potatoes, Growing Trees*. Vol. 3. Telford: The Tolkien Society, 48-52.

throwing our Ring (*plainly* attachment) back into the Crack of Doom! And that's not all. Take Elbereth – clearly modelled on the feminine Bodhisattva of Compassion: Kuan-yin, Kannon or Avalokiteshvara (her Japanese, Chinese and Tibetan names respectively). As for the map of Middle-earth, have you ever tried superimposing it on one of India? Now Bodhgaya, where the Buddha attained enlightenment, falls *exactly* ...

Well, I could go on; and on. But apart from poking a little fun at some of the literary criticism that Tolkien has indeed been subjected to, I am trying to make a serious point. That I can find some genuine Buddhist truths in the work of a man who never went anywhere near the subject is possible because his work has potentially universal significance; so every human culture and concern can find itself reflected therein. The reason is simply that it addresses universally *human* themes, like death, and loss, and love. And food; and irritating in-laws; and by implication, at least, mobile phones on trains, drum machines below hotel rooms ... (By the way, that includes religion – but only insofar as it too is a fundamentally human preoccupation. Where I part company with Tolkien's religious interpreters is when they reverse that order of priorities. Not all do, of course.)

Now, within that vast range, I actually do want to say something about a tiny but interesting bit of it which I don't recall anyone else much remarking. (In so doing I shall, as usual, avail myself of a liberal portion of "applicability".) Attention has been rightly paid to the pairs (or splits) of Frodo/Gollum, and within the latter, Gollum/Sméagol. But what I want to bring out here – using Bilbo, reasonably enough, as Everyman and Everywoman – is the irreducible tension between one's *Baggins* side and one's *Took* (or in Frodo's case, Brandybuck) side.

The Baggins position is encapsulated in Bilbo's considered (but, appropriately enough, unspoken) reply to the Eagle's rhetorical question, "What is finer than flying?": "A warm bath, and late breakfast on the lawn afterwards." I have always felt a profound affinity with that sentiment. And indeed, the virtues of good food, bed, and hot water are rightly praised throughout Tolkien's books. (Or, for that matter, just plain water as such; which takes us into the ecological domain, where – having already banged on about it at length in print – I am not going to go tonight.) But we should also note that taken *alone*, the Baggins virtues and their adherents tend to descend into the stuffy, provincial and boring materialism and respectability that neither Tolkien, Bilbo nor Frodo admired or liked. And materialism and respectability have always returned the favour, to Tolkien and hobbits alike.

In the case of these particular hobbits, however, there was little danger of that fate. For whenever *bourgeois* (or perhaps I should say, middling) security became too strong – and therefore always unexpectedly – the Took side grew restless, and found or engineered a crisis that involved one of those "nasty, disturbing, uncomfortable things" that always make you late for dinner: an adventure. And that's the thing about adventures – the odds can be shortened or lengthened, but there really are no guarantees that they will turn out well. (That's what makes them adventures.) But without them, there wouldn't have been much to say in *The Hobbit* or *The Lord of the Rings* or *The Silmarillion*, would there? By the same token, the story of our own lives would be dead boring; or rather, perhaps, just dead. And there is really something to be said for living while you are alive. In addition, of course, there is what Gildor pointed out to Frodo: "The wide world is all about you: you can fence yourselves in, but you cannot for ever fence it out."

There is also a danger with being just a Took, however. Flying loses its savour, and even sense, if you can never alight and stop for a while. Perhaps, like me, you have known someone who has been at it so long that their life has become a desperate flight from everything: love as well as loss. Similarly, it is little appreciated that just as the unfulfilled soul of a Took longs for the Mountains or the Sea, to an undernourished Baggins the "woods and fields and little rivers" of the Shire can be a prospect more intoxicating than any paradise complete with ambrosia and *houris*. That is perhaps why I have always found the opening chapters of *The Lord of the Rings*, which strike some readers as twee, very affecting. (I am also reminded of an immortal remark of Peter Cook's about the theatre: "I don't want to see plays about rape, sodomy and drug addiction … I can get all that at home.")

As so often, therefore, the essential skill is to be able to move between these two apparently incompatible domains. It is the paradoxical combination of

Baggins and Took in one life and one person that works best – to the extent that anything does, and to the extent that such a difficult feat can be mastered. (I personally think it can – but not always, and never easily.)

However – as a Baggins by temperament who, a couple of years ago, found himself willy-nilly embarked on a new adventure, called "my life" – I want to explore the Took side of things a little more closely, before I end. It seems to me to have a close affinity with what Tolkien called "Enchantment", and thus Elves, the pre-eminent practitioners of Enchantment. Now Tolkien was very clear that *Faërie* is a "Perilous realm". This was no mere conceit; the state of Enchantment, and its exemplars in human form, are indeed perilous, especially from the Baggins point of view. Every important encounter between a human and an elf in the history of Middle-earth – and particularly where one is male and the other female – was intense to a clinically dangerous degree, and fraught with profound sorrow as well as joy. Elves are not, and never can be, human (that's what makes them Elves ... among other things) and, equally to the point, *vice-versa*. Compared to humans Elves are, as Tolkien pointed out, *super*-natural. You may interpret this how you will, in terms of Jungian archetypes, angelic beings or whatever, but it remains true. So however fruitful their intercourse (in the broadest sense), it is a serious mistake to confuse the two. And although it is often in relationships this sort of thing occurs, that point also applies more impersonally to *the* Elvish, i.e. *Faërie*; because it can happen that an idea, in whatever form it may take, casts a dangerously creative, obsessively inspiring spell.

Therefore, if you should chance (as we say in Middle-earth) to meet someone or something who for you embodies, perhaps literally, Tolkien's definition of Enchantment – "the realisation of imagined wonder" – beware! It would be much the most sensible course of action to look, and walk, the other way. And yet ... would you? And should you be blamed, if you do not? In an essay of Montaigne's, he describes the extraordinary courage, even cheerfulness, with which various Christian martyrs bore the most horrible tortures; and then he adds that although this is indeed admirable, yet there is also something less than human – or more, but in any case, something *in*human – about these men. I think the same is true in this case.

Granted, you may get to a point where the advice of Randy Newman becomes sound: "Forget your foolish dreams and schemes that things will work out in the end / And put some real mileage between you & the object of your love, my friend." But to succumb to Enchantment from the beginning – no matter how it ends – is "only", as they say, human. Just don't expect (as I did) to be able to go back to everything as it was, when the spell breaks (as it will); because by then, "everything" will have changed. So the vital work then becomes to make room in your life once again for all those local, mundane and grounding, not to say earthy, Baggins virtues, and to re-establish some balance. Until, of course, you meet her, or him, or it, again. Or start to wish you would …

Thank you. And good luck!

Walking Tree Publishers
Zurich and Jena

Walking Tree Publishers was founded in 1997 as a forum for publication of material (books, videos, CDs, etc.) related to Tolkien and Middle-earth studies.

Please also visit our web pages:
http://www.walking-tree.org

Cormarë Series

The *Cormarë Series* collects papers and studies dedicated exclusively to the exploration of Tolkien's work. It comprises monographs, thematic collections of essays, conference volumes, and reprints of important yet no longer (easily) accessible papers by leading scholars in the field. Manuscripts and project proposals are evaluated by members of an independent board of advisors who support the series editors in their endeavour to provide the readers with qualitatively superior yet accessible studies on Tolkien and his work.

News from the Shire and Beyond. Studies on Tolkien
Peter Buchs and Thomas Honegger (eds.), Zurich and Berne 2004, Reprint, First edition 1997 (Cormarë Series 1), ISBN 978-3-9521424-5-5

Root and Branch. Approaches Towards Understanding Tolkien
Thomas Honegger (ed.), Zurich and Berne 2005, Reprint, First edition 1999 (Cormarë Series 2), ISBN 978-3-905703-01-6

Richard Sturch, *Four Christian Fantasists. A Study of the Fantastic Writings of George MacDonald, Charles Williams, C.S. Lewis and J.R.R. Tolkien*
Zurich and Berne 2007, Reprint, First edition 2001 (Cormarë Series 3), ISBN 978-3-905703-04-7

Tolkien in Translation
Thomas Honegger (ed.), Zurich and Jena 2011, Reprint, First edition 2003 (Cormarë Series 4), ISBN 978-3-905703-15-3

Mark T. Hooker, *Tolkien Through Russian Eyes*
Zurich and Berne 2003 (Cormarë Series 5), ISBN 978-3-9521424-7-9

Translating Tolkien: Text and Film
Thomas Honegger (ed.), Zurich and Jena 2011, Reprint, First edition 2004 (Cormarë Series 6), ISBN 978-3-905703-16-0

Christopher Garbowski, *Recovery and Transcendence for the Contemporary Mythmaker. The Spiritual Dimension in the Works of J.R.R. Tolkien*
Zurich and Berne 2004, Reprint, First Edition by Marie Curie Sklodowska, University Press, Lublin 2000, (Cormarë Series 7), ISBN 978-3-9521424-8-6

Reconsidering Tolkien
Thomas Honegger (ed.), Zurich and Berne 2005 (Cormarë Series 8), ISBN 978-3-905703-00-9

Tolkien and Modernity 1
Frank Weinreich and Thomas Honegger (eds.), Zurich and Berne 2006 (Cormarë Series 9), ISBN 978-3-905703-02-3

Tolkien and Modernity 2
Thomas Honegger and Frank Weinreich (eds.), Zurich and Berne 2006 (Cormarë Series 10), ISBN 978-3-905703-03-0

Tom Shippey, *Roots and Branches. Selected Papers on Tolkien by Tom Shippey*
Zurich and Berne 2007 (Cormarë Series 11), ISBN 978-3-905703-05-4

Ross Smith, *Inside Language. Linguistic and Aesthetic Theory in Tolkien*
Zurich and Jena 2011, Reprint, First edition 2007 (Cormarë Series 12),
ISBN 978-3-905703-20-7

How We Became Middle-earth. A Collection of Essays on The Lord of the Rings
Adam Lam and Nataliya Oryshchuk (eds.), Zurich and Berne 2007 (Cormarë Series 13), ISBN 978-3-905703-07-8

Myth and Magic. Art According to the Inklings
Eduardo Segura and Thomas Honegger (eds.), Zurich and Berne 2007 (Cormarë Series 14), ISBN 978-3-905703-08-5

The Silmarillion - Thirty Years On
Allan Turner (ed.), Zurich and Berne 2007 (Cormarë Series 15),
ISBN 978-3-905703-10-8

Martin Simonson, *The Lord of the Rings and the Western Narrative Tradition*
Zurich and Jena 2008 (Cormarë Series 16), ISBN 978-3-905703-09-2

Tolkien's Shorter Works. Proceedings of the 4th Seminar of the Deutsche Tolkien Gesellschaft & Walking Tree Publishers Decennial Conference
Margaret Hiley and Frank Weinreich (eds.), Zurich and Jena 2008 (Cormarë Series 17), ISBN 978-3-905703-11-5

Tolkien's The Lord of the Rings: Sources of Inspiration
Stratford Caldecott and Thomas Honegger (eds.), Zurich and Jena 2008 (Cormarë Series 18), ISBN 978-3-905703-12-2

J.S. Ryan, *Tolkien's View: Windows into his World*
Zurich and Jena 2009 (Cormarë Series 19), ISBN 978-3-905703-13-9

Music in Middle-earth
Heidi Steimel and Friedhelm Schneidewind (eds.), Zurich and Jena 2010 (Cormarë Series 20), ISBN 978-3-905703-14-6

Liam Campbell, *The Ecological Augury in the Works of JRR Tolkien*
Zurich and Jena 2011 (Cormarë Series 21), ISBN 978-3-905703-18-4

Margaret Hiley, *The Loss and the Silence. Aspects of Modernism in the Works of C.S. Lewis, J.R.R. Tolkien and Charles Williams*
Zurich and Jena 2011 (Cormarë Series 22), ISBN 978-3-905703-19-1

Rainer Nagel, *Hobbit Place-names. A Linguistic Excursion through the Shire*
Zurich and Jena 2012 (Cormarë Series 23), ISBN 978-3-905703-22-1

Christopher MacLachlan, *Tolkien and Wagner: The Ring and Der Ring*
Zurich and Jena 2012 (Cormarë Series 24), ISBN 978-3-905703-21-4

Renée Vink, *Wagner and Tolkien: Mythmakers*
Zurich and Jena 2012 (Cormarë Series 25), ISBN 978-3-905703-25-2

The Broken Scythe. Death and Immortality in the Works of J.R.R. Tolkien
Roberto Arduini and Claudio Antonio Testi (eds.), Zurich and Jena 2012
(Cormarë Series 26), ISBN 978-3-905703-26-9

Sub-creating Middle-earth: Constructions of Authorship and the Works of J.R.R. Tolkien
Judith Klinger (ed.), Zurich and Jena 2012 (Cormarë Series 27),
ISBN 978-3-905703-27-6

Tolkien's Poetry
Julian Eilmann and Allan Turner (eds.), Zurich and Jena 2013
(Cormarë Series 28), ISBN 978-3-905703-28-3

O, What a Tangled Web. Tolkien and Medieval Literature. A View from Poland
Barbara Kowalik (ed.), Zurich and Jena 2013 (Cormarë Series 29),
ISBN 978-3-905703-29-0

J.S. Ryan, *In the Nameless Wood*
Zurich and Jena 2013 (Cormarë Series 30), ISBN 978-3-905703-30-6

From Peterborough to Faëry: The Poetics and Mechanics of Secondary Worlds
Thomas Honegger & Dirk Vanderbeke (eds.), Zurich and Jena 2014
(Cormarë Series 31), ISBN 978-3-905703-31-3

Tolkien and Philosophy
Roberto Arduini and Claudio R. Testi (eds.), Zurich and Jena 2014
(Cormarë Series 32), ISBN 978-3-905703-32-0

Patrick Curry, *Deep Roots in a Time of Frost. Essays on Tolkien*
(Cormarë Series 33), ISBN 978-3-905703-33-7

Paul H. Kocher, *The Three Ages of Middle-earth*
Zurich and Jena, forthcoming

Beowulf and the Dragon

The original Old English text of the 'Dragon Episode' of *Beowulf* is set in an authentic font and bound in hardback creating a high quality art book. Illustrated by Anke Eissmann and accompanied by John Porter's translation. Introduction by Tom Shippey. Limited first edition of 500 copies. 84 pages.

Selected pages can be previewed on:
www.walking-tree.org/beowulf

Beowulf and the Dragon
Zurich and Jena 2009
ISBN 978-3-905703-17-7

The Monster Specialist

Sir Severus le Brewse, among the least known of King Arthur's Round Table knights, is preferred by nature, disposition, and training to fight against monsters rather than other knights. After youthful adventures of errantry with dragons, trolls, vampires, and assorted beasts, Severus joins the brilliant sorceress Lilava to face the Chimaera in The Greatest Monster Battle of All Time to free her folk from an age-old curse. But their adventures don't end there; together they meet elves and magicians, friends and foes; they join in the fight to save Camelot and even walk the Grey Paths of the Dead. With a mix of Malory, a touch of Tolkien, and a hint of humor, The Monster Specialist chronicles a tale of courage, tenacity, honor, and love.

The Monster Specialist is illustrated by Anke Eissmann.

Edward S. Louis, *The Monster Specialist*
Zurich and Jena 2014 (Tales of Yore Series No. 3), ISBN 978-3-905703-23-8

Tales of Yore Series (earlier books)

The *Tales of Yore Series* provides a platform for qualitatively superior fiction that will appeal to readers familiar with Tolkien's world.

Kay Woollard, *The Terror of Tatty Walk. A Frightener*
CD and Booklet, Zurich and Berne 2000, ISBN 978-3-9521424-2-4

Kay Woollard, *Wilmot's Very Strange Stone or What came of building "snobbits"*
CD and booklet, Zurich and Berne 2001, ISBN 978-3-9521424-4-8

Information for authors

Authors interested in contributing to our publications can learn more about the services we offer by reading the "services for authors" section of our web pages.

http://www.walking-tree.org/authors

Manuscripts and project proposals can be submitted to the board of editors (please include an SAE):

Walking Tree Publishers
CH-3052 Zollikofen
Switzerland

e-mail: info@walking-tree.org

Walking Tree Publishers, Zurich and Jena, 2014

CPSIA information can be obtained
at www.ICGtesting.com
Printed in the USA
BVHW04s1409020418
512065BV00012B/23/P